UNDERSTANDING & USING

CHALLENGING EDUCATIONAL THEORIES

KARL AUBREY AND ALISON RILEY

Los Angeles | London | New Delhi
Singapore | Washington DC | Melbourne

Los Angeles | London | New Delhi
Singapore | Washington DC | Melbourne

SAGE Publications Ltd
1 Oliver's Yard
55 City Road
London EC1Y 1SP

SAGE Publications Inc.
2455 Teller Road
Thousand Oaks, California 91320

SAGE Publications India Pvt Ltd
B 1/I 1 Mohan Cooperative Industrial Area
Mathura Road
New Delhi 110 044

SAGE Publications Asia-Pacific Pte Ltd
3 Church Street
#10-04 Samsung Hub
Singapore 049483

Editor: James Clark
Assistant editor: Rob Patterson
Production editor: Tom Bedford
Copyeditor: Andy Baxter
Proofreader: Camille Bramall
Indexer: Silvia Benvenuto
Marketing manager: Dilhara Attygalle
Cover design: Sheila Tong
Typeset by: C&M Digitals (P) Ltd, Chennai, India
Printed by: CPI Group (UK) Ltd, Croydon, CR0 4YY

Library of Congress Control Number: 2016950055

British Library Cataloguing in Publication data

A catalogue record for this book is available from the British Library

ISBN 978-1-4739-5579-0
ISBN 978-1-4739-5580-6 (pbk)

At SAGE we take sustainability seriously. Most of our products are printed in the UK using FSC papers and boards. When we print overseas we ensure sustainable papers are used as measured by the PREPS grading system. We undertake an annual audit to monitor our sustainability.

UNDERSTANDING & USING
CHALLENGING
EDUCATIONAL
THEORIES

Sara Miller McCune founded SAGE Publishing in 1965 to support the dissemination of usable knowledge and educate a global community. SAGE publishes more than 1000 journals and over 800 new books each year, spanning a wide range of subject areas. Our growing selection of library products includes archives, data, case studies and video. SAGE remains majority owned by our founder and after her lifetime will become owned by a charitable trust that secures the company's continued independence.

Los Angeles | London | New Delhi | Singapore | Washington DC | Melbourne

CONTENTS

ABOUT THE AUTHORS

Karl Aubrey is a Senior Lecturer on the Applied Studies in Education programmes, as well as a tutor with postgraduate students, at Bishop Grosseteste University. Prior to this Karl was the Programme Leader for a range of initial teacher education and professional development programmes at a large city further education college. Between 2003 and 2005 he was seconded to the DfES Standards Unit as a learning and teaching practitioner in the East Midlands. Karl has contributed to the *Oxford Dictionary of Education*. His doctoral thesis explored the reforms in further education teacher education from 2000 to 2010, from the viewpoint of teacher educators. Karl's research interests include inclusion, education policy, pedagogy and work-based learning.

Alison Riley is the Academic Co-ordinator for the BA(Hons) Early Childhood Studies degree at Bishop Grosseteste University, she has also worked on a number of educational-related programmes at the university including initial teaching training courses. Prior to joining Bishop Grosseteste University Alison spent sixteen years working in primary education, as a classroom teacher, deputy head teacher and finally head teacher of a large junior school. Alison has been involved in a number of collaborative projects, and has recently been involved in an EU-funded project researching 'Creativity in Early Science and Mathematics Education'. Alison has recently commenced doctoral studies in which she is researching the journey of students entering higher education with alternative qualifications.

ACKNOWLEDGEMENTS

SAGE would like to thank the following people whose comments helped to shape this book:

Catherine Ashdown, Canterbury Christ Church University;

Lynn Boyle, University of Dundee;

Karan Vickers-Hulse, University of the West of England.

INTRODUCTION

WHY A BOOK ABOUT THEORISTS WHO CHALLENGE EDUCATIONAL THINKING AND PRACTICE?

This is a companion volume to our *Understanding and Using Educational Theories* (2016) and, as such, aims to complement the theories already covered. Similar to our previous volume, the purpose of this book is to introduce students to theories and enable them to link theory with practice. The difference is that this book contains what could be perceived as *challenging* theories. We have used the word *challenging* in an eclectic sense. For example, characters like Bourdieu, Foucault, Giroux, Bernstein and Mezirow could be considered challenging because of the supposed complexities of their ideas. Maslow and Rogers are quite established educational thinkers, but this volume aims to explore the wider aspects of the thinkers and explore other features of their work in addition to their well-known concepts. Neill, Holt and hooks are perhaps challenging in the sense of their radical approach to teaching and schooling (or indeed non-schooling). Stenhouse, Goodlad, Darling-Hammond and Noddings offer alternate ideas on the curriculum, schooling, teacher professionalism and moral education, respectively.

We contend, as we did in the last book, that current education policy and resultant practices are being ideologically driven with the object of competing in the global marketplace. Consequently, the principal purpose of education, to foster personal growth and fulfilment, is being neglected. This book adds to the breadth and depth of evidence from these contemporary theorists which counter the increasingly prescriptive and competence-based notion of education championed by educational policy-makers. As such, the book offers readers the opportunity to adopt a critically analytical approach to their understanding of education generally, schooling, teaching, and culture that encompasses the learning process, both for adults and children.

We reiterate the point that this book is not intended as a comprehensive appraisal of each of the theorists' work, rather it acts as more of an introduction into the way of their thinking and possible applications of their ideas. However, we argue that these theories, based upon empirical research, augment those of the previous book and allow readers to challenge current policy and practice. The book provides a valuable foundation for students who wish to explore the theories in more depth, it also makes links between the different ideas of the educational thinkers. Finally, it is hoped that the book will provide food for thought about creating meaningful learning opportunities in practice.

We continued to find deciding which theorists to include problematic. Again we sought opinions from colleagues and students, including postgraduate students, and finally considered that the conditions for inclusion would be that firstly all thinkers should have a degree of 'challenge' in their ideas as we have explained, and secondly we thought they should be reasonably contemporary. Finally, we wanted an international and cultural blend, and with diverse areas of focus. Therefore, we have included theorists from mainland Europe, Britain, Canada and the United States – with, for example, focuses in social reproduction and power, the morality and freedom of schooling, alternate ways of forming curricula, race, teacher professionalism, and humanistic approaches to teaching and learning. Once more, grudgingly, we have omitted the social reformers and classical educational thinkers.

WHO WOULD FIND THIS BOOK RELEVANT?

We hope this book has a use and appeal for a variety of readers with an interest in education and learning, whether formal or informal. Our aim is that it will be of assistance in bridging the gaps between theory and practice and in enhancing readers' own professional development. We also have a goal that it will enable students to advance their skills in critical analysis, synthesis and evaluation in their research and assignment submissions, regarding perhaps those thinkers they may have already been aware of but need additional ideas and further reading about. Furthermore, our desire is that it will be of benefit to both undergraduate, and more than the first book, postgraduate students (many postgraduates wished they had been introduced to some of these *challenging* ideas). Once more our aspiration is that this book will be valuable for those who are concerned with all sectors of education from early years, formal stages of schooling to further, higher, adult and offender education, as well as informal education such as youth work. Again this will include students on work-based degrees and their progression routes, as well as those undergraduates undertaking teacher education for all sectors of education – schools, further and higher education and youth work. It is our hope that teachers and practitioners, whether studying or not for formal programmes might find this volume of interest.

ORGANISATION AND STRUCTURE OF CHAPTERS

Chapters in the book are sequenced in an approximate chronological order, starting with Abraham Maslow and finishing with Linda Darling-Hammond. We have adopted this arrangement so that readers can follow how educational thinking has evolved over time, and in relation to the characters' focuses of concern. Furthermore, the sequence makes it possible for the reader to make links, not only between the theorists included here, but between other significant thinkers they may wish to explore further. We have avoided organising this book in a manner which places the thinkers into theoretical categories such as constructivists, behaviourists and humanists, as we feel this is too simplistic and does not reflect the complexity and the multidirectional nature of many of their ideas; we consider in their own way they are *challenging*.

Each chapter considers a particular theorist and follows a common arrangement of sections. Firstly, the learning outcomes indicate what readers should be able to do having read the chapter; this is followed by a list of key words which are pertinent to the theorist's work. The introduction aims to set the scene, by outlining the significance and impact of the theorist's work, before briefly considering their biography. The next section explores the theories in greater detail, and then links these theories with other educational thinkers. This is then followed by a critical examination of their ideas, based upon evidence from other theorists and other academic sources. The subsequent section offers suggestions for ways that that particular theorist's ideas could be applied in the reader's practice. Then, ahead of the summary, readers are invited to reflect upon the chapter and complete a task which ventures to consolidate theory with their current or future practice. Each chapter ends with suggestions for further reading which readers can follow for further in-depth study, as well as a list of references that have been cited in the chapter.

As we have noted, the opening chapter starts with Abraham Maslow's concept of the humanistic approach to education. Chapter 2 then goes on to Rogers' idea of learner-centred teaching. Chapter 3 focuses on Neill's freedom to learn in the quite radical environment of Summerhill School. Chapter 4 explores Goodlad's concept of schools and teaching from Goodlad's North American point of view. Chapter 5 considers Bernstein's ideas on social class, pedagogy and the curriculum. Chapter 6 concerns Bourdieu's theory of society from an educational viewpoint, whereas Chapter 7 outlines Foucault's notion of power and control in education. Chapter 8 contemplates the notion of moral education in Noddings' thinking. In Chapter 9 we look at Stenhouse's thoughts on linking the curriculum with theory, research and practice. Chapter 10 is an opportunity to consider the radical aspects of Giroux's thoughts on critical pedagogy. Chapter 11 investigates Gardner's ideas on multiple intelligences. In Chapter 12 we learn about Holt's idea of unschooling or home schooling. Chapter 13 examines bell hooks' work on education as a practice of freedom. The ideas of Mezirow's transformational learning are reviewed in Chapter 14. Finally, Darling-Hammond's ideas for reforming schools and teachers are considered in Chapter 15.

USING THE BOOK

We have followed the previous book in suggesting how to use this book. There are a number of ways in which this book can be read. Perhaps you could read it as a whole entity where you start from the introduction and finish at the end – which would offer you a sequential and chronological order of the theories as they evolve. However, it is suggested that it would be more beneficial if you chose the chapters and theorists that interest you so you can begin to know, or refresh your understanding of their ideas, to consider the criticisms of them and how they link to others and how to apply their ideas in practice. Furthermore, you could track the links with other like-minded theorists as well as use the references and further reading to delve deeper. We again also suggest that readers use the reflective tasks to consider and reflect on their ideas and practice, which hopefully will develop future practice and understanding. Nevertheless, regardless of the way you use this book it is our deepest hope that it will help with your understanding of the ideas of these theorists, and add to your criticality for your practice and your assignments.

REFERENCE

Aubrey, K. and Riley, A. (2016) *Understanding and Using Educational Theories*. London: SAGE.

1

ABRAHAM MASLOW

THE FATHER OF AMERICAN HUMANISM

INTRODUCTION

Abraham Maslow is perhaps one of the best-known educational theorists in the field of humanist psychology. Despite initially studying in the field of behaviourist psychology and having renowned behaviourist Harry Harlow as a mentor, Maslow quickly turned his attention to contributing to a new school of thought, humanism, believing this to be a more positive way of viewing people.

Maslow is best known for his hierarchy of needs, a diagrammatic representation of the physiological and psychological needs which humans must pass through on the path to self-actualisation. Maslow theorised that all humans aspired to be the best they could be, stating that 'What a man can be, he must be. This we call self-actualization' (Maslow, 1954: 93). Maslow presented his ideas in the form of a pyramid, with physiological needs forming the base. These he called basic needs, or deficiency needs, and he theorised that these must be met before a person could aspire to the growth needs further up the pyramid. By its very nature the pyramid became less stable the further one ascended, thereby illustrating the importance of setting a firm foundation.

While Maslow was later criticised for the methods employed in developing his theory, particularly when defining what it meant to be self-actualised (see the 'Critiquing the theory' section in this chapter), it cannot be denied that he played an important role in encouraging a view of the whole person, taking account of all the factors required to develop a psychologically and physiologically healthy individual. O'Connor and Yballe (2007) observe that Maslow sought to build an appreciative understanding of human beings at their best, and was instrumental in taking a positivist stance towards psychology at a time when the focus was traditionally based around what was wrong with the human psyche.

Leontiev (2008) sees Maslow as a visionary, and suggests that rather than being afraid of the mistakes he made, Maslow used these as a basis for continually developing and refining his theories, Leontiev (2008) suggests that this is why Maslow's work endures in the psychologies of today. Hoffman (2004) suggests that Maslow saw himself as a psychological pioneer, 'exploring new territories of human experience' (2004: 442). In his later years Maslow turned his attention to management theory, supporting managers in the workplace to help motivate the workforce to increase productivity.

Maslow himself led a simple life, he maintained an interest in humanity up until his untimely death in 1970, sadly leaving behind a host of unfinished projects, but also a legacy which has endured to the present day.

ABRAHAM MASLOW, THE PERSON

It is unsurprising that Maslow spent a lifetime theorising on the conditions under which human beings thrived best, given his own difficult childhood experiences. The eldest of seven children, Maslow was the son of Russian immigrants, Samuel and Rose

Maslow. Maslow's parents were uneducated, but hardworking people, who sought a better life economically for their children (Hoffman, 1992). However, Maslow's upbringing was not a happy one; born in Brooklyn in 1908 Maslow had a poor relationship with his parents, he was at odds with his father for much of his childhood, and was documented to have loathed his mother, a relationship that was never reconciled. To further add to his unhappy and lonely childhood Maslow's parents were Jewish immigrants and Maslow found himself the target of anti-semitic hatred, being the sole Jewish boy in his community; this increased his feelings of isolation and loneliness,

> I was a little Jewish boy in the non-Jewish neighborhood. It was a little like being the first Negro enrolled in an all-white school. I was isolated and unhappy. I grew up in libraries and among books, without friends. (Maslow cited in Hall, 1968: 37)

Maslow, then, sought solace in the local library where he immersed himself in books, thus beginning a lifelong love of learning.

Maslow attended the Brooklyn Boys High School where he became an active member of several academic clubs, in addition to editing the school's Latin magazine and the school's physics paper for a year. Hoffman observes that like many youngsters coming from a background of hardship Maslow's early education experiences 'inexorably shaped his world view' (1992: 440), and saw him seeking an intellectual route which would ultimately lead to 'overcoming religious and ethnic prejudices to create a world based on economic justice and universal education' (Hoffman, 1992: 440).

Despite his animosity towards them, Maslow initially sought a route which would satisfy his parents, especially his father. Therefore, on leaving school Maslow went on to study law at City College, New York. However, he struggled with his studies and after only three semesters he transferred to Cornell University, before transferring back to City College and then proceeding to graduate school at the University of Wisconsin. During this time Maslow also married his first cousin, Bertha Goodman, against his parents' wishes. Maslow saw his marriage as giving him, 'a feeling of love and belongingness' (Bayer and Mottarella, 2005: 814). This period also saw Maslow find an academic path which suited him better than law, and as he began to pursue the study of psychology he also started to achieve much greater academic success. During his time at the University of Wisconsin Maslow gained three degrees in psychology; a bachelor degree in 1930, followed by a masters in 1931 and a doctorate in 1934.

Maslow was initially drawn to behaviourism, a strand of psychology which was prevalent at the time through the work of renowned psychologists such as Watson and Skinner. However, on transferring to the University of Wisconsin he became influenced by the work of Alfred Adler, and Harry Harlow who later became Maslow's doctoral advisor, which led him to an interest in a more practical, socially orientated approach to psychology (Hoffman, 1992). Maslow began teaching at Brooklyn College in 1931, a role he continued in until 1951 when he became Chair of the Psychology

Department at Brandeis University until 1969. During his time at Brooklyn College Maslow came into contact with, and was influenced by, a number of European intellectuals who were immigrating to the United States, the most notable being Gestalt psychologist Max Westheimer and anthropologist Ruth Benedict. It was his observations of these 'two favourite mentors' (Hoffman, 1992) that led him to his ground-breaking studies of self-actualising people. This work was also influenced by the Second World War, since while Maslow himself was ineligible for the military draft, he was horrified by what he saw through the media, and was convinced that a better understanding of what motivated people would help to bring peace to the world. In a 1992 interview with Edward Hoffman Maslow states:

> It was at this moment that I realised that the rest of my life must be devoted to discovering a psychology for the peace table. That moment changed my whole life. (Hoffman, 1992)

Throughout the 1940s Maslow developed and refined his hierarchy of inborn needs, attempting to understand and explain human motivation. However, despite first proposing his theory of needs hierarchy in the 1943 paper 'A theory of human motivation', his findings were not formally published until 1954 when his landmark book *Motivation and Personality* was released, documenting fifteen years of theorising about human nature. Maslow's work at this time was ground-breaking since it offered a view of psychology which focused on the positive side of human nature rather than the negatives,

> The science of psychology has been far more successful on the negative than on the positive side ... it has revealed much to us about man's shortcomings, his illness, his sins but little about his potentialities, his virtues, his achievable aspirations, or his psychological health. (Maslow, 1954: 354)

It was during the 1960s that Maslow's work really took off. He was elected as President of the American Association for Humanist Psychology in 1961 and published his second book on human needs, *Towards a Psychology of Being*, in 1962. Maslow found himself receiving accolades from colleagues and former students, and was in demand from managers and entrepreneurs who saw the potential in his work for motivating the workforce.

Unfortunately, Maslow's work was interrupted in 1967 following a major heart attack, and despite having suffered with heart problems for most of his adult life he suddenly found himself constrained by a lengthy period of convalescence. Maslow became increasingly frustrated by his slow recovery and had to put on hold future plans for research, lectures and travel; it was at this time that he began to think about his own mortality and 'began to ponder his career accomplishments and his unrealised goals' (Hoffman, 1992). Following his heart attack Maslow relocated to the San Francisco Bay area, with Bertha, in the hope that the milder climate would help with his health problems, and while his health troubles persisted Maslow continued to write, teach and consult. Abraham Maslow died from a fatal heart attack in 1970 at the age of 62, leaving behind a lifelong legacy devoted to maximising human potential.

THE HIERARCHY OF NEEDS AND SELF-ACTUALISATION

Maslow is most well-known for his hierarchy of human needs and his theory of self-actualisation; however, in order to fully understand the context of this work it is necessary to consider the influences behind this theory.

Maslow, along with other eminent humanist psychologists, including Carl Rogers, is credited with developing what was referred to as the 'third force' in psychology. In looking for an alternative theory to the prevalent psychologies of the time, behaviourism and psychoanalysis, humanist theory was born with a focus on the positive side of human nature. Maslow saw behaviourism as the first force in psychology, with the emphasis on human behaviour being influenced and controlled by the manipulation of the external environment. Alongside this he referred to psychoanalysis as the second force where human behaviour was controlled almost totally by internal, unconscious forces (De Marco and Tilson, 1998). Maslow rejected the idea that behaviour could be controlled by either external or internal forces; he felt stifled by the very nature of behaviourism and believed that 'humans were more than billiard balls on the pool table of life' (O'Connor and Yballe, 2007: 741). Instead Maslow was keen to develop a theory which combined aspects of both behaviourism and psychoanalysis, but which embraced an appreciation of human beings at their best, looking at the farthest reaches of human nature.

Humanist theory, then, has a focus on the healthy individual, rejecting in particular the Freudian psychology, common at the time, which Maslow believed placed far too much emphasis on the unhealthy side of the human condition (Weinberg, 2011). Maslow set out a vision and purpose for his new psychology stating that, 'Freud supplied to us the sick half of psychology, and we must now fill it out with the healthy half' (Maslow, 1962: 7), thus commencing a life's work establishing the physiological and psychological human needs required for a person to function fully and productively. It is through this study that Maslow's hierarchy of needs evolved.

In developing his theory Maslow focused his attention on psychologically healthy individuals; this marked a change from previous studies in which the focus was most frequently on damaged individuals (Weinberg, 2011). It also broke away from traditional thinking as Maslow sought to determine what factors brought about a state of good psychological health. Maslow was concerned with the factors which motivated people, and identified two kinds of motivation: *deficiency motivation*, which demanded the need to reduce physiological tensions such as hunger or thirst, and *growth motivation*, which was concerned with the satisfaction of needs such as the need to be loved and belong. Maslow noticed that needs tended to fall into specific patterns, which he arranged into a hierarchy, these needs he believed were inborn into everyone regardless of culture and were genetic in origin (DeMarco and Tilson, 1998). At the base of the hierarchy Maslow placed physiological needs such as sleep, rest, food, drink and shelter; this was then followed by safety and security needs such as feeling safe from harm, being secure in home and life, financial security and routine. Maslow's theory proposed that in order to meet those needs higher up the pyramid then an individual must first, at least partially, satisfy these lower-level basic needs.

Maslow identified that as people progress up the pyramid then the need for belongingness, love and esteem becomes more prevalent, and while these are still referred to as deficiency needs these become more about personal growth with individuals seeking acceptance and affection, as well as respect and personal esteem. Maslow identified good self-esteem as being,

> soundly based on real capacity, achievement and respect from others … satisfaction of self-esteem needs leads to feelings of self-confidence, worth, capability and adequacy of being useful and necessary in the world. (1943: 382)

While Maslow believed that most individuals are aspiring towards this feeling of good self-esteem and high self-worth he also acknowledged that as an individual ascends the pyramid then the relative strength of each need is reduced (Snowman and Biehler, 2006), and at any point in the hierarchy an individual might stop striving towards a higher need if a lower-level need is activated.

Maslow theorised that these steps on the pyramid were important stages in a person becoming self-actualised, which, for Maslow, was the pinnacle of the pyramid and, ideally, the ultimate goal of every individual. However, Maslow is also well-documented as stating that for most people the goal of self-actualisation will never be achieved simply because progress is all too often disrupted by a failure to fully meet lower-level needs. Maslow suggested that only 1 in 100, or between 1 and 2 per cent of the population, become fully self-actualised, and this may partly be the result of societies' tendency to reward motivation based on esteem, love and social needs – in which case where is the motivation to become fully actualised?

For individuals who are fully actualised Maslow created clear defining criteria, in his own words

> Self-actualising people have a wonderful capacity to appreciate again and again, freshly and naively, the basic goods of life, with awe, pleasure, wonder, and even ecstasy, however stale those experiences have become to others. Thus, for such a person any sunset may be as beautiful as the first one, and flowers may be of breath taking loveliness, even after he has seen a million flowers. The thousandth baby he sees is just as miraculous a product as the first one he saw. He remains as convinced of his luck in marriage thirty years after his marriage and is as surprised by his wife's beauty when she is sixty as he was forty years before. For such people, even the casual workaday, moment-to-moment business of living can be thrilling, exciting and ecstatic. (Maslow, 1959: 43)

In essence then, the self-actualised individual is not just fulfilled, having achieved everything he is capable of, but has also a feeling of euphoria, joy and wonder in every aspect of his life. While Maslow initially believed that self-actualisation would automatically follow all other needs, he revised this theory after identifying individuals who did not follow this pattern. In this respect Maslow later typified self-actualisers as those who hold certain values such as truth, goodness, beauty, justice, autonomy and humour (Feist and Feist, 2001), it is such values that enable self-actualised people to stand apart from those who only meet their esteem needs.

In his later years Maslow began to consider a fourth force of psychology which saw a shift in emphasis to a more transpersonal psychology. Initially Maslow's new direction showed influences from eastern philosophies, emphasising meditation as a means of developing a higher level of consciousness, capturing phenomena such as epiphanies, peaks, revelations and transformative moments. However, Maslow abhorred the hippy culture of the time and was keen not to be associated with the mysticism prevalent in some areas of 1960s American culture (Hoffman, 2008). This may, then, account for Maslow's later work which saw a focus on personal mission, choice and self-investment (Leontiev, 2008), since he 'ultimately felt far more comfortable studying entrepreneurs and business organisations than mystics, sages and exalted states of consciousness' (Hoffman, 2008: 442).

LINKS WITH OTHER THEORISTS

Maslow was a humanist in the truest sense; as such, links can be perceived with other theorists in the field of humanism such as Carl Rogers and Alfred Adler. Like Maslow, Rogers developed his own theory of self-actualisation; however, rather than basing his theories on personal views Rogers used empirical evidence from his own clinical observations to develop his theory. Unlike Maslow, Rogers (1951) considered the obstacles to self-actualisation, and looked at the characteristics of the fully functioning person when developing his own definition of self-actualisation. Rogers also looked at supporting the individual to help them achieve self-actualisation whereas Maslow believed that this would happen automatically once all other needs had been met. Both Maslow and Rogers did, however, believe that gaining acceptance was far more important than gaining self-actualisation.

Maslow was heavily influenced by the work of Alfred Adler who, like Maslow, had also dismissed the work of Freud. Initially one of Freud's first disciples, Adler became one of the first dissidents of psychoanalysis, creating his own psychoanalytical school which he called individual psychology to distinguish it from Freud's school (Chiriac, 2003). Adler was keen that when viewing humans it should be done from a holistic perspective, rather than through bits of their personalities such as the id and ego, he also suggested that the physical and social environment were also important factors in the development of the individual. Adler postulated that the driving force behind all human behaviour was to strive for perfection, which he saw as the desire to fulfil one's potential; it is not difficult to see the similarity here with Maslow's theory of self-actualisation. However, whereas Maslow saw this as being an individual endeavour, Adler believed that a driving force behind achieving one's potential was through social interest, and thereby achieving a sense of solidarity with humanity and the local community. This is in opposition to Maslow who saw the self-actualiser as one who could resist social conformity.

As we saw earlier in the chapter, Maslow's later work was seen to influence practice in business organisations, with managers looking to Maslow's theory to help motivate their workforce. In this respect, then, it is possible to see links between Maslow's work and that of Frederick Herzberg (1964), who developed his own two-factor motivation theory related to satisfaction in the workplace – also referred to as Herzberg's motivation-hygiene theory. Herzberg sought to identify the factors in the workers' environment which caused satisfaction and dissatisfaction, suggesting that by eliminating the factors which caused dissatisfaction an increase in work motivation would be achieved. Herzberg identified a set of hygiene factors, or maintenance factors which were required before workers experienced job satisfaction. Herzberg's hygiene factors, including achievement, recognition, responsibility and advancement are in parallel to Maslow's growth needs. It could be argued that Maslow's work was then the stimulus for Herzberg's theory.

CRITIQUING THE THEORY

Maslow was heavily criticised for the elitist elements in his theories, particularly in relation to those people he considered to be self-actualisers, which some believe to be unrepresentative of real individuals, living in real society with real jobs (Pearson 1999). Indeed, it could be argued that Maslow's work on self-actualisation was somewhat subjective, since his choice of subjects when defining the criteria for self-actualisation was very much based on his own personal observations and choice. This suggests that he had already selected his criteria and was looking to find subjects that formed a best fit to the observations he had already made.

The methodology used by Maslow when defining the characteristics of the self-actualised individuals was called into question since this relied largely on biographical analysis, and his sample size for making these generalisations was small in number, consisting of only eighteen individuals whom Maslow himself decided were self-actualised people. Drawing from people of esteem, such as Abraham Lincoln and Albert Einstein, and including his own mentors Ruth Benedict and Max Westheimer, Maslow has been criticised for selecting only the most highly educated, and predominantly white, males to develop his theory. As such, it is difficult to see where people from lower social classes or different ethnic groups fit into his theory.

A further criticism of Maslow's theory lies in the hierarchical nature of the needs, since if we interpret the hierarchy literally then it would follow that only once the deficiency needs have been met can people strive towards high self-esteem and self-actualisation. However, if this were the case then it could be argued that artists such as Van Gogh, for example, may never have reached the heights of their creative endeavours, since the very fact that they lived in poverty for most of their lives should, according to Maslow, have stifled their creative ability (Tay and Diener, 2011). Similarly, it is quite possible that a person living in poverty may well feel tired and hungry, yet may still feel love and belonging.

O'Connor and Yballe (2007) suggest, however, that Maslow may well have been misrepresented and misunderstood, and they question whether the positive message which Maslow was trying to promote was undermined by too much emphasis on the invalid research methods employed. They suggest that Maslow did not intend to suggest that people move through the hierarchy in a series of stages, and in fact may well move between levels at different periods of their life. Maslow never considered self-actualisation to be an end point, rather an ongoing process requiring life choices, which were often associated with risk and required courage (O'Connor and Yballe, 2007).

APPLYING MASLOW IN PRACTICE

Maslow's work is eminently applicable to the classroom and, not surprisingly, it can frequently be seen reflected in a variety of teaching and classroom management practices in use today. Maslow himself did not set out to influence classroom practice, so it is testament to his work that his theory has been adopted in educational settings, albeit unconsciously in many cases.

As we have seen, Maslow's work centred on human motivation, and the conditions required to maximise the human experience, including the desire to learn. At its simplest level then, the role of the educator must be to ensure that everything possible is done to ensure that learners' physiological needs have been addressed, since, 'even the most inspirational educator will not be able to reach a student whose lower-level needs are not being met' (DeMarco and Tilson, 1998: 93) and it cannot be assumed that a learner entering the classroom has already had these needs met.

In recent years in Britain we have seen an increased focus on the holistic needs of the child, particularly for those children at the primary level of education. This was almost certainly prompted by the introduction of the *Every Child Matters* agenda (DfES, 2003), a green paper following the investigation into the abuse and subsequent death of Victoria Climbié. While the objectives of the paper were predominantly to ensure that child protection processes in England and Wales were strengthened, a further focus on five specific outcomes (be healthy, stay safe, achieve economic well-being, enjoy and achieve, and make a positive contribution) reflected strongly the deficiency needs as theorised by Maslow. All settings which held responsibility for children aged from zero to nineteen years were tasked with the challenge of meeting the holistic needs of their pupils, through a range of initiatives which were designed to ensure the basic needs of children were met, thereby ensuring the foundations for learning were set.

Such initiatives saw, for example, the introduction of breakfast clubs into schools, an increased focus on healthy and nutritional hot school meals, and extended school provision, to name but a few. While subsequent UK governments have failed to acknowledge the *Every Child Matters* agenda in its original form, the legacy of these initiatives has prevailed with a continued emphasis on the needs of the child being seen through more recent government policies, such as Pupil Premium and the introduction of hot school meals for Key Stage 1 pupils in schools in England, which have essentially targeted vulnerable pupils and those from disadvantaged backgrounds.

While not directly linked to Maslow's work it can be seen therefore that there is an increasing awareness that learning can be seriously compromised if deficiency needs are not met. However, it is perhaps more pertinent to look at needs further up the pyramid to consider how practitioners can more effectively influence student motivation through their own actions. Assuming all psychological needs have been met, the next two tiers on Maslow's hierarchy are concerned with matters related to safety and belongingness and love. We need look no further than the physical layout of the learning environment to consider how it might promote the safety of the learner, and policies related to visitors in school. Health and safety practices around the use of classroom policies can certainly contribute to both the child and family feeling confident in the physical safety of the child.

In early years settings, provision includes ensuring that each child has a key person in the setting who is responsible for their individual needs. The most recent Early Years Foundation Stage (EYFS) framework, applicable in England, makes clear that,

> each child must be assigned a key person. Their role is to ensure that each child's care is tailored to meet their individual needs … to help the child become familiar with the setting, offer a settled relationship for the child and build a relationship with the parents. (DfE, 2014: 21)

While the 'key person' concept is more reflective of the theories of Bowlby (1969), Ainsworth (1964) and, more recently, Elfer et al. (2003), there are also clear parallels with the safety and belonging needs as theorised by Maslow. Indeed, the EYFS framework also makes clear the importance of developing a safe, suitable and appropriate environment, as well as attending to a child's health needs.

The importance of a child feeling welcome and a part of the classroom remains throughout the period of statutory education. Maslow (1987) theorised that belonging was an essential and prerequisite human need which needed to be met before one could ever achieve a sense of self-worth. Therefore, the role of the classroom practitioner should be to ensure that individuals develop a feeling of belonging, for example through ensuring that children's views are heard, listening and responding positively to individuals, and being seen to act on their suggestions and opinions. On a wider scale the development of school councils has been a positive move forward in allowing pupil voice to be heard, and in encouraging students to take a more active role in the development of the school community.

According to Maslow's theory, students are more likely to aspire to the growth needs at the top of the pyramid if their deficiency needs have been met; in contrast a student who does not feel that their teacher cares about them or what they do is more likely to give up trying, feeling their efforts will not be appreciated (Snowman and Biehler, 2006). This emphasises the important role of the practitioner in ensuring that students feel supported in their endeavours; as suggested by DeMarco and Tilson (1998) students need to be told, 'you've done a good job' otherwise their needs become frustrated and the student begins to feel inferior. At the same time it is essential that the practitioner creates a learning experience which sets appropriate challenge for the learner, but which allows each to succeed at their own level, in this way the practitioner is assisting the learner in developing a feeling of self-worth and accomplishment.

A student who has developed a high level of esteem is, according to Maslow's theory, most likely to achieve self-actualisation, or to maximise their potential, although as we saw earlier Maslow believed only a small number of the population will ever fully reach the top of the pyramid. It is also highly unlikely that self-actualisation will be seen within the educational setting since in Maslow's theory this is defined as the full use and exploitation of one's talents, capacities and potentialities (Maslow 1954), and in this respect it could be argued that the educational journey is preparation for self-actualisation, and only once the student has left formal education can their true potential be realised. If this is indeed the case, then the role of the educator becomes even more important in setting the developmental foundations for self-actualisation to be fully realised.

REFLECTIVE TASK

When defining self-actualisation Maslow looked to the individual characteristics of people, including: human centredness, sense of personal autonomy, dignity, spontaneity, creativity and solitude.

Do you think these values still hold true in the fast-paced world of today, when success is often measured by material resources, or do you think Maslow's work is outdated?

SUMMARY

Maslow can be credited with putting human beings at the centre of psychology. At a time when the focus was on what was wrong with the human psyche Maslow developed a theory which looked at the positive side of human nature. In so doing Maslow established a hierarchy of needs which is instantly applicable to any given situation, and which practitioners can use as a guide to developing practice, and ensuring that individuals are given the best conditions possible for success to occur.

For Maslow the key to his work was in establishing what it meant to be self-actualised, and while he identified that all humans had basic needs that were innate, such as hunger and thirst, he also acknowledged that self-actualisation was much harder to achieve. In defining what it meant to be self-actualised Maslow chose people who he himself believed to be self-actualised and it is for this that his work received the most criticism, since its very nature showed a degree of subjectivity which made it difficult to generalise his concepts.

Nevertheless, despite this criticism Maslow continued to develop his theories; he accepted that his methods had flaws and sought to find further ways of establishing his ideas particularly around what motivates people, this led him to apply his works to management situations where he advised managers on how to motivate their workforce.

Maslow left a legacy which is still as applicable today as it was when he was alive. He applied a common sense approach to psychology in a format which could be practically applied in most formal situations. Any theory which seeks to establish the most favourable conditions to promote the best in people must surely be one worthy of note.

 ## FURTHER READING

Goble, F.G. (2004) *The Third Force: The Psychology of Abraham Maslow*. Florida: Maurice Bassett Publishing.
A condensation of Maslow's ideas from his books and publications, presented in a user-friendly format.

King, P.W. (2009) *Climbing Maslow's Pyramid: Choosing Your Own Path through Life*. Leicester: Matador.
An examination of how individuals can use their life experiences to change the person they are using aspects from Maslow's hierarchy of needs.

Maddi, S.R. and Costa, P.T. (2009) *Humanism in Personology: Allport, Maslow and Murray*. New Jersey: Transaction Publishers.
A summary of the works and their applicability to the development of personality.

McGuire, K.J. (2011) *Maslow's Hierarchy of Needs: An Introduction*. Norderstedt: Books on Demand.
Maslow's hierarchy of needs as applied to the workplace, an evaluation of how Maslow's work can motivate the workforce.

REFERENCES

Ainsworth, M.D. (1964) 'Patterns of attachment behavior shown by the infant in interaction with his mother'. *Merrill-Palmer Quarterly of Behavior and Development*, 10: 51–8.
Bayer, M. and Mottarella, K.E. (2005) in: Salkind, N.J. *Encyclopaedia of Human Development*. London: SAGE.

Bowlby, J. (1969) *Attachment and Loss*. New York: Basic Books.

Chiriac, J. (2003). *Freud versus Adler*. AROPA. www.freudfile.org/freud_adler.pdf.

De Marco, M.L. and Tilson, E.R. (1998) 'Maslow in the classroom and the clinic'. *American Society of Radiologic Technologists*, 70: 91–4.

DfE (Department for Education) (2014) *Early Years Foundation Stage*. Crown Copyright.

DfES (Department for Education and Skills) (2003) *Every Child Matters*. Green Paper. Crown Copyright.

Elfer, P., Goldschmied, E. and Selleck, D. (2003) *Key Persons in the Nursery: Building Relationships for Quality Provision*. London: David Fulton.

Feist, J. and Feist, G.J. (2001) *Theories of Personality* (fifth edition). Dubuque: McGraw-Hill.

Hall, M.H. (1968) 'A conversation with Abraham Maslow'. *Psychology Today*, July: 35–7, 54–7.

Herzberg, F. (1964) 'The motivation-hygiene concept and problems of manpower'. *Personnel Administrator*, 27: 3–7.

Hoffman. E. (1992) *Overcoming Evil: An Interview with Abraham Maslow, Founder of Humanistic Psychology*. www.psychologytoday.com/articles/199201/abraham-maslow.

Hoffman, E. (2004) 'Abraham Maslow's life and unfinished legacy'. *Japanese Journal of Administrative Science*, 17: 133–8.

Hoffman, E. (2008) 'Abraham Maslow: A biographer's reflections'. *Journal of Humanist Psychology*, 48: 439–43.

Leontiev, D. (2008) 'Maslow yesterday, today and tomorrow'. *Journal of Humanist Psychology*, 48: 451–3.

Maslow, A.H. (1943) 'A theory of human motivation'. *Psychological Review*, 50: 370–96.

Maslow, A.H. (1954) *Motivation and Personality*. New York: Harper & Row.

Maslow, A.H. (1959) 'Cognition of being in the peak experiences'. *The Journal of Genetic Psychology*, 94: 43–66.

Maslow, A.H. (1962) *Towards a Psychology of Being*. New York: Harper & Row.

Maslow, A.H. (1987) *Motivation and Personality* (third edition). New York: Harper & Row.

O'Connor, D. and Yballe, L. (2007) 'Maslow revisited: constructing a road map of human behaviour'. *Journal of Management Education*, 31: 733–58.

Pearson, E.M. (1999) 'Humanism and individualism: Maslow and his critics'. *Adult Education Quarterly*, 50: 41–55.

Rogers, C. (1951) *Client-centered Therapy: Its Current Practice, Implications and Theory*. London: Constable.

Snowman, J. and Biehler, R. (2006) *Psychology Applied to Teaching*. Boston: Houghton Mifflin.

Tay, L. and Dicner, E. (2011) 'Needs and subjective well-being around the world'. *Journal of Personality and Social Psychology*, 101: 354–65.

Weinberg, D.R. (2011) 'Montessori, Maslow and self-actualization'. *Montessori Life*, 23: 16–21.

2

CARL ROGERS

THE FATHER OF CLIENT-CENTRED THERAPY

LEARNING OUTCOMES

Having read this chapter you should be able to:

- Appreciate how Rogers' upbringing led to his development of psychoanalytical theories of development
- Recognise the impact of Rogers' work on the psychotherapy movement in America
- Understand Rogers' theory of self-actualisation when applied in educational settings

KEY WORDS

Client-centred therapy; self-actualisation; facilitator; self-direction; self-image; unconditional positive regard; conditional positive regard; ideal self; congruence

INTRODUCTION

Renowned psychologist Carl Rogers is best known for his work in the field of client-centred psychology and counselling. However, his influence has been far-reaching in sectors outside of clinical psychology, including in the areas of education and health (Smith, 2004), making him one of the most influential psychologists of the twentieth century.

Rogers had a diverse education, which saw him studying in the fields of agriculture, religion and education, before he finally settled on clinical and educational psychology as his area of specialism. It could be argued that this journey into the field of psychology exposed him to a range of influential ideals and philosophies which ultimately led him to developing his own theory of client-centred therapy. Rogers was able to draw on the work of Otto Rank and John Dewey (through W.H. Kilpatrick) and, through linking together elements of their work, he took their notions of the human as a whole being capable of possibilities and applied his own therapeutic insight. From this Rogers developed his own theory which advocated the idea that the client usually knows better than the theorist in how to proceed with their treatment. At a time when psychologists such as Freud were trying to 'cure' the human psyche this was seen as a revolutionary approach to therapy.

Rogers had a career that spanned over fifty years, beginning in child psychology as director of the Society for the Prevention of Cruelty to Children, he then undertook numerous roles working predominantly in the academic field. Rogers was able to use his roles in academia to undertake scientific research, an approach which Kirschenbaum (1979) suggests was still underutilised in the field of psychotherapy, possibly due to therapy still being in its infancy. It is perhaps for this reason that Rogers' work really resonated with other professionals.

Rogers published numerous articles and books in which he recorded his findings from the research undertaken; however, he is perhaps best known for his text, *On Becoming a Person* (1961), in which he first set out his theory that people have the resources for self-healing and growth which formed the basis for his client-centred therapy, later to become person-centred therapy. Rogers' theory was widely accepted in the field of therapy, and was subsequently applied to other person-facing professions such as education and nursing. Smith (2004) suggests that Rogers was both an accomplished communicator and committed practitioner who was able to draw from his own experiences. It is perhaps for these reasons that his work was so widely accepted and enduring, along with the fact that his work had relevance to a number of professional fields.

CARL ROGERS, THE PERSON

Carl Ransom Rogers was born in 1902 in Oak Park, Illinois. Rogers was one of six children born to Walter and Julia Rogers, a staunchly religious and uncompromising couple who could trace their lineage far back into US history (Thorne, 1992). Rogers' father, a college graduate of the University of Wisconsin, had already established himself as a businessman in the engineering field when Rogers was born, and his mother too had a college education, and came from a family who 'had made notable contributions to the community and to the development of the new country over more than 300 years' (Thorne, 1992: 1). Thorne suggests, then, that Rogers was not a European emigrant like many of his contemporaries, but a 'genuine product of Midwestern America' (1992: 1).

Rogers was brought up in a Christian household, where the family were strict observers of the faith; as such, the emphasis was on family life, with close-knit family ties, and a strict adherence to a moral code. Rogers grew up then, having little social life outside of the immediate family, and even within this his social life did not extend to such frivolities as theatre visits, dancing or card games. Likewise, the drinking of alcohol was strictly prohibited. Rogers had a somewhat lonely childhood, perceived by his family as a 'sickly child who was prone to be over-sensitive' (Thorne, 1992: 2), he spent his formative years seeking solace in books, which Thorne believed served as the starting point to his scholarly endeavours.

Given his Christian upbringing it is perhaps unsurprising that Rogers eventually opted to study theology at university, becoming convinced that his calling was to be a Christian minister. However, his journey to this calling was not straightforward, nor was it enduring. In fact, when he first became a student at the University of Wisconsin in 1919 it was to study the field of scientific agriculture, the result of time spent on the family farm where his father encouraged him, and his brothers, to take on responsibility for various ventures. It was at Wisconsin that Rogers became familiar with scientific methodology, and learned about what it entailed to set up valid experiments (Thorne, 1992). Indeed it seemed that the satisfaction he gained from this was in some way seen as a substitute for the human intimacy he so yearned for.

While Rogers' early ambition was to eventually manage his own farm using the most scientific methods possible, Thorne (1992) acknowledges that his experience of university was a profound period of personal change and development, which ultimately saw him changing his major from agriculture to religion. The turning point came when he joined a Sunday morning group for agriculture students, and influenced by the leader Professor George Humphrey, Rogers began to see a world outside of the family circle. This also led to a reaffirmation of the Christian values he had grown up with, and convinced him of a calling to the ministry.

Rogers' renewed interest in religion saw him move away from his evangelical upbringing, into one which focused on the possibility of personal freedom, this was further affirmed during a visit to Beijing for the World Student Christian Federation Conference where Boeree (1998) observes that Rogers broadened his thinking to the extent that he began to doubt some of his basic religious views. We can see then that Rogers had a somewhat ambiguous relationship with religion, and his ambition to enter the ministry was shaken once again following his attendance at a student-led seminar, at the Union Theological Seminary, entitled 'Why am I entering the Ministry?'. Rogers was later to comment that such a class should not be taken unless you want to change your career, and observed that most of the participants who attended 'thought their way right out of religious work' (Boeree, 1998).

Boeree (1998) observes that religion's loss was psychology's gain, as Rogers switched to the clinical educational psychology programme at Columbia University where he received his PhD in 1931. During his time at Columbia Rogers undertook clinical work at the Rochester Society for the Prevention of Cruelty to Children, where he became influenced by the work of Otto Rank and John Dewey, through the work of W.H. Kilpatrick. Reflecting on their techniques and theories Rogers was able to apply his own techniques to clinical psychology through his own clinical practice (this will be expanded on further in the next section of this chapter).

Following on from his tenure at Columbia, Rogers was offered a full professorship at Ohio State in 1940; here he found a certain amount of freedom, which he attributed to the fact that he had not had to work his way up through the university faculty, entering the academic world at professorial level (Thorne, 1992). While at Ohio Rogers was able to undertake some lecturing, but was also afforded the opportunity to write numerous articles, serve on committees and, perhaps most importantly, establish a 'practicum in counselling and psychotherapy' (Thorne, 1998: 11). He also published his first book *Counselling and Psychotherapy* (1942) while at Ohio, followed in 1951 by his renowned work *Client Centered Therapy* (1951), in which he outlined his basic theory (Boeree, 1998).

Rogers returned to the University of Wisconsin in 1957; however, this was not a successful move since he had returned at a time of great conflict in the psychology department (Boeree, 1998), and while he was able to carry out one of his major research projects there, he soon became disillusioned with higher education. Rogers did, however, publish his most influential work *On Becoming a Person* (1961) while at Wisconsin, which 'catapulted him into the limelight and brought him more fame and influence than he could ever have hoped for' (Thorne, 1998: 11). It was the success of this book that gave Rogers the confidence to move out of established institutions, and accept a research position at La Jolla, California. Rogers remained there, giving speeches, providing therapy and writing, up until his death in 1987.

THE THEORY

Rogers could be viewed as a humanist theorist, having much in common with Maslow when considering the conditions needed by humans to grow and develop. However, Thorne observes that Rogers himself 'was highly suspicious of theories' (1992: 24), preferring to view himself as a pioneer, rejecting the idea of trying to apply theories to a situation, and instead working individually with his clients, in identifying what worked best for them.

Rogers is most well-known for his work on client-centred therapy in which he expounded the belief that therapy works best when the client is at the centre. The foundations of his belief are reflected in the fact that he used the term 'client' rather than 'patient', preferring not to think of the person as having a condition to be cured. Whereas contemporaries of Rogers, such as Freud, sought to establish what was wrong with the human psyche, Rogers based his work on the belief that people were essentially good and healthy. The therapist, according to Rogers, should be empathetic and non-judgemental, and should support the client in overcoming any personal challenges in their quest to reach self-actualisation.

Boeree (1998) suggests that Rogers' theory is both simple and elegant, being built on one single 'force of life', which he called *the actualising tendency*. DeRobertis explains that Rogers saw the actualising tendency as 'the innate tendency of the organism to develop all of its biological and psychological capacities in ways that serve to maintain or enhance itself' (2006: 179). For Rogers the organism sought to increase its autonomy through lessening the influence of external forces, a tendency he believed to be present from birth. As the child develops through infancy they seek more and more control over their environment, which is the early development of the 'self'; Rogers saw this as 'the capacity of the individual, in a growth promoting environment, to move towards self-understanding and self-direction' (1986: 128).

For Rogers, not only did the organism seek to maintain itself through its interactions within the environment, but it also sought to 'move towards the constructive accomplishment of its potential' (Thorne, 1992: 26). It is not enough to survive, to achieve satisfaction the organism must feel it has maximised its own potential. Rogers recognised that this was influenced by the environment that the organism grew up in; an unfavourable environment would undoubtedly stunt the growth of the actualising tendency (Thorne, 1998).

Rogers suggested that the human organism instinctively knows what is good and bad for them, a capacity he referred to as *organismic valuing* (Boeree, 1998), and from this he coined the term *positive regard*. Rogers used this as an umbrella term to describe behaviour such as love, affection and nurture, which he believed organisms needed to survive. Alongside this he identified *positive self-regard* as being developed as a result of others' positive regard towards an individual, from this he suggested that the individual gained self-esteem and self-worth, all important factors in the quest to self-actualisation. For the developing child the most influential positive self-regard would ideally come from the main caregiver, and through the early interactions and responses to certain behaviours, as Rogers stated:

> The parent who is able (1) genuinely to accept ... feelings of satisfaction experienced by the child, and (2) to fully accept the child who experiences them, and (3) at the same time to accept his or her own feelings that such behaviour is unacceptable in the family, creates a situation for the child very different from the usual one. The child in this relationship experiences no threat to his concept of himself as a loved person. He can experience fully and accept ... himself. (1951: 502)

To put this simply, the caregiver who provides positive and consistent interactions with the developing child is setting the foundations for the development of good positive self-regard, since the child will come to view themselves as good and worthy of love (Rogers, 1951). On the other hand, the child who experiences inconsistent parental interactions, in which behaviour is often disapproved of, is likely to develop negative self-worth, feeling they are not worthy of love. Rogers saw this as a threat to the development of the self, since the child in seeking parental approval will moderate and change their behaviour. Rogers suggested that where an organism denies and distorts their own experience in favour of introjected values, then 'self-concept becomes increasingly alienated from the organism' (Rogers, 1951: 505).

Rogers believed that a child who experiences positive self-regard is most likely to develop the *real self*, that is, the person they were meant to become; however, he also recognised that society was frequently out of sync with the actualising tendency (Boeree, 1998), in which case it was necessary for the organism to make compromises. Rogers referred to this as the development of the ideal self, something he categorised as being not real, 'something that is always out of our reach, the standard we can't meet' (Boeree, 1998). Rogers referred to the gap between the real self and the ideal self as incongruity, and believed that the wider the gap the greater the incongruity, which could lead to problems in later life, as the organism became out of sync with itself.

Rogers had a firm commitment to the development of the healthy individual, which he referred to as the *fully functioning person*. Rogers recognised that only a few could aspire to this since it required the individual to have experienced the most ideal environment for developing self-actualisation. Rogers saw the psychologically healthy person as one who has, 'been fortunate enough to live in contexts that have facilitated the emergence of self-concepts which allow them to be in touch for at least part of the time with their deepest experiences and feelings' (Thorne, 1992: 32). Nevertheless, for those who had been fortunate enough to become a fully functioning person he identified five specific attributes, these being:

- *openness to experience*, an ability to listen to one's self and others, as well as an ability to experience what is happening without feeling threatened;
- *existential living*, to live fully in the present, being attentive to each moment as it is lived and trusting each experience rather than feeling fearful of it;
- *organismic trusting*, regarding experiences as what feels right as the most valid sources of information, to trust their own judgement rather than deferring to others;
- *experiential freedom*, to accept responsibility for determining actions and consequences;
- *creativity*, the sense of being a free agent, adjusting or adapting to changing conditions to produce creative ideas or to initiate imaginative projects.

(adapted from Thorne, 1998: 34)

Rogers believed that the fully functioning person was not trapped by the conventions of society; however, they are still able to take their place fully in that society, being neither ostracised nor seen as an eccentric or radical extremist (Thorne, 1992).

Rogers' theoretical observations came predominantly from his work with individuals in his client-centred therapy. Initially referred to as non-directive therapy, Rogers based his work on the notion that the client should direct the progress of the sessions, with the therapist taking on the role of facilitator. He later changed the name to client-centred therapy following his observations that the client still looked to the therapist as a guide, in this respect he believed that the client themselves should seek to identify what was wrong and determine their own conclusion (Boeree, 1998). Rogers identified three specific qualities which the therapist should demonstrate: congruence, empathy and respect.

While Rogers' enduring work was in the field of therapy we will see in the following sections that many of his ideas can be applied to the field of education, particularly when considering the importance of creating the most favourable environments for self-actualisation to develop, which each individual should be aspiring towards.

LINKS WITH OTHER THEORISTS

Rogers was influenced by the work of Otto Rank. Formerly a pupil of Sigmund Freud, Rank disassociated himself from Freud's theory, which focused on a patient's past experience, and developed his own therapeutic process which looked at the present condition. Rogers developed Rank's patient-centred philosophy to establish his own client-centred therapy, although while Rank utilised artistic creativity to support his patients, Rogers developed his work around the therapeutic relationship of authenticity, empathy and unconditional positive regard.

Rogers' work can be linked to that of Abraham Maslow in that they both sought to study the positive side of human nature, looking for the good in people as opposed to trying to put right what was wrong. Like Maslow, Rogers believed that in order to be fully satisfied a person must become self-actualised, or in Rogers' terms – a fully functioning person. Maslow developed his theory around a set of needs to be met built on a hierarchy, in which self-actualisation was positioned at the pinnacle. For self-actualisation to occur all needs on the pyramid must first be met. For Rogers the self-actualising tendency was the key motive of the organism, and is what drives the individual. In his writings Rogers openly admits that the actualising tendency was not unique to his own theoretical viewpoint and notes the work of Maslow in his own reflections (Thorne, 1992).

In looking at Rogers' humanistic view on child development parallels can be seen with his work and that of Karen Horney (DeRobertis, 2006). DeRobertis suggests that both Rogers and Horney made observations about child development through a reconstruction of their patients' childhoods. For both Horney and Rogers the development of self is key to their theories of development, and while they differed in their conceptions of 'self' they both agreed that it was fundamental to the social and emotional development of the child.

When considering Rogers' views on education, parallels emerge with the work of John Dewey, particularly in respect of his focus on experience as a basis for learning. Rogers was influenced by Dewey's progressive view of education, which advocated the importance of a student-centred approach to learning. Rogers and Dewey were both critical of an education system which stifled creativity and prevented the teacher from developing learning experiences which were informed by the pupil, both believing that the child knew what he needed to learn, and would direct his own learning accordingly. This too is in accordance with the work of John Holt and A.S. Neill, who also believed that the formal education system supressed rather than encouraged learning.

CRITIQUING THE THEORY

Rogers' insistence that individuals should seek to find their own answers to their problems has attracted much criticism in recent years (Thorne, 1992). Thorne suggests that at a time when people are looking for swift answers to their problems, Rogers' focus on the person-centred approach has been somewhat usurped in favour of more cost-effective techniques which lead to quicker results. Additionally, it could be argued that it is irresponsible to ask a person to find their own way forward when dealing with some of the more challenging issues related to the human condition, and could reflect a somewhat naïve view of the human psyche.

Despite his own Christian upbringing, and his early religious studies Rogers was heavily criticised by Paul Vitz, a Christian professor of psychology (Vitz, 1977, in Thorne, 1992). Vitz argued that Rogers made no allowances for human nature, seeing only the good, and not the bad, in people. In this respect Rogers' work was out of sync with the Christian ethos, which is based around the philosophy of redemption. Rogers' belief that humans were fundamentally good meant that there was no place for good and evil in the world, this was a significant challenge to the Christian belief.

It is perhaps Rogers' optimistic view of human nature which has attracted the most criticism of his work, particularly since he applied this not just to his client-centred therapy, but also to other aspects of his work, such as education. Rogers had an idealistic view of the education system, which saw him promoting the idea of the teacher acting as facilitator, and the learner initiating their own learning (Rogers, 1951). In this model he believed that self-assessment and self-criticism were the most important forms of feedback, and any external assessment was inconsequential. In such a model Rogers is assuming that the individual has the capacity for such self-assessment, and that a curriculum would be flexible enough for learner-initiated work. In reality this is an ideal which is unlikely to be realised due to curriculum constraints and the measurement of success through formal assessment processes.

APPLYING ROGERS' THEORY TO EDUCATION

As we have already seen Rogers' work was carried out in the field of clinical psychology. However, Rogers himself was a gifted teacher (Smith, 2004), and in his text *Freedom to Learn* (1969), he documented how he applied the role of facilitator, as seen in his client-centred therapy, to his role in the classroom. In *Freedom to Learn* Rogers focused on the attitudes of the teacher, rather than on methods or techniques to be applied (Patterson, 1977). He believed that successful teaching was based on the relationship between student and teacher, stating that 'the facilitation of significant learning rests upon certain attitudinal qualities which exist in the personal relationships between facilitator and learners' (Rogers, 1969: 19).

Rogers raised a number of philosophical, social and psychological questions which he believed education should be responding to, suggesting that education should be seen as a vehicle for preventing potential crises. In this respect, for Rogers, education was not merely about knowledge exchange or cognitive and intellectual development, but focused increasingly on the areas of personal development and interpersonal relationships (Patterson, 1977). In this he was applying his notion of the importance of personal growth and the development of the whole person, or the fully functioning person.

Rogers identified two distinct types of learning: rote learning, typified by facts to be learned and memorised, which he considered to be meaningless; alongside the more beneficial learning which came from the everyday experiences which students had. Rogers believed that the traditional classroom teaching methods, in which the formal curriculum was followed, through methods which required the learner to be a passive recipient of knowledge, lacked any personal meaning to the student, neither responding to feelings nor the whole person – he referred to this as 'being educated from the neck up' (Patterson, 1977: 18). On the other hand, learning which came from a person's first-hand experience, experiential learning, had meaning and personal relevance (Patterson 1977). Such learning, he said, was more easily retained.

Rogers recognised that although the education system promoted the type of learning which fostered the passive learner, he also recognised that, for the most part, teachers would prefer the style of teaching which actively promoted experiential learning. Rather than just theorising this, Rogers made suggestions as to how this type of learning might be realised. Rogers believed that in order for learning to be centred on the experiences of the learner, then the traditional roles of teachers and students needed to be re-evaluated. Using his own teaching experiences as a model he explored the notion of teacher as facilitator, theorising that 'we cannot teach another person directly; we can only facilitate his learning' (Rogers, 1951: 389). He also believed that traditional learning conditions could prove potentially threatening to the individual and suggested that the organism becomes rigid under threat, thereby restricting learning. For Rogers:

> The educational situation which most effectively promotes significant learning is one in which 1) threat to the self of the learner is reduced to minimum, and 2) differentiated perception of the field of experience is facilitated. (1951: 123)

Alongside the teacher facilitating learning, Rogers also expressed the notion that the learner should set their own objectives, believing that this is the most effective way of motivating the learner, and reducing threat. By its very nature, if a student is setting their own agenda then learning will proceed at a pace. Rogers believed that humans had a natural propensity to learn, and where the student can see the value of the subject matter to their own personal growth then learning would be a natural progression. However, we can see here a tension, since if Rogers is suggesting that learning cannot be taught, then this begs the question as to whether there is indeed a role for the teacher. Rogers himself mused. 'it seems to me that anything that can be taught to another is relatively inconsequential and has little or no significant influence on behaviour' (Kirschenbaum and Henderson, 1989: 302), and in his own personal reflections he suggests that even where teaching appears to succeed it leads to the individual distrusting his own experience and stifling significant learning (Patterson, 1977).

Rogers' ideals create a significant challenge for teachers, and these would not be easy to apply in the current education system which relies so heavily on the outcome of tests and assessments. Indeed, Rogers himself identified that the education system should do away with examinations since they measure only inconsequential learning, and likewise grades and credits should be outlawed for the same reason (Rogers, 1951). It is unlikely that such radical measures would ever be considered, particularly given a government agenda which emphasises the importance of more traditional means of measuring success. It is perhaps unthinkable then that teachers might adopt the style of teaching which Rogers advocated.

Nevertheless, we should not discount some of the ideas which Rogers presented regarding the relationship between student and teacher, and there is merit here in respect of the mutual respect which should be formed. Rogers raises the concept of a community of learners, where students share rather than hoard information, and where the development of skills outside of the cognitive domain should be encouraged (Patterson, 1977). In this model cooperation and not competition is encouraged and in this way positive self-concept is developed leading to a positive regard and respect for others. It is hard not to show a commitment to the establishment of such an ethos even within a standards-driven culture.

Rogers believed that teacher education and administration should change, with teacher education encouraging the adoption of facilitation over teaching and administration accepting this as a possibility. In this way the climate for self-directed learning might begin to exist (Patterson, 1977). Collins et al. (2002) suggest that the three basic qualities, which Rogers identified in effective counselling as being key to warm 'person-centred' relationships, could equally be applied to learning. They suggest that the three qualities of acceptance, genuineness and empathy are in common with the reflective teacher who should demonstrate 'an open-mindedness and a whole hearted commitment to the learner' (2002: 21). Teachers should reflect on the powerful discourse between learner and teacher, and should create a learning environment conducive to the development of 'self' even within the constraints of a curriculum-led system.

REFLECTIVE TASK

When I try to teach, as I do sometimes, I am appalled by the results, which seems a little more than inconsequential, because sometimes the teaching appears to succeed. When this happens I find that the results are damaging. It seems to cause the individual to distrust his own experience, and to stifle significant learning. Hence, I have come to feel that outcomes of teaching are either unimportant or hurtful. (Rogers 1961: 276)

Why was Rogers concerned that 'the teaching appears to succeed'? What is this statement saying about the relationship between teacher and learner?

SUMMARY

Thorne (1992) observes that person-centred scholars and therapists no longer have the same standing in the field of academic psychology that they once had, appearing as 'naïve enthusiasts from a former age' (1992: 64). It is then testament to Rogers' work that his writings have endured, and certainly in the world of clinical psychology Rogers' work remains a significant force, with a 1982 survey of American psychologists revealing him to be the most influential figure in twentieth-century psychotherapy (Kirschenbaum and Henderson, 1989: xiii). Thorne (1992) suggests that he has become 'an idealised figure symbolising a "purity" of approach and a hopefulness about both people and therapy' (1992: 64).

For others outside of the arena of clinical psychology Rogers has encouraged a new way of thinking, opening up questions about the relationship between groups of people. Rogers firmly advocated that his core conditions for therapy – congruence, acceptance and empathy – could be applied to other situations where relationships were being formed, such as between student and teacher, and sought to change some of the more traditional roles of individuals. Ultimately, Rogers believed that all human beings were seeking self-actualisation, and therefore it was the role of the practitioner to support them in becoming the fully functioning person they aspired to be.

Rogers had a genuine interest in the human psyche and his life's work was to promote those conditions which allowed for human growth, be that through the counselling he developed, or in his writings on education and health in which he encouraged the development of an increasingly person-centred approach. Rogers increased the popularity of humanistic theory, particularly in the field of psychology, and did much to encourage thinking around the whole person, focusing on goals and aspirations, rather than merely treating symptoms.

 ## FURTHER READING

Cohen, D. (2000) *Carl Rogers: A Critical Biography*. London: Robinson.
A 'warts and all' account of the life and works of Carl Rogers including some of his own challenges set against the background of his work.

Farber, B.A., Brink, D.C. and Raskin, P.M. (1996) *The Psychotherapy of Carl Rogers: Cases and Commentary*. New York: The Guilford Press.
An opportunity to look at some of Rogers' work with complete transcripts of ten cases alongside commentary from other notable psychotherapists.

Kirschenbaum, H. (2007) *The Life and Works of Carl Rogers*. Herefordshire: PCCS Books.
The second edition of Kirschenbaum's biography of Carl Rogers, which includes the period prior to his death, which was one of the most important stages of his career. The book gives a personal and professional account of the life and works of Carl Rogers.

REFERENCES

Boeree, C.G. (1998) *Carl Rogers*. http://webspace.ship.edu/cgboer/Rogers.html.
Collins, J., Harkin, J. and Nind, M. (2002) *Manifesto for Learning*. London: Continuum.
DeRobertis, E.M. (2006) 'Deriving a humanistic theory of child development from the works of Carl R. Rogers and Karen Horney'. *The Humanist Psychologist*, 34(2): 177–99.
Kirschenbaum, H. (1979) *On Becoming Carl Rogers*. New York: Delacorte Press.
Kirschenbaum, H. and Henderson, V.L. (Eds) (1989) *The Carl Rogers Reader*. New York: Houghton Mifflin.
Patterson, C.H. (1977) 'Carl Rogers and humanistic education'. In: *Foundations for a Theory of Instruction and Educational Psychology*. New York: Harper & Row.
Rogers, C.R. (1942) *Counseling and Psychotherapy*. New York: Houghton Mifflin.
Rogers, C. (1951) *Client-Centered Therapy: Its Current Practice, Implications and Theory*. London: Constable.
Rogers, C.R. (1961) *On Becoming a Person: A Therapist's View of Psychotherapy*. New York: Houghton Mifflin.
Rogers, C.R. (1969) *Freedom to Learn: A View of What Education Might Become*. Columbus: Merrill.
Rogers, C.R. (1986) 'Rogers, Kohut and Erikson'. *Person Centred Review*, 1: 125–40.
Smith, M.K. (2004) *Carl Rogers, Core Conditions and Education*. http://infed.org/mobi/carl-rogers-core-conditions-and-education.
Thorne, B. (1992) *Carl Rogers*. London: SAGE.

3

A.S. NEILL

FREEDOM TO LEARN

LEARNING OUTCOMES

Having read this chapter you should be able to:

- Appreciate Neill's background and his contribution to education and child development
- Understand and identify his educational philosophies
- Be aware of the origins of his theories and how his ideas influenced others within education
- Critically evaluate Neill's works and theories
- Recognise how his ideas could be used in practice

KEY WORDS

Summerhill School; free child; self-regulating child; self-government; repression; conscious/unconscious; psychoanalysis

INTRODUCTION

Alexander Sutherland Neill (1883–1973) was arguably the most progressive, and possibly the most controversial, educator of the twentieth century, whose philosophy centred upon democratic free schooling and a child-centred approach to learning and teaching. He was also the founder of 'that dreadful school' Summerhill (Croall, 1983). His philosophy was no doubt a response to his own strict Scottish Calvinist childhood and education. He felt that children should not be exposed to a set of values and morals dictated to them by adults, nor should children be frightened or threatened by the imposition of traditional forms of school discipline. Neill's ideas on education were radical to say the least and have drawn attention from a worldwide audience, including teachers and parents, who have been appalled, elated or enthused by his many writings and talks.

Neill is synonymous with Summerhill School, which he established in 1921; a school which is renowned throughout the world and where Neill's radical philosophy of democratic, child-centred learning was put into practice. Summerhill is still very much a functioning school today and still based upon Neill's ideas. It has received considerable criticism since its inception, especially from some sections of the press who consider it a 'school without rules' and a place of 'all play and no work' (Howlett, 2013: 163). However, Neill endeavoured to create an environment where children could find happiness. He believed they could only find true happiness if they were free from external repression from adults in authority; such repression he felt created unhappiness and hostility. Neill's ideas were influenced by Freud, who argued that since hostility could not be articulated to the adult by the child, the hostility became owned by the child, which then turned into self-loathing and ultimately into anti-social behaviour. A number of children who displayed such anti-social behaviour ended up at Summerhill where they were: 'cured, Neill maintains, by the application for the first time in their lives of freedom' (Hobson, 2001: 2).

It is without doubt that Neill's ideas on education are of great consequence even today but are at the same time controversial. The concept of Summerhill has been imitated throughout the world. Neill's writing spread over a considerable number of years and spanned an era of massive social change where established and traditional methods of learning and teaching were being challenged. The notion of the 'free child' who is essentially wise, who if left by themselves without adult imposition can grow with confidence and happiness, continues to interest parents and teachers alike. His many writings still attract attention. Aspects of Neill's philosophy along with the criticisms it has endured, and the application of his ideas, will be explored later in this chapter.

NEILL, THE PERSON

Neill was born in the town of Forfar, Scotland. His father was a teacher in the nearby village of Kingsmuir at the school where Neill himself was taught. Howlett suggests that it was Neill's unhappy childhood experience at school, where the response to any form of misbehaviour by pupils was the use of corporal punishment without any regard for the emotional welfare of the child, which sowed the seeds of his own educational philosophy (2013). After leaving school he had a number of jobs before he was taken on as an apprentice school teacher in 1899. He eventually achieved matriculation to Edinburgh University studying the arts and graduated in 1905 after reading English literature. Following graduation he taught in government schools in Scotland for twelve years (Hobson, 2001). In 1917 Neill enlisted in the British Army, but he was neither a competent nor an enthusiastic soldier. He found the class divisions within military life abhorrent. He also loathed the requirement for the lower ranks to comply without question to orders from their superiors. This, together with his earlier experience of authority, as a school pupil and as a teacher, had reinforced his aversion to coercion (Croall, 1983).

Following the war, and with a growing dislike of the traditional forms of education, Neill's career direction changed, which enabled him to follow the interests of his embryonic philosophy. Firstly, he taught at King Alfred School in London which was a new experimental establishment, and then in 1921 he became, for a short duration, assistant editor for the radical New Education Fellowship. He then took up a position at a progressive school in Dresden, Germany, where he stayed until 1923 when the school was moved to Vienna, Austria. Neill came back to England in 1924 and set up his own progressive school in Lyme Regis with the aid of Frau Neustatter, a co-worker from the schools in Dresden and Vienna. The new school was Summerhill and Neill became the head teacher. Neill and Frau Neustatter were married in 1927 and in the same year the school's location was moved to Leiston in Suffolk, where it remains today (Hobson, 2001).

From the earliest days at Summerhill Neill began to start putting his notions of pupil freedom into practice by stripping away the trappings of teacher authority. Even though the pupil enrolment was low the school became well-known mainly because of Neill's prolific writing: he wrote some twenty books. Neill's seminal work *Summerhill* (1960), which collates much of his noteworthy ideas and their application, is especially sought after as required reading by undergraduate and postgraduate students in relevant fields such as education, psychology and sociology (Howlett, 2013; MacBlain, 2014). However, because he wrote so many books, and in a style which was often one-dimensional, it is difficult to condense and codify exactly his educational philosophy, as Croall who wrote an influential text on Neill and Summerhill states:

> I found Neill's best books a delight to read. Fresh, humorous, provocative, they were often inspiring in their profound common sense. Yet Neill could also be infuriatingly simple-minded or evocative when tackling certain issues. I had constantly to bear in mind the fact that, though in many respects he was a brilliant publicist for his own ideas, he was also a propagandist, intent on convincing an often puzzled or hostile world of the value and practicality of his revolutionary ideas about children. (1983: 3)

Yet his books continued to sell globally, which not only generated widespread interest in his ideas but also brought many visitors to Summerhill who were keen to imitate his ideas in their own countries. His 1960 work *Summerhill* sold two million copies. Most of his works explored and promoted his revolutionary ideas of child development; however, *Neill! Neill! Orange Peel! A Personal View of Ninety Years* (1973) is also an account of his early influences regarding the notions of self-regulation and self-government. These notions were the cornerstone of Neill's philosophy of a democratic and pupil-centred education, which he considered was of vital importance in providing a happy childhood for those children in his care at Summerhill; a philosophy which, essentially, is present in Summerhill to this day. When Neill died in 1973, the school was run by his second wife Ena until her retirement in 1985. Their daughter Zoë then took over the reins, which at the time of writing, is still the situation. Neill's philosophy is both inspirational and controversial in its extremes yet it has certainly stood the test of time.

NEILL'S PHILOSOPHY

Neill's philosophy has had little impact on educational policy or much bearing upon initial teacher education practices because his ideas were considered to be too rebellious (Croall, 1983). However, Neill's thoughts about education drew an immense degree of interest from educators and parents who were interested in his revolutionary democratic approach to child development. In his 1960 work *Summerhill: A Radical Approach to Child Rearing*, Neill set out the principles of his philosophy, which can be summarised as:

- A faith in the goodness of the child.
- The aim of education is to work joyfully and to find happiness.
- Education is about both intellectual and emotional development.
- Education needs to match the psychic needs of the individual child.
- Discipline and punishment is harmful to child development.
- Freedom does not mean licence – respect needs to be a two-way process.
- Learning and development needs to be free from guilt.

These aspects will be interwoven in this section, which will cover aspects of Neill's principles and philosophies such as freedom and repression, guilt, sex, religion, democracy and the curriculum.

Firstly, it should be acknowledged that the basis for Neill's ideas of child development and education emanated from Freud and psychoanalysis. Freud considered that children's inhibitions, anxieties and problems originate from sexual repression and the resultant feelings of guilt. He also argued that the *unconscious* is more crucial to child development than the *conscious* – children are more likely to be happier if they are free to act on their own instincts rather than be subject to the censures and punishments imposed by adults (MacBlain, 2014). For Neill an important aspect of Freud's thinking was the notion of freedom in their development and their education: the free child and the free school. For children to be truly happy they needed to feel they had negligible repression, only then could they feel free. At Summerhill, he endeavoured to create an all-round education which provided such freedom; unlike a conventional school which 'makes the mistake of exalting the intellect over the emotions with the result that children may know a lot of facts but lack inner contentment and fulfilment' (Hobson, 2001: 2).

Neill strongly contended that freedom was related to his belief in the inherent goodness of children; that 'a child is innately wise and realistic' (Neill, 1960: 20). He could not countenance the idea of original sin where a child is born with in-born wickedness. However, 'if left to himself without adult suggestion of any kind, he will develop as far as he is capable of doing' (Hobson, 2001: 2). He also stressed how important it was that children experience freedom at an early age, and how freedom is linked to love from the parents: 'No amount of freedom at school can completely counteract the influence of a bad home. Character acquired in the first months or years of life can be modified by freedom, but it can never be completely changed' (Neill, 1953: 36). Furthermore, he argues that 'there is only one truth about children, that if they are loved and free they become good and honest' (Neill, 1953: 86–7). On the other hand and by way of caution: 'by continually correcting children we must make them feel inferior; we injure their natural dignity' (Neill, 1953: 107). Neill's opinion on the effect of free schools reflects not only his philosophy but also the aim of Summerhill:

> If all schools were free and all lessons were optional, I fancy that children would find their own level, and indifferent scholars who, under discipline, scrape through college or university and become unimaginative teachers and doctors and lawyers. (Neill, 1953: 34)

Freedom for Neill gave children courage and tolerance and enabled them to meet difficult challenges with confidence. Freedom also helped create the self-regulated child, where the child's conduct is governed by the child themselves and not from adult imposition. Conversely, a 'moulded child has no self; he is only a replica of his parents' (Neill, 1967: 9). There is a danger, recognised by Neill that outright freedom of action could lead to a chaotic and unjust environment; freedom then at Summerhill 'means doing what you like so long as you do not interfere with the freedom of others' (Neill, 1967: 19). He thought there was a fine dividing line between freedom and licence, which was balanced by the practice of mutual respect between teachers and pupils. Neill's view of freedom originated from the appreciation that a child was adept at self-regulation. Repression by adults, Neill felt, hindered and indeed harmed, the natural development of children.

Unfree children, Neill contested, were greatly hampered by guilt which he thought served the manifestations of authority. Guilt, he argued, was an obstruction to independent thought and actions as well as creativity. Feelings of guilt 'start a cycle which oscillates constantly between rebellion, repentance, submission, and new rebellion' (Neill, 1960: xiii). Guilt is related to conscience and the fear that non-compliance with the conventional moral standards will result in punishment. Punishment for a child, especially at the time of Neill's writings could be in the form of physical harm such as beatings, or emotional harm such as the withholding of love from a parent or being ignored. Neill had a great deal of experience in what he called 'curing' children who had been damaged by adults who induced guilt and fear into their young lives. He considered that only hate could thrive in an environment of guilt and the fear of punishment.

Sex and indeed religion played a major part in contributing to a child's fear and sense of guilt, here Neill emphasises his thoughts:

> To a frightened child sex *is* everything! Yes, the child uses sex as the chief peg on which to hang his fears. For he has been told that sex is wicked. The child with night terrors is often the child who is afraid of his sex thoughts. The devil may come and take him to hell, for is he not a sinful boy who deserves punishment? The bogeyman, the ghost, the goblin are only the devil in disguise. Fear comes from a guilty conscience. It is the ignorance of the parents that gives the child his guilty conscience. (Neill, 1960: 121–2)

Neill also found that many of the more difficult and challenging children he had worked with had, like himself, undergone a strict religious upbringing. It was, he felt, this strict background and the moralistic teachings of religion which gave sex an inflated status that increased the guilt and fear in children, and he considered that this was because many religions acknowledged the notion of original sin. Although Summerhill did not have religious education as part of the curriculum, Neill thought Jesus would have favoured the manner in which children were treated: 'In Summerhill, we give children love and approval' (Neill, 1960: 373).

Neill's philosophy of democracy and freedom was applied in Summerhill, which was, and still is, a self-governing school, democratic in structure and organisation. All matters associated with communal and social life, including the awarding of punishments for social wrongdoings, being decided by vote at the weekly school meeting. Teachers and pupils had one vote each, including Neill, and the majority of votes carried the day. It created a democracy where children and their opinions were listened to, prized and valued (Howlett, 2013). When it came to dealing with a wrongdoer at these weekly meetings, Neill thought children were more judicious and astute than adults in comparable circumstances (Croall, 1983).

Democracy in the form of pupil choice played a large, and controversial, part in Neill's philosophy and is linked very closely to the curriculum at Summerhill. There was no compulsion for children to attend lessons, some newly arrived pupils at Summerhill spent weeks and even months playing before attending lessons, and even then only those which they wanted to. As we have seen, Neill felt that children were capable of developing, both intellectually and emotionally, without guidance from adults. He argued that children would eventually find out what interests them without imposition and they were the best judge, a notion based on the idea that children are born inherently good.

The usual academic subjects were on offer at Summerhill but were not unduly promoted. Instead great emphasis was placed on aesthetic subjects which promoted creativity such as art, craft, drama and dance. Neill thought that these subjects helped foster children's emotional welfare; they also offered an opportunity for non-academic pupils to shine (Hobson, 2001). Play, especially outside and undirected by adults, was also encouraged. Neill considered play vital for children's all-round development, where they could live out their fantasies. However, Neill had certain misgivings about team sports. His main worry was that those who were particularly gifted in sport would be considered heroes:

> I take it that the underlying motive for encouraging team games is the wish to cultivate team spirit... In Summerhill the team spirit arises out of a self-government in community living. Hence no child is ever a hero or heroine with us. Games prowess means nothing and brilliance in lessons also means nothing. Free children do not worship. (Neill, 1967: 31)

The growing concern over exam results and the inclination to label children as academic or not from an early age were an anathema to Neill. Following his death the introduction of the National Curriculum (in England and Wales) in the 1980s meant that schools were disinclined to follow Summerhill's progressive approach to the curriculum, particularly with the increased authority given to the school inspection organisation Ofsted. However, Summerhill's successful legal rebuff following a damning Ofsted report in 1999 does offer some hope for Neill's philosophy being carried forward well into the future (Brighouse, 2006).

LINKS WITH OTHER THEORISTS

Most of those educational thinkers associated with Neill, as can be imagined, have progressive philosophies regarding child development. It should be recognised that Neill came from a background in psychology and psychoanalysis, and he strongly believed that child psychology should be at the core of educational thinking (Neill, 1973). As we have already seen Neill was influenced by Freud and in how he 'linked education to an unconscious problem of learning for love' (Britzman, 2011: 20–1). Neill's belief that there was no such thing as original sin was also shaped by Rousseau's naturalism. But whereas Rousseau was concerned with the mind, Neill was concerned with both the mind and body. There are strong connections with early educational thinkers such as Steiner who stressed the importance of play without adult intervention, as well as Froebel who encouraged notions of children exploring and learning through nature.

Neill approved of some of Montessori's notions, specifically that children should be free to play without the imposition of adults. Though other ideas he considered to be abhorrent. He thought she lacked emotion and that her methods were too scientific and controlling. Furthermore, Neill was very uneasy with Montessori's religious principles, which underpinned much of her work (Croall, 1983). Pestalozzi also has some very close links to Neill's view of a free education. He contested that children should be encouraged to pursue their own particular interests and make their own discoveries; and emphasised the role nature played in these discoveries. For Pestalozzi, and Neill, allowing children such freedom was important in their development and progress into the adult world. Moreover, Pestalozzi also felt education placed too much emphasis on intellectual matters and paid too little attention to practical and emotional issues (Howlett, 2013). John Dewey's philosophy is similarly linked with Neill's ideas. Dewey's Laboratory School in Chicago explored the best conditions for childhood development and he emphasised that children should be encouraged to foster skills and activities centred on their own interests instead of being directed by teachers (Croall, 1983).

Neill's ideas on self-regulation and self-governance were influenced by Wilhelm Reich and Homer Lane. Indeed it was a visit to Homer Lane's Little Commonwealth School for young offenders, in Dorset, which inspired Neill's work at Summerhill. At Homer Lane's school he found that once quite hardened youngsters were given freedom in a community of self-government, where the adults were on the side of the children, many steadily progressed into balanced and respected citizens (Neill, 1960). In his influential 1969 book *How Children Fail*, John Holt noted that schools could be places of fear and negate any inherent aspiration to learn, and like Neill he criticised overt motivation such as awards and hero worship because it might underline a child's fear of failure (Williams, 2004). Carl Rogers, an American psychologist and advocate for humanistic methods in education, who we discussed in Chapter 2, also argued that children intuitively knew what they wanted, and suggested teachers should facilitate these desires. Many progressive teachers and thinkers have endeavoured to follow Neill's philosophy, although his ideas have also attracted considerable criticism.

CRITIQUING THE THEORY

Neill's philosophy, and undeniably his practice, at Summerhill have invited both praise and criticism, which have been poles apart in their nature. Much of the condemnation Neill received came from exaggerated responses from the conservative press because of their perception of Summerhill as 'all play and no work', and as such may, to some extent, be discarded. Nevertheless, there are a number of aspects of Neill's work which do appear susceptible to censure, particularly as he pushed the limits of even the most progressive educational thinkers, who themselves had attracted criticism for their pupil-centred views (Hobson, 2001; Howlett, 2013). Specific aspects of Neill's work can be questioned, such as: Do children actually know what is best for them socially and educationally? Should education be centred on practical rather than intellectual matters? Will children be able to use their given freedom without a fundamental intellectual background when making significant decisions about their future? (Hobson, 2001).

Arguably the most fundamental criticism could be that his educational thinking was not underpinned by any methodical or logical philosophy, or significant concept of knowledge. Neill's thinking mainly originated from his 'experiences and observations, supplemented with some study of psychological (especially psychoanalytic) theory' (Hobson, 2001: 3). Although, it could be said experience is a significant factor in forming an educational philosophy, the lack of a substantial theoretical base does weaken its credibility. This paucity of theory is evident in his very readable books, which focus on the practicalities of child development and include many unsubstantiated and embellished claims. At times he is apt to generalise and simply state aspects of his thinking rather than explore in-depth the philosophical rationale of his declarations. This is particularly the case in relation to the difference between *freedom* and *licence*, which are complex and important issues that have significant impact for the application of his ideas (Hobson, 2001).

Another area for criticism is whether children when unrestrained from the guidance of adults and the norms of civilisation would choose violence and spitefulness. It is interesting to note that Neill acknowledged that a number of children who arrived at Summerhill presented such behaviour, but this behaviour he contested was caused by the discipline imposed upon them by their parents or their earlier experience of education. According to Neill 'savagery and barbarism in humanity was caused by an abundance of civilization and not seemingly by its lack!' (Howlett, 2013: 174). It is perhaps that Neill's view of civilisation and indeed education has become outdated. During Neill's early career, industry, mainly heavy industry, was at the forefront of the economy and the vast majority of the population worked and earned a wage and some self-respect but not much more. Recently, there have been vast changes in technology and a growth in the creative industries, which offer greater opportunities and these have in turn altered the way in which education is preparing young people for the world of work and life. More is known about how the brain develops, which has helped to improve methods of learning and teaching and enhanced the life chances for all children regardless of background (Brighouse, 2006). Equally, Neill's views on religious and moral education could also appear old-fashioned; today such subjects are introduced through debate, and with consideration for cultural differences (Hobson, 2001).

APPLYING NEILL'S IDEAS IN PRACTICE

In spite of the numerous and substantial criticisms of Neill's philosophy there are a number of his philosophies which can, even in today's highly regulated classrooms, be applied in practice. It may appear that the approaches used at Summerhill would

have very little place in schools. This is particularly the case perhaps when Neill himself states: 'I am criticised because I do nothing to help teachers practically... I am not
interested in organisation or exams or methods of teaching' (1973: 162). Yet his underpinning beliefs and philosophies of tolerance, his understanding and genuine love of
children have, and continue, to enlighten the practice of many teachers in both the
private and state sectors (Brighouse, 2006). In accordance with Neill's philosophy this
section will explore features such as respect, pupil voice, creativity and teaching
approaches which could be employed in practice.

A major aspect for Neill was the notion of respect for children. Whether teachers
realise that they are directly implementing Neill's core concepts or not, respect for a
child's individual distinctiveness is greater today than in the more didactic and sub-
missive classroom of the past. Teachers endeavour to discover as much as possible
about the children they are responsible for, and take into account and value the ever-
changing differences in 'culture and racial identities of their mobile multilingual,
multi-faith, increasingly inclusive pupil population arriving from all parts of the
world' (Brighouse, 2006: 3). For Neill, respect not only involved getting to know the
child but doing so without judgement and without attempting to shape the child
(Neill, 1973). A core feature of respect is that of listening to children's interests and
concerns. Currently, pupil voice is highly valued in forms such as school councils and
many schools utilise pupils to evaluate lessons and even to voice their opinion on
the employment of new members of staff. Views are also sought from children by
the use of anonymous questionnaires to evaluate areas of concern about school life
and to gather ideas for areas of possible school improvements. Some schools involve
children in making judgements about accusations of bullying. All these practices are
akin to Neill's notion of self-governance (Brighouse, 2006).

Even though Neill would have scoffed at employing formal learning and teaching
activities, there are a number of suggestions, now acclaimed as pupil-centred practice,
which would have been close to Neill's thinking. Although these practices are now
commonplace, they are worth reinforcing here if only to propose that perhaps Neill's
ideas were far ahead of his time. Listening and displaying enthusiasm for children's
ideas, even if they seem offbeat, builds trust and lessens the fear of derision. By adopting a conversational and informal style when replying to children's questions adults
help create a much safer setting. Also, allowing children plenty of time to give
responses to questions reduces their anxieties. Underpinning all these points, and
aligned with Neill's thinking, is the need for adults to get to know the individual children by discovering the things they think are important and which interest them; and
use these interests to plan and inform learning activities (Williams, 2004).

Key to the learning experience at Summerhill was the focus on creativity. This
was underpinned by Neill's thinking that the more children develop creative and
contrary approaches to learning the more they will disregard negative thoughts of
failure so often associated with the more traditional subject-based teaching and
learning. As Gilbert argues, we should not only use 'creative-strategies, we need to

encourage them to have the sort of levels of hope that will keep them optimistic in the face of apparent failure' (2002: 166). Providing occasions for creative thinking gives children the confidence to respond to questions without fear of censure and gives everybody an opportunity to achieve. This includes planning time in lessons for pupil responses and to use these to inform lessons and the use of open-ended questions to stimulate discussion and debate (Neill, 1973). Neill was fond of drama to encourage creativity: at Summerhill a form of dramatic art called spontaneous acting was very popular with most pupils. He felt that the performing of already written plays lacked the opportunity for creativity and was merely imitation, whereas performing plays written and produced by the children fostered resourcefulness and imagination. Imagination and creation were also encouraged through dance – 'the joy of dancing is the joy of invention. When invention is left out, dancing becomes mechanical and dull' (Neill, 1960: 74).

Play involving the visual arts, and practical creative activities allow children the freedom to explore aspects of personal interests and also experience success. Furthermore, symbolic play where children take on the role of adults (according to Neill children at Summerhill enjoyed playing gangsters), gives children opportunities to explore their own feelings and experiment with language. It also supports socialisation, cooperative learning and imagination (Cohen et al., 2004). It is also possible to enthuse children's imagination within their written work; for example, here is one of Neill's methods of doing this: 'I once said to a class. This is the first line of an essay or story … "Bloody hell' cried the bishop," Carry on' (Neill, 1967: 65). Although it is suggested you do not actually use this particular example, for obvious reasons, the essence of Neill's strategy does offer a way of stimulating children's imagination in their written work.

Similar to much of the learning in schools today, learning at Summerhill was activity-based. According to Kyriacou: 'active learning refers to any activities where pupils are given a marked degree of autonomy and control over the organisation, conduct and direction of the learning activity' (1991: 42). Neill probably would have preferred total autonomy for the children; however, it is unrealistic to advocate such freedom in schools with such constraints as the national curriculum and the pressures of examinations. Nevertheless, active learning, which often includes problem solving and research, could be either an individual or a collaborative project. The advantages of active learning approaches are that they are enjoyable, less stressful than teacher-led approaches, and the collaborative projects foster imaginative outcomes (Kyriacou, 1991).

The fundamental aspects of Neill's ideas, where children opt out of attending lessons and make decisions about what subjects are taught, will probably never be on the agenda for other schools, especially state schools. Yet there is now an acknowledgement of the needs of the whole child, and not just the intellectual child. Schools are increasingly providing support for children's emotional and physical needs in the form of pre- and after-school clubs (Brighouse, 2006: 3). Children's intellectual interests are also now taken into account through personalised learning and intervention group work and differentiated practice, although Neill would probably not have been totally in favour of such impositions.

> **REFLECTIVE TASK**
>
> One of Neill's key principles was that education should match the cognitive needs and interests of the individual child (Neill, 1960). List the practices which are in place in your setting, classroom or in placement settings to ensure this is achieved. Then list any other practices that could be adopted to enhance matching children's needs and interests even further.

SUMMARY

There is little doubt that Neill has had a major impact on the thinking behind child development and education. His ideas on the free and self-regulating child have drawn extremes of both criticism and praise. Although not many would align with Neill's notions on total child freedom, present-day thinking on learning and child development is underpinned by a greater wish for honesty and inclusion than in the past. Perhaps his greatest influence was not his prolific writing on education 'but the unconditional love of children which he both exemplified and demanded' (Howlett, 2013: 175).

Neill will always be linked with Summerhill, a school which is still going strong over forty years after his death. Summerhill still follows his philosophy and attracts pupils from all over the world. For Neill it was the environment of Summerhill which made an impact on the children rather than him as an individual. However, former pupils and colleagues who worked with him felt it was Neill's 'humanity and understanding that produced the results' (Croall, 1983: 407). It is fitting to close this chapter with a quote from Neill's 1960 *Summerhill* which encapsulates his philosophy:

> If Summerhill has any message at all it is: Thou shalt not opt out. Fight world sickness, not with drugs like moral teachings and punishments but with natural means – approval, tenderness, tolerance … love. (Neill, 1960: 13)

 ## FURTHER READING

Hemmings, R. (1972) *Fifty Years of Freedom: A Study of the Development of the Ideas of A.S. Neill.* London: Allen & Unwin.
This book traces the development of Summerhill and Neill's ideas aligned to the political and social context of the period as well as making connections with other progressive thinkers.

Neill, A.S. (1966) *Freedom Not License!* New York: Hart.
Neill's offer of advice on child rearing to American parents.

Stronach, I. (2006) 'Inspection and justice: HMI and Summerhill School'. In: Vaughan, M. (Ed.) *Summerhill and A.S. Neill*. Maidenhead: Open University Press.
Stronach outlines the story of the famous Ofsted inspection of Summerhill and the following legal battle with the Department for Education and Employment.

REFERENCES

Brighouse, T. (2006) Introduction. In: Vaughan, M. (Ed.) *Summerhill and A.S. Neill*. Maidenhead: Open University Press.
Britzman, D. (2011) *Freud and Education*. London: Routledge.
Cohen, L., Manion, L. and Morrison, K. (2004) *A Guide to Teaching Practice* (fifth edition). London: RoutledgeFalmer.
Croall, J. (1983) *Neill of Summerhill: The Permanent Rebel*. London: Routledge and Kegan Paul.
Gilbert, I. (2002) *Essential Motivation in the Classroom*. London: RoutledgeFalmer.
Hobson, P. (2001) 'A.S. Neill, 1883–1973'. In: Palmer, J. (Ed.) *Fifty Modern Thinkers on Education: From Piaget to the Present*. London: Routledge.
Holt, J. (1969) *How Children Fail*. Harmondsworth: Penguin.
Howlett, J. (2013) *Progressive Education: A Critical Introduction*. London: Bloomsbury.
Kyriacou, C. (1991) *Essential Teaching Skills*. Oxford: Blackwell.
MacBlain, S. (2014) *How Children Learn*. London: SAGE.
Neill, A.S. (1953) *The Free Child*. London: Herbert Jenkins.
Neill, A.S. (1960) *Summerhill: A Radical Approach to Child Rearing*. New York: Hart.
Neill, A.S. (1967) *Talking of Summerhill*. London: Gollancz.
Neill, A.S. (1973) *Neill! Neill! Orange Peel! A Personal View of Ninety Years*. London: Weidenfeld & Nicholson.
Williams, J. (2004) *Great Minds: Education's Most Influential Philosophers*. London: A *Times Education Supplement* Essential Guide.

4

JOHN GOODLAD

THE RENEWAL OF TEACHING AND LEARNING, SCHOOLS AND TEACHER EDUCATION

LEARNING OUTCOMES

Having read this chapter you should be able to:

- Appreciate the life and ideas of John Goodlad
- Identify and understand Goodlad's thoughts on non-grading, curriculum inquiry, schooling, teacher education and educational renewal
- Critically evaluate Goodlad's ideas
- Appreciate the links between his work and other educational thinkers
- Appraise how Goodlad's concepts are related to education and practice

KEY WORDS

Non-grading; curriculum inquiry; schooling; teacher education; educational renewal (not reform); morals, ethics and democracy in education

INTRODUCTION

John Goodlad, the North American leading progressive educational thinker, scholar and researcher died in 2014 aged ninety-four. For more than sixty years his work had an important influence on schooling, education and teacher education, particularly in the United States (Soder, 2014). He was a tireless campaigner for a more humanistic approach to education. The focuses of his work in education were many but he had a profound impact on the discourse surrounding the role and function of schools. Goodlad's overarching aspiration was that schools facilitate children to become free and full contributors in a democratic world by encouraging them to embrace learning and appreciate their civic responsibilities (Goodlad, 2004). This humanistic ideal was not only central to his work but also underpins his optimism and sense of fair play in the education process. Ethics and morals are core aspects of the teaching process. For Goodlad, 'teaching the young has a moral dimension … because education – a deliberate effort to develop values and sensibilities as well as skills – is a moral endeavour' (Goodlad et al., 1990: xii).

Goodlad's empirical research and writings can be identified as falling into the following major individual themes: non-grading, curriculum inquiry, schooling, teacher education and educational renewal (rather than reform). These themes evolved over the span of his long career and are very much interconnected. Shen, writing in 2001, clearly asserts the breadth and depth of Goodlad's work:

> As an educator, Goodlad is unique in the sense that he is a researcher, an activist and a philosopher. He conducts empirical studies on schooling and education, engages in putting his innovative ideas into practice, and reflects philosophically upon the social phenomenon called 'education'. The combination of being an empirical researcher, a philosophical thinker and an activist of educational renewal is uncommon in education. (Shen, 2001: 123)

Goodlad wrote numerous books many of which have been translated into other languages such as Japanese, Italian, French, Chinese, Hebrew and Spanish. His most seminal work *A Place Called School: Prospects for the Future* (1984) was a landmark text which explored the effectiveness of public schooling in the United States. The data for the book were collected from 27,000 teachers, parents and pupils in schools across the United States. The book was given the Outstanding Book of the Year Award from the American Educational Research Association and the Distinguished Book of the Year Award from Kappa Delta Pi (Harmon, 2014). His other major works include: *The Dynamics of Educational Change: Toward Responsive Schools* (1975), *What Schools Are For* (1979), *Teachers for Our Nation's Schools* (1990), *Educational Renewal: Better Teachers, Better Schools* (1994), *In Praise of Education* (1997), *Romances with Schools: A Life in Education* (2004), and with his associates *Curriculum*

Inquiry: The Study of Curriculum Practice (1979). To appreciate fully Goodlad's works, we need to have an insight into his background, and an overview of his long career as a teacher and academic.

GOODLAD, THE PERSON

John Goodlad grew up in Vancouver, British Columbia, Canada during the time of the Great Depression. At school, in spite of his advanced reading ability, his parents were advised that he should repeat a year. His father, however, insisted that he progressed to the next level without hindrance, which he did and he even skipped forward a year later on in his schooling. The Great Depression and the requirement that pupils should repeat levels in their schooling were two factors which would have a lasting effect on his career. His first teaching post was in a rural one-room, multi-graded school – Woodward's Hill School in a rural setting in British Columbia. He quickly became exasperated by the set curriculum and inflexible grading processes. He began to adopt pioneering teaching methods using inventive resources. He did this to help engage pupils so that they could enjoy the learning process, because many of his pupils had to repeat grades as they failed the required tests for promotion to the next grade (Goodlad, 2004; Amrein-Beardsley, 2012).

His second teaching post was at the British Columbia Industrial School for ('delinquent') Boys – a 'reform' school. The word reform, as we shall see, features significantly in Goodlad's works. The school was near the town of Port Coquitlam and was known, for succinctness, as 'BISCOQ – pronounced *bisco* … a fortresslike prison' (Goodlad, 2004: 156). His experience at his multi-graded first school stood him in good stead for BISCOQ. Many of his charges had already repeated a minimum of two grades and he could not be certain of the students' actual grade classifications. This notion of students not being promoted from one grade to another, and having to repeat grades, he found a fruitless and personally damaging process. At BISCOQ he found this led to an 'ethos of defeat' for the boys and many of the staff (Goodlad, 2004: 178). His experiences at BISCOQ stimulated the focus for his PhD thesis: a study of the effects of promotion and non-promotion.

Goodlad's education leading to, and including, his masters degree was completed in Canada. He attained his doctorate at the University of Chicago in 1949, from there he held a number of academic and leadership roles in higher education. He was a professor at Emory University, the University of Chicago, the University of California at Los Angeles (UCLA) and the University of Washington. The many leadership positions which he held include: the Director of the University Elementary School (UES) and the Dean of the Graduate School of Education, both at UCLA; the Director of the Centre for Teacher Education at the University of Chicago; the Director of the Centre for Educational Renewal at the University of Washington; and the President of the

Institute for Educational Inquiry in Seattle. He was also the President of both the American Educational Research Association, and the American Association of Colleges for Teacher Education (Shen, 2001; Soder, 2014).

GOODLAD'S IDEAS

Goodlad's thoughts on non-grading, curriculum inquiry, schooling, teacher education, and his overriding quest for educational renewal will be explored at this point. Also considered here will be his mission to create a moral, ethical and democratic form of education. Non-grading is an aspect of Goodlad's work which interested him professionally since his first teaching days at Woodward's Hill School and BISCOQ; this interest was to be maintained throughout his career as a researcher. For Goodlad, the grading process was harmful, both academically and morally:

> If kids don't pass some arbitrary standard of what a grade means, you punish them twice. They've already experienced failure, an enormously debilitating experience, and then you tell them they have to do it all over again. (Goodlad, in Goldberg, 2000: 83)

Goodlad was an avid campaigner for non-graded elementary schools. He was also instrumental in setting up, and leading, UCLA's University Elementary School, which practised the principle of non-grading. His research from his PhD and postdoctoral work enabled him to build a convincing argument for championing non-grading for moral, psychological, economic and pedagogical reasons (Shen, 2001).

His involvement in curriculum inquiry was far-reaching, with the ultimate aim of improving students' lives so they could discover their own meanings of the world.

Curriculum inquiry, for Goodlad, was the study of all the facets of curriculum practice, such as 'context, assumptions, conduct, problems, and outcomes' (Goodlad and associates, 1979: 17). His notion of curriculum inquiry involved three aspects:

> The first is *substantive* and has to do with goals, subject matter, materials, and the like – the commonplaces of any curriculum. Inquiry into their nature and worth. The second is *political-social*. Inquiry involves the study of all those human processes through which some interests come to prevail over others... The third is *technical-professional*. Curriculum inquiry examines those processes ... through which curricula are improved, installed, or replaced. (Goodlad and associates, 1979: 17)

Goodlad, then, argued that the curriculum was a complex and multi-faceted entity which merited in-depth inquiry for it to be developed. He was frustrated by those who thought that curricula could be built by authors of curriculum textbooks or even by teachers in their schools. For Goodlad, the curriculum was a living thing; it could not be built as it already exists (Goodlad, 1984). He contended that the curriculum was constantly changing in all schools. The reasons for these changes were many and include: students continually reconstructing how they saw themselves; students differing from one year to the next; and the evolution of technology and its uses in schools. These changes are usually small, but for Goodlad they merit inquiry so that teachers can be informed in their pursuit of improving the students' learning experience (Stake, 1987).

Goodlad was dismayed by the notion that schools should concentrate explicitly on the influence that teachers have on pupil learning. He thought schooling should also embrace and interact with families and the community to enhance the learning experience (Amrein-Beardsley, 2012). Schools, for Goodlad, should be extending their role, to include less restricted hours of opening, and encouraging all age groups in the community to be involved so 'the school becomes the centre for community education, recreation, and education-related human services' (Goodlad, 1984: 350). He also argued that when schooling is seen as contributory to the economy, 'the scope of education provided will continue to narrow, to the detriment of childhood' (Goodlad, 2000: 89). In a similar vein he felt that schooling should not be solely focused on preparing children for employment. He contested that a young person with a broad and grounded education would be readily equipped to assimilate the skills of a particular work role when needed (Goodlad, 2000).

His research into schooling was extensive and included aspects of the classroom environment, the history of schools and early years schooling. He also addressed the questions of the aims, functions and goals of schools. In particular, the goals of schools are quite interesting in that they encapsulate Goodlad's personal philosophy of the purpose of schooling. His idea was that the goals of schools form four separate, yet interwoven, categories; these are:

1. *academic*, embracing all intellectual skills and domains of knowledge;
2. *vocational*, geared to developing readiness for productive work and economic responsibility;
3. *social and civic*, relating to preparing for socialisation into complex society; and
4. *personal*, emphasising the development of individual responsibility, talents and free expression.

(Shen, 2001: 124)

Another major theme of Goodlad's work was teacher education. He railed against the 'increasing technification of teacher education' and called for the inclusion of the 'moral dimensions of teaching and moral mission of schooling' (Shen, 2001: 125). Goodlad thought that teacher education focused too much on matters of

psychological considerations which emphasise such things as human development and teaching methods at the expense of the sociological and cultural phenomena as well as the functioning of the school. (Wideen, 1987: 8)

Teacher education departments in universities should also be closely linked with schools, a model similar to that practised at UES. His thoughts, and those of his associates, on teacher education are explored in *Places Where Teachers Are Taught* (1990) (Shen, 2001).

Educational renewal is central to Goodlad's thinking, and the focus of his research, on schools and teacher education. He stressed the need for the school to be at the heart of renewal and the head teacher the lead in such renewal. Goodlad contested that

> for renewal to occur, there must be some combination of internal responsiveness and external stimulation; for renewal to continue, there must be some continual, productive state of tension between these two essential sets of forces. (Shen, 2001: 125)

He uses the term renewal rather than educational 'reform'. For Goodlad, the term reform is a disgrace as he felt it reflected all that was wrong with the American system of public schooling, as it was 'a linear model of inputs and outputs, prescribed by well-meaning outsiders, whose initiatives show just how out of touch they are' (Coffield and Williamson, 2012: 70).

He became exasperated with those who readily used the term reform. He recalled his days at BISCOQ, which was also known as a reform school, where the perceptions from the public and many of the staff were that the boys were bad. It was also assumed that the staff at BISCOQ would do something with these boys to make them law-abiding citizens, that they would comply with the staff's directions; but this seldom happened. Indeed many pupils filled cells in the adult prison system after leaving BISCOQ. He argued that this was a shocking model to use for schools and education generally (Goodlad, 1999, 2004). Furthermore, he considered that reform is 'a nasty concept that suggests bad people and bad conditions that must be reformed in somebody else's image' (Goodlad, 2000: 83).

Goodlad thought such reforms were driven by political and market forces and did not provide a genuine learning experience for all children. He called for a Bill of Educational Rights and an Educational Constitution which would ensure a process of educational renewal. Goodlad contested that these two measures would assure that the children receive the education that they deserve. It would also ensure that education would embrace the 'freedoms, responsibilities, and justice embedded in its democratic principles' (Goodlad, 2004: 330). Conversely, he argued that the current system of schooling was more fitting 'to the packaging, distribution and standardisation of milk products than the development of thoughtful, responsible, caring members of a social and political democracy' (Goodlad, 2004: 280).

Goodlad stressed that questions regarding public schooling were indeed moral questions, and that teaching was a moral ethical undertaking. He stated that teaching practice is itself an ethical and difficult function. Good teaching should encompass these complex moral and ethical issues rather than the evidence from test results, performativity and technical indicators (Goodlad et al., 1990). These issues in teaching involve matters of caring for pupils and the community, a regard for social justice, a high level of competence in teachers' subject knowledge, and the engagement in collegiate inquiry. Goodlad and his contemporaries felt strongly that teachers need these attributes to enable them to act ethically:

> A non-intellectual and/or non-reflective classroom environment is hardly conducive to a thoughtful engagement with information and knowledge beyond rote learning. Teachers who lack competence in their disciplines and/or who teach outside their areas of competence, as well as those who conspire in such practices disgrace the very concept of pedagogy and are engaged in clearly unethical activities. (Sirotnik, 1990: 311)

The democratic, moral and ethical aspects of Goodlad's ideas, together with his thoughts on non-grading, curriculum inquiry, schooling, teacher education and educational renewal have close associations with a number of other educational thinkers.

LINKS WITH OTHER THEORISTS

As Goodlad's work is so far-ranging it would be feasible to make connections between his ideas and numerous other educational thinkers. Primarily though it is with other North American progressive educators, particularly those with a strong sense of social justice, where the closest links can be made. There is clear evidence of John Dewey's work in the notions developed by Goodlad in a number of ways. Both thought that education should be about developing children to become caring human beings in the broadest sense (Goodlad, 1984). Also, education should not be focused and driven solely for economic reasons, rather it requires a broader more social and critical aim, which

> enables people to think for themselves and debate with others, to respect them and to engage with political life of their societies and not merely their own local communities, is a necessary requirement of a healthy democracy. (Coffield and Williamson, 2012: 22)

There is also a close association with the manner in which both Dewey and Goodlad put into practice their thoughts and philosophies. Dewey's Laboratory School at the University of Chicago for observing children and developing teaching and learning methods served as a centre for exemplary practice. This is similar to the role and function of UES, which was started and led by Goodlad at UCLA (Goodlad, 1984). Furthermore, UES has since been renamed UCLA Lab School (Harmon, 2014). Similarly, there are ties between Goodlad and a number of other North American progressive educational thinkers most notably Nel Noddings, Michael Apple and Linda Darling-Hammond.

Noddings was also drawn to the aspects of curriculum inquiry and the adverse effects of political imposition on schooling. However, it was her commitment to encouraging teachers to adopt an ethical and caring approach to their teaching which was most in tune with Goodlad's ideas. Noddings argued that 'caring is a moral attitude' and urged teachers to embrace this approach in their practice (Flinders, 2001: 214). Resembling Goodlad's notion of educational renewal and the imposition of education policy from politicians, Apple contested that those people with close links to the realities of schools such as pupils, parents and teachers should have a greater say in the process of education. Apple's work also involved the relationship between culture and power in education, as well as the increasingly economically driven character of the school curriculum. Like Goodlad, he argued that schools should adopt democratic practices which reflect the democratic principles in society as a whole (Torre, 2001). For the most part it would appear that there are a number of associations between Goodlad and Darling-Hammond: both worked tirelessly on matters of research, fairness, schooling and teacher education, and her formation of Professional Development Schools has similarities with UES. However, there are two major differences: (1) their different standpoints on assessment, but (2) more significantly, between Goodlad's notion of renewal and Darling-Hammond's work in educational reform as a policy-maker.

The English educator Basil Bernstein was likewise interested in matters of the curriculum. He was also, more poignantly, interested in the democratic notion that all young people experience a rich education. Bernstein called for a democratic set of three rights for students, and that schools guarantee these rights. These are the rights of enhancement, inclusion and participation (Bernstein, 2000). Another English educational thinker with close connections with Goodlad was Lawrence Stenhouse. Stenhouse was embedded in curriculum research and he also thought those closely connected with school practice should have a greater say in the development and content of the curriculum. Stenhouse's views were that the curriculum was overly influenced by the dominant class and culture in society, his Humanities Curriculum Project (HCP) endeavoured to explore this concept. Like Goodlad, Stenhouse also encouraged, through the HCP, close partnership working between teachers in schools and academics in university schools of education (Stenhouse, 1975). There are other educational thinkers who could be associated with Goodlad. Most of these thinkers would loosely belong to a progressive genre of educators, and as such this would be the foundation of some of the criticisms his work attracted.

CRITIQUING GOODLAD'S IDEAS

Firstly, criticism of Goodlad's work relates to the impracticability of some of his ideas because of the political and market-driven approach to education in the United States and in other developed countries. Secondly, parts of his work are somewhat contradictory. Thirdly, his concept of renewal being driven from school head teachers and teachers is considered an unrealistic option.

Similar to Dewey, conceivably one of the most influential thinkers in education even today, Goodlad's ideas of renewal and school democracy were considered too revolutionary for the United States government, educational policy-makers and even most of parents. The drive to create an economy-focused and skill-based education system by many countries appears to be the current pattern where, unfortunately, the needs of the market override the humanistic aspects of a democratic progressive education system. Despite the innovative ideas Goodlad pursued, and centres of advanced practice, such as UES, it has proved that implementing renewal, and sustaining its concept, is a remarkably difficult undertaking. Even those teachers who began to use democratic and ethically based classroom practice eventually returned to traditional methods of teaching (Gibbons and Norman, 1987). His notion of non-graded schools grounded on pupils' interests, particularly in a skill-based and economically driven education system, is an example of the impracticability (Amrein-Beardsley, 2012).

Goodlad's inclusive ideas on schools – involving and encouraging all of the community, regardless of age, to take part in the learning process – is rather at odds with his 'age-four-to-sixteen model [of schooling which was] better suited to the developmental characteristics of the young' (Goodlad, 2004: 323). He contended that the presence of students between sixteen and eighteen years of age had a detrimental effect on the younger children. For example, he offers the view that exposure to and use of alcohol and drugs increased markedly in the culture of the sixteen-and-over age groups, and therefore questions whether 'they are best suited to remain as role models for their younger schoolmates?' (Goodlad, 2004: 323).

The idea of head teachers and teachers being the instigators of educational renewal is a worthy concept and he argues his case very passionately. However, within the increasingly demanding environment evident in schools, it is a challenging and unrealistic prospect. As he admitted himself, renewal 'requires motivation, dedication, systematic and systemic evolution, and *time*, and it is not possible in the current educational system' (Goodlad et al., 1990: 25). Furthermore, it is possibly naïve to expect that all teachers and head teachers will possess the revolutionary zeal to implement and sustain the renewal that was envisaged by Goodlad. It is accepted that many will take up this call for renewal and endeavour to make decisions themselves for change while others will be content to comply and carry out directions imposed from above (Coffield and Williamson, 2012). In a similar way it is idealistic to consider that the successes of exemplary schools such as UES can be replicated more widely. Nevertheless, it is argued that such idealism and optimism should be an inspiration to policy-makers and educators when they consider the way in which they think about and apply Goodlad's ideas.

GOODLAD'S IDEAS IN RELATION TO EDUCATION AND PRACTICE

Some of Goodlad's work relates to education in its broadest sense, which encompasses such conceptual notions as the function of schools, democracy and social justice. While other areas of his work are related to practice, it is recognised that his ideas are quite progressive and could be tricky to apply within the current constraints in formal educational settings. However, it is argued that the spirit underpinning his ideas is student-centred, meaningful and positive, and as such they are worth pursuing where possible. This part of the chapter will offer ideas relating to Goodlad's work in the broader aspects of education, schools and communities, teacher education and teaching.

Goodlad's vision of educational renewal was based upon the foundations of an ethical, moral and democratic set of principles. The key actors in this renewal were to be an alliance of school educators and other interested members of the community. This would be a school and community endeavour, because it was these people who knew the area, school and the cultural context of the locality; with head teachers taking the leading role. The reason why he felt this was significant was because he thought the politically driven concept of educational reform was 'the perpetuation of myths … [implemented by outside] … policy makers, who are currently bogged down in determining matters of teaching, learning, and assessment for which they are unqualified' (Goodlad, 1999: 38).

Coffield and Williamson (2012) agree with the sentiments behind Goodlad's concept of educational renewal rather than reform. However, they argue that for such renewal to work, particularly in the context of the UK education system, the head teacher of the school (or college principal, or university vice-chancellor) is not in the best position to advance the cause of renewal. Leaders of schools, colleges and universities are hindered in carrying out this renewal leadership role:

> Their time is absorbed in responding to the latest round of government initiatives and changes in funding, the ensuring of survival and growth in their institutions, and the day-to-day running of huge, complex social organisations. (Coffield and Williamson, 2012: 70)

Nevertheless, Coffield and Williamson offer a way in which renewal can be implemented in practice that is still within the spirit of Goodlad's concept. For them the impetus for renewal needs to come from teachers and tutors who are excited about a more democratic educational system, curriculum and classroom practices. Like Goodlad, they champion the cause of building alliances with the community, employers, and between other teachers in the larger community (Coffield and Williamson, 2012).

Practical ideas for realising his ideas of the age-four-to-sixteen model of schooling were founded on his thoughts on what best matched the developmental needs of the young. His ideas are of interest as they begin to set out the sequential and developmental content of a renewed educational system – possibly a brief outline for a renewed curriculum – the proposal was

> for there to be three small four-year units, each with differentiated educational functions … the early unit devoted to romantic exploration of children's close-at-hand world, extended through stories of other times and places; the middle unit of greater precision, connecting with the larger and human and natural environment; and the third emphasising generalisation and application. (Goodlad, 2004: 323)

For schools to be truly effective within his concept of educational renewal, they needed to be 'richly textured environments guided by caring, competent, and professional teachers' (Goodlad, 1998: 2). He argued that children thrive intellectually when they are born into invigorating sensory surroundings. This development is enhanced if the children enrol in schools in prosperous communities, with a wealth of teaching resources, and which attract and keep teachers of note. Such schools are schools of choice and often oversubscribed (Goodlad, 1998). However, in his vision for renewal this correlation between affluence and an enhanced intellectual development need not occur; all schools could benefit all children. Included in Goodlad's vision was the age-four-to-sixteen model, with the three small four-year units of development, which has been described. There would no longer be the need in schools for choice, or for specialist schools, because arts, sports and sciences would be included in the education for all pupils (Goodlad, 1999).

Goodlad set out his vision of the ideal school based upon his empirical research carried out and published in his seminal 1984 text *A Place Called School: Prospects for the Future*. His ideal school was clearly articulated in an interview:

> The ideal school is small. The only valid argument for enlarging schools is to provide a broader curriculum, which runs out very quickly with increasing size. This [increasing size should be limited to] … 400 youngsters in elementary school, 600 in middle school, and 800 in secondary school. (Goodlad, 1999: 38)

To support his vision of the ideal school he also advocated that schools should embrace the concept of professional development centres to provide teachers with leadership skills. These centres would also enable teachers to be closely involved with other public service professionals in areas such as health and welfare (Goodlad, 1999). Another aspect which he encountered in his research into schooling, was the difference in the classroom environments between the early years and secondary schools. Mostly, he found the early years' classroom contained stimulating, informative and colourful displays and artefacts. Whereas, in contrast, the secondary classrooms were drab, cramped for space and devoid of wall displays. Goodlad felt a stimulating classroom environment was just as important for students as they progressed through the latter grades of schooling (Goodlad, 1984).

Goodlad was an enthusiastic advocate for a mode of teacher education which was less prescribed and technically orientated. He strove to promote a more intellectually and morally based form of teacher preparation, and continuing teacher professional development. With this in mind, his practical ideas for improving teacher education centred on closer relationships between faculties of teacher education (or schools of education) in universities and schools themselves, a notion which was prompted by his experiences as the director of UES. He was particularly interested in creating schools which could be designated as centres of innovation and best practice. Goodlad explains his concept of who would be involved and, the role and function of such schools:

To them [centres of innovation and best practice], outstanding career and head teachers are to be drawn. Beginning teachers are to be interned *only* in these schools. University faculty members orientated to research and development in school organisation, curriculum, and teaching are to be provided with space in these schools and here carry out their scholarly inquiries, sharing their expertise with the school faculty. The head teachers and a few highly gifted teachers will serve as clinical faculty in the schools of education... Research, school improvement, in-service education of experienced teachers, and preservice teacher education will proceed hand in hand. (Goodlad, 1984: 316)

For Goodlad, an effective teacher education programme 'lies not in classroom competence, but the development of a professional commitment within which each competence is based' (Goodlad et al., 1990: 244). He argued that a crucial task for teacher educators was to transform the required professional commitment into workable approaches for those learning to teach. This task, he felt, included five core factors: first, motivation to want to teach; second, creating an ethos of professional behaviour; third, building and negotiating proficiencies with parents; fourth, acquiring a spirit of acceptance of criticism through reflective practice; and fifth, developing professional partnerships within, and outside, the profession (Goodlad et al., 1990).

The primary duty of teachers is to establish and maintain an environment which will foster learning for all of their pupils. A central part of this, both morally and pedagogically, is that teachers need to believe that each of their charges is able to learn. It is the teacher's role to plan, make choices in creating a learning environment and reflect on the effectiveness of those choices. Goodlad contended that there were fundamental conditions that teachers needed to demonstrate for pupils' learning to occur. These included 'motivation and encouragement, knowledge of subject matter, opportunity to learn, time, space, appropriate curricula materials, clear instruction, and methods of measuring student learning progress' (Goodlad et al., 1990: 261). Interestingly, he goes further by arguing that if just one of these conditions is absent or lacking, 'learning is compromised, and the teacher is not fulfilling his or her moral responsibility' (Goodlad et al., 1990: 261).

Goodlad observed some excellent teaching during his research into classroom practice. For example, he came across a teacher who expended less energy than other teachers in controlling students. This teacher was observed to be fair and demonstrated a caring persona, and set tasks for the students that were challenging but not too difficult. Goodlad, also noticed that in this class the pupils had more respect for each other, and worked cooperatively with each other and the teacher (Goodlad, 1984). This observation also indicates some of the benefits of teachers creating cooperative and collaborative classroom environments, where pupils learn to change effortlessly between talking with their fellows and the teacher (Moore, 2000).

Goodlad argued that teachers should have the freedom to choose topics which matched the interests of pupils. Furthermore, that they should use all the teaching methods, activities and resources available to encourage their charges to be creative. He felt that it was better for pupils to learn fewer topics and to know them thoroughly, than to cover lists of topics just for regurgitation. For Goodlad, the quest 'is for understanding and for the processes basic to acquiring this understanding' (Goodlad, 1984: 339). What was paramount for Goodlad and in his thoughts on teaching was that teachers should work collaboratively, and in doing so exercise their democratic status as professionals (Coffield and Williamson, 2012).

Goodlad's research and his work is located within the context of US education; nevertheless, it is contested that his notions of moral and democratic education together with his ideas of non-grading, curriculum inquiry, schooling, teacher education and educational renewal certainly have relevance for educators in other countries.

REFLECTIVE TASK

Goodlad stated that school goals should have four interlinking categories: academic, vocational, social and civic, and personal. Thinking about your own practice setting, list the opportunities that are *currently* provided for learners for the social and civic, and the personal categories. Then, having read and reflected on Goodlad's ideas in this chapter, list any further opportunities that could be offered to students for these same two categories.

SUMMARY

John Goodlad's long and distinguished career as an educator and academic has influenced the way educators think about schooling and education in the United States and internationally. His sense of fairness and the quest for a democratic, ethical and moral system of education is evident throughout his works. His main themes of interest, however, were non-grading, curriculum inquiry, schooling, teacher education and the overarching concept of educational renewal. These themes were explored in his numerous articles and books. Apart from being an educator and academic he was also the leader of a number of higher education institutes, and innovative projects such as UES. These leadership roles enabled him to apply his ideas and to encourage others to adopt humanistic practices.

Goodlad and Dewey both shared a belief in the concept of a democratic education. They both created exemplar schools to observe and develop teaching and learning practice. Other North American progressive educators have similar ideas to Goodlad. Noddings' thoughts on a caring and ethical approach to teaching are aligned with Goodlad's ideas. There are also parallels between Apple's thoughts on culture and power in education, economy and the curriculum, and democracy. Darling-Hammond's and Goodlad's ideas are similar on a number of counts; however, her involvement in educational reform would be at odds with Goodlad's renewal. There are two British educators with close connections with Goodlad: firstly, Bernstein and his democratic rights for students; secondly, Stenhouse, regarding curriculum research, and the call for greater links between schools and universities.

Goodlad's work has attracted criticism because of the impracticability and unsustainably of some of his ideas, particularly in the political and economy-driven approach to educational policy-making. There are also some contradictions in his work. Furthermore, the notion that head teachers lead and nurture the changes he advanced in schools is unrealistic in terms of time and their current roles and responsibilities. Yet there are a number of areas where Goodlad's ideas can be put into practice. Some of these include: schools involving the whole community in their activities in more innovative ways; thinking more about the social and civic, and personal aspects of schooling; and providing for closer links between university schools of education and individual schools for professional development and research opportunities. Goodlad's work provides a refreshing, optimistic and caring foundation for practice and reflection.

 ## FURTHER READING

Goodlad, J. and associates (1974) *Looking behind the Classroom Door.* Worthington: Charles A. Jones Publishing.
A report on a far-reaching observational study of the organisation, curriculum and pedagogy of numerous elementary schools in the United States.

Goodlad, J., Mantle-Bromley, C. and Goodlad, S. (2004) *Education for Everyone: Agenda for Education in Democracy.* Indianapolis: Jossey-Bass.
The forefathers of the United States looked upon education as providing an understanding and a practical preparation of democracy. This book argues for a universal system of education to make schools safe and democratic environments.

Oakes, J. and Goodlad, J. (2005) *Keeping Track: How Schools Structure Inequality* (second edition). New Haven: Yale University Press.
An exploration of how grouping students according to ability levels mirrors the class and racial inequalities in the United States.

Sirotnik, K. (1999) 'On inquiry and education'. In: Sirotnik, K. and Soder, R. (Eds) *The Beat of a Different Drummer: Essays on Educational Renewal in Honor of John, I. Goodlad.* New York: Peter Lang Publishing.
A review of Goodlad's positive contribution in advancing schooling as an important factor for human and social well-being.

REFERENCES

Amrein-Beardsley, A. (2012) *Inside the Academy*, video with Dr John Goodlad. http://insidetheacademy.asu.edu/john-goodlad.
Bernstein, B. (2000) *Pedagogy, Symbolic Control, and Identity: Theory, Research, and Critique* (revised edition). London: Taylor & Francis.

Coffield, F. and Williamson, B. (2012) *From Exam Factories to Communities of Discovery: The Democratic Route*. London: Institute of Education, University of London.

Flinders, D. (2001) 'Nel Noddings, 1929–'. In: Palmer, J. (Ed.) *Fifty Modern Thinkers on Education: From Piaget to the Present*. London: Routledge.

Gibbons, M. and Norman, P. (1987) 'An integrated model for sustained staff development'. In: Wideen, M. and Andrews, I. (Eds) *Staff Development for School Improvement: A Focus on the Teacher*. London: Falmer Press.

Goldberg, M. (2000) 'Leadership for change – interview with John Goodlad'. *Phi Delta Kappan*, 82(1): 82–5.

Goodlad, J. (1975) *The Dynamics of Educational Change: Toward Responsive Schools*. New York: McGraw-Hill.

Goodlad, J. (1979) *What Schools Are For*. Bloomington: Phi Delta Kappa.

Goodlad, J. (1984) *A Place Called School: Prospects for the Future*. New York: McGraw-Hill.

Goodlad, J. (1990) *Teachers for Our Nation's Schools*. San Francisco: Jossey-Bass.

Goodlad, J. (1994) *Educational Renewal: Better Teachers, Better Schools*. San Francisco: Jossey-Bass.

Goodlad, J. (1997) *In Praise of Education*. New York: Teachers College Press.

Goodlad, J. (1998) 'Schools for all seasons'. *Phi Delta Kappan*, 79(9): 670–1.

Goodlad, J. (1999) 'Interview: Educational renewal'. *Phi Delta Kappan*, 36(1): 35–8.

Goodlad, J. (2000) 'Education and democracy'. *Phi Delta Kappan*, 82(1): 86–9.

Goodlad, J. (2004) *Romances with Schools: A Life in Education*. New York: McGraw-Hill.

Goodlad, J. and associates (1979) *Curriculum Inquiry: The Study of Curriculum Practice*. New York: McGraw-Hill.

Goodlad, J. and associates (1990) *Places Where Teachers Are Taught*, San Francisco: Jossey-Bass.

Goodlad, J., Soder, R. and Sirotnik, K. (Eds) (1990) *The Moral Dimensions of Teaching*. San Francisco: Jossey-Bass.

Harmon, J. (2014) *In Memoriam: John Goodlad, Former Dean of the UCLA Education School*. Los Angeles: UCLA.

Moore, A. (2000) *Teaching and Learning: Pedagogy, Curriculum and Pedagogy*. London: RoutledgeFalmer.

Shen, J. (2001) 'John I. Goodlad, 1920–'. In: Palmer, J. (Ed.) *Fifty Modern Thinkers on Education: From Piaget to the Present*. London: Routledge.

Sirotnik, K. (1990) 'Society, schooling, teaching, and preparing to teach'. In: Goodlad, J., Soder, R. and Sirotnik, K. (Eds) *The Moral Dimensions of Teaching*. San Francisco: Jossey-Bass.

Soder, R. (2014) *John Goodlad – Obituary*. www.uwyo.edu/wsup/_files/docs/john goodlad obituary.doc.

Stake, R. (1987) 'An evolutionary view of programming staff development'. In: Wideen, M. and Andrews, I. (Eds) *Staff Development for School Improvement: A Focus on the Teacher*. London: Falmer Press.

Stenhouse, L. (1975) *An Introduction to Curriculum Research and Development*. Oxford: Heinemann Educational.

Torre, C. (2001) 'Michael W. Apple, 1942–'. In: Palmer, J. (Ed.) *Fifty Modern Thinkers on Education: From Piaget to the Present*. London: Routledge.

Wideen, M. (1987) 'Perspectives on staff development'. In: Wideen, M. and Andrews, I. (Eds) *Staff Development for School Improvement: A Focus on the Teacher*. London: Falmer Press.

5

BASIL BERNSTEIN

LANGUAGE CODES, SOCIAL CLASS, PEDAGOGY AND THE CURRICULUM

LEARNING OUTCOMES

Having read this chapter you should be able to:

- Appreciate how Bernstein's background led to his work on language and social class in relation to education
- Identify and understand Bernstein's notions of language codes, classification and framing, and pedagogy
- Recognise the links between Bernstein's ideas and those of other educational and sociological thinkers
- Critically appraise his works
- Identify which facets of Bernstein's works could be applied to the classroom

---

KEY WORDS

Restricted and elaborate language codes; classification and framing; collection and integrated types of curriculum; visible and invisible pedagogies; democratic pedagogy

INTRODUCTION

Basil Bernstein, who died in 2000, was the most renowned British social theorist in the field of the sociology of education; his work was of intellectual substance and significance and his ideas will be of consequence in the future (Moore, 2006). It was through his many papers that social scientists of the 1960s and 1970s became conscious of the possibilities of sociolinguistics. He demonstrated a stimulating insight into the associations between social and cultural groupings and the manner in which culture was assumed (Giglioli, 1972). Bernstein became an active member of a growing group of sociologists of the time whose principal aim was to explore and expose the effects of social class and regionalism in British schooling. Within this group of sociologists 'Bernstein was, by far, the most persuasive, generative and articulate of his generation' (Goodson, 2001: 163). His work was known to, and often cited by, linguists, sociologists and educators throughout the world, as well as being the focus of interest and contention (Atkinson, 1985).

Throughout his academic life Bernstein strove to analyse one of society's great afflictions, that of the recurrence of disadvantage in the educational system. He viewed schools as being active purveyors of privilege and disadvantage – his aim was to make schools fairer environments for all, regardless of class background. He examined how language, family, and the complex systems and processes of education influenced social and educational inequalities (Goodson, 2001; Sadovnik et al., 2013). He found that many children with average levels of intelligence finished their compulsory education labelled as failures. The prevailing thought from many was 'society has given them the opportunity, and they have failed to respond to it'; this perception, in Bernstein's view, was hurtful and wrong; he wanted to know why these young people were identified as failures and then rectify the causes (Halliday, 1973: ix).

Bernstein's work spanned three evolving and interrelated major themes. The first theme in his earlier work was mainly concerned with language codes, the second theme focused on classification and framing and the construction of the curriculum, the third theme explored pedagogic practice (Goodson, 2001). All three of these themes were, for Bernstein, connected with issues of social class. It is arguably the first theme of language and social class that Bernstein is most noted for. He contended that social class and family socialisation produce characteristic types of speech. For him, working-class students learn and use 'restricted' language codes, while middle-class children learn and use 'elaborated' language codes. He thought that schools, as a rule, tend to devalue students who use restricted language codes, but reward students who use the elaborated codes of the middle class (McLaren, 2003).

These evolving themes are reflected in the chronological sequencing of his major texts. These books are really a collection of individual papers which were loosely concerned with the development and reinforcement of his ideas. The titles and subtitles of each are a true indication of the progression of his thinking. These are: *Class, Codes and Control: Theoretical Studies towards a Sociology of Language*, Vol. 1. (1971);

Class, Codes and Control: Theoretical Studies towards a Sociology of Language, Vol. 2. (1973); *Class, Codes and Control: Theoretical Studies towards a Theory of Educational Transmission*, Vol. 3. (1975); *Class, Codes and Control: The Structuring of Pedagogic Discourse*, Vol. 4. (1990); and *Pedagogy, Symbolic Control, and Identity: Theory, Research, and Critique* (2000). The latter text is sometimes referred to, unofficially, by many as volume 5 even though it is the only one of this series without *Class, Codes and Control* in the title (Bernstein and Solomon, 1999). To achieve a better understanding of how his thinking developed, we need to explore his early life and experiences as a teacher and how his academic career as an educational sociologist developed.

BERNSTEIN, THE PERSON

Born in 1925 to a Jewish family, Bernstein had experienced the hardships of working-class education in the 1930s. He left school at fourteen and joined the Royal Air Force at an early age, spending the latter years of the Second World War as a bomb-aimer in Sunderland flying boats (a type of seaplane) above the West African coast (Inglis, 2001). Following the war, Bernstein accepted a post as resident worker at the Bernhard Baron Settlement in Stepney, in the East End of London. He remained in this post for three years. While at the settlement he took part in the running of boys' clubs, with ages ranging from nine to eighteen. The settlement was a religious institution based upon Reform Judaism, whereas the community it served was Orthodox. This in turn introduced Bernstein to the interrelationships between social class and religion. Furthermore, during this time he was also involved with family casework, which had a profound influence on his life: 'It focused and made explicit an interest I always seemed to have had in the structure and process of cultural transmission' (Bernstein, 1971: 2).

Following his time at the settlement, Bernstein read sociology at the London School of Economics (LSE). In his characteristically honest reflection he admits 'I did not obtain what is called a "good" degree: my work was too undisciplined and I had agonising difficulties in expressing what I was trying to grasp' (Bernstein, 1971: 5–6). However, he was at the LSE along with a number of sociologists who were researching the impact of social inequality in fields such as health, welfare and education (Goodson, 2001); Bernstein chose education. After the LSE he enrolled on a postgraduate certificate in education (PGCE) at Westminster College of Education, which he completed in 1954, and he was then appointed as a grade 'A' teacher at the City Day College, London where he stayed until 1960 (Bernstein, 1971).

His role at the City Day College involved teaching students released for the day from their particular industry. The students that Bernstein taught had been failed by the formal, compulsory school system. He has written about these experiences of working with students from different trade and industrial backgrounds. He struggled with the significant lack of interest shown by his students in arithmetic, English and liberal studies in contrast to their captivation with practical topics (Inglis, 2001). This rift between theory and practice 'must have been especially fascinating in his class on car mechanics: Bernstein had been a life-long non-driver, so theory must have led to practice here' (Goodson, 2001: 163). His practical experience of teaching these students exposed Bernstein to the impact of social class differences. Furthermore, this experience also enabled him to explore the fields of linguistics and the 'problematic status of educational contents (curriculum) [which] provided further grist to Bernstein's mill' (Atkinson, 1985: 12).

His attraction to language and its association with social class was to lead to a two-year study at the Department of Phonetics at University College London in the early 1960s (Goodson, 2001). Bernstein started his doctoral studies, also at University College London, in 1960 where he obtained his doctorate in linguistics. After completing his PhD he moved to the Social Research Unit at the London Institute of Education, where he stayed for his whole academic career, eventually becoming the Karl Mannheim Chair of Sociology (Goodson, 2001). During his career Bernstein's contribution to the theory of linguistics and its link with social class and education was profound.

BERNSTEIN AND HIS KEY THEMES

In this section Bernstein's key themes of language codes, classification, framing and the curriculum, and pedagogic practice will be considered. These key themes do overlap and all are underpinned by Bernstein's concern with social class and the power, or lack of power, associated with class. To highlight the significance of the restricted and elaborated codes in relation to the educational possibilities and limitations they may have for the speakers, it is fitting that we start with Bernstein's definition of the codes:

> They can be defined, on a linguistic level, in terms of the probability of predicting for any one speaker which syntactic elements will be used to organize meaning. In the case of an elaborated code, the speaker will select from a relatively extensive range of alternatives and therefore the probability of predicting the pattern of organizing elements is considerably reduced. In the case of the restricted code the number of these alternatives is often severely limited and the probability of predicting pattern is greatly increased. (Bernstein, 1971: 77)

In short, the elaborated code has a greater range of vocabulary and reasoning power in comparison with the restricted code. He also linked these codes with two other distinctive forms of language, 'formal language' (elaborated code) and 'public language' (restricted code). In general, 'a middle-class child could speak in both languages, while working-class children were restricted in codes of public language' (Goodson, 2001: 164).

For Bernstein, then, these language distinctions indicate the different levels of attainment which could be achieved by working-class and middle-class children. He argued that language is a crucial element of social structure which can advantage, or disadvantage, children in their schooling. 'According to this position, language does not simply reflect the world but actively organizes the world into categories of experience' (Bartlett et al., 2001: 183). As such, different language codes mirror specific forms of social experience peculiar to their cultural environments. Therefore, when children arrive in school from different social and cultural backgrounds their use of language may not correspond with the language expected in schools, which favours the dominant elaborated language code. Hence, children who use a restricted code may encounter isolation in school because of their language. Whereas those who use the elaborated language code connected with 'standard English' are more in tune with the linguistic environment of schooling' (Bartlett et al., 2001: 183).

What is important to consider about the restricted code, from Bernstein's point of view, is that schools require children to use an elaborated language code which is without context, clear and universally understood. He argues that it is not that some children lack the aptitude to use this language required in school, rather, he contends, that when the 'task is set for them in school they understand the task as being one in which a restricted code is sufficient, and this is clearly in conflict with what is expected in school' (Scott, 2008: 75). This difference between what the learners bring with them in the form of experience and culture, and what the school expected, was of great interest to Bernstein throughout his career. As such, he sought to answer the question 'how are forms of experience, identity and relation evoked, maintained and changed by the formal transmission of educational knowledge and sensitivities?' (Bernstein, 1971: 202).

For Bernstein, such formal educational knowledge could be analysed through three 'message systems': curriculum, pedagogy and evaluation; he then defines each of these message systems and introduces his notions of classification and framing:

> Curriculum defines what counts as valid knowledge, pedagogy defines what counts as valid transmission of knowledge, and evaluation defines what counts as a valid realization of this knowledge on the part of the taught. The term 'education knowledge code' … refers to the underlying principles which shape curriculum, pedagogy and evaluation … the form this code takes depends upon social principles which regulate the classification and framing of knowledge made public in educational institutions. (Bernstein, 1971: 203)

Classification denotes the boundaries between curriculum types, where a strong classification signifies a curriculum that is clearly segregated into traditional subject knowledge. A weak classification signifies an integrated curriculum with very loose borders. These two types of curricula are respectively termed as collection and integrated. Framing, on the other hand, refers to the transmission of what matters as educational knowledge through pedagogic practice in schools. Framing involves the amount of control that teachers and students have over the choice and organisation of educational knowledge and the pace of teaching. A strong framing restricts the choices, whereas a weak framing means a wider choice and flexibility (Goodson, 2001). Bernstein, explains further these two notions: 'Classification, here, does not refer to *what* is classified, but the *relationships* between the contents [and] [f]rame refers to the form of the *context* in which knowledge is transmitted and received' (Bernstein, 1971: 205).

Bringing classification and framing together with the two curriculum types, the following brief outline is offered to give these notions context. The collection curriculum type is strongly classified and has differentiated and separate boundaries. Students have to satisfy certain admission needs, enrol for examinations and select a number of different subjects, modules and credits; therefore, students begin to construct their own educational knowledge by creating their own sets of modules and subjects. Hence, it is suggested that the framing is also strong and teachers and students have less choice in how and what is taught, and the pace at which it is taught. Conversely, in the integrated curriculum type the subjects and the content are interrelated and the isolating borders are weak (Atkinson, 1985). The integrated curriculum has similarities with the cross-curricular mode adopted by primary schools in England, as for 'primary teachers the boundaries between knowledge and disciplines are blurred rather than defined' (Robertson, 2000: 191). The framing is also, apart from the increasing restrictions required by the national curriculum, relatively weak.

The links between Bernstein's themes of the curriculum and pedagogic practice are clear and they still have the underlying theme of the advantages and disadvantages of social class. In his later writings, Bernstein explored the disparities in curricula and teaching in different regions of England. Generally, he found that schools in working-class districts tended to have authoritarian and teacher-centred pedagogic practices as well as, in secondary schools, having more vocationally based curricula. On the other hand, in schools in middle-class areas there was more evidence of student-centred teaching. The curricula in these middle-class schools included more liberal, humanistic and arts subjects; students were also coached in preparation for further and higher education. Furthermore, he found that upper-class students attended private schools, experienced an authoritarian form of teaching, and at secondary level a classical and humanistic curriculum which also helped students prepare for further studies (Sadovnik et al., 2013).

Bernstein, in his 1990 work *Class, Codes and Control: The Structuring of Pedagogic Discourse*, Vol. 4, outlined two generic types of pedagogic practice: visible pedagogies (normally found in traditional education) and invisible pedagogies (normally found in progressive education). Visible pedagogies stress the importance of performance, where the student learns to set criteria, and are found in working-class schools. Furthermore, with visible pedagogies, each student achieves a graded outcome thus creating hierarchical differences between students. Invisible pedagogies are more subtle in nature (and initially invisible to the student) and do not focus on a 'gradable' performance but rather concentrate on the competence of the acquirer attaining cognitive, linguistic, affective and motivational processes (Bernstein, 1990: 71). Bernstein maintained that invisible pedagogies were more likely to be found in middle-class schools, while the visible pedagogies were more likely to be evident in working-class schools. He contended that such class differences related to pedagogic practices are the consequence of different purposes for different social groups. Therefore, because such differences are possibly caused by sociological influences they may be significant in 'understanding the differences in academic achievement between groups' (Sadovnik et al., 2013: 298).

The final aspect of his pedagogic practices is Bernstein's call for a democratic form of pedagogy. He felt that education must be focused on guaranteeing the 'empowerment of every individual, on developing a real sense of involvement and control of the social context of one's life' (Kelly, 2004: 89). To achieve this Bernstein, in his last major work *Pedagogy, Symbolic Control, and Identity: Theory, Research, and Critique* (2000), wrote about the democratic need to safeguard three interconnected rights for students in educational institutes. These rights are: enhancement, inclusion and participation. Bernstein sees the first right as 'experiencing boundaries, be they social, intellectual or personal … it is the right to the means of critical understanding and new possibilities'. The second right is 'the right to be included socially, intellectually and personally'. The third right 'is the right to participate in construction, maintenance and transformation of order' (Bernstein, 2000: xx). Each of these three rights has corresponding social conditions for involvement and levels of operating, which are:

Rights	*Conditions*	*Levels*
Enhancement	Confidence	Individual
Inclusion	Communities	Social
Participation	Civil discourse	Political

(adapted from Bernstein, 2000: xxi)

Bernstein's key themes of language, curriculum and democratic pedagogy are shared with sociological and educational thinkers, particularly those with radical and socio-cultural viewpoints.

LINKS WITH OTHER THEORISTS

There is little doubt that Bernstein was heavily influenced by the French sociologist Emile Durkheim (1858–1917). He was particularly inspired by Durkheim's analysis of the evolution of education in France, which began with the 'discourse, social structure and social relations of the medieval university … which provided the dynamics of the development of the university' (Bernstein, 2006: 119). Durkheim also demonstrated how the structure of societies could be broken down into classifications and frames to uncover the distribution of power and the norms of social control. Bernstein also felt that Durkheim's work provided an impressive understanding of social relationships, social orders and the structuring of experience (Bernstein, 1971). There are also clear associations between John Dewey, who promoted the notion of democracy in schools, and Bernstein's democratic pedagogies and his idea of the three democratic rights in education: enhancement, inclusion and participation (Bernstein, 2000).

According to Ball (2001) Bernstein's ideas on linguistics originated from the continental sociology of the time, 'it is now difficult to read Bernstein and not see resonances with Bourdieu and Foucault' (Ball, 2001: 41). Like Bernstein, Bourdieu viewed social class and culture as playing a large part in deciding educational success or failure. In particular, Bourdieu felt that the failure of working-class children in education was directly associated with a systematic bias in schools which is primarily concerned with the dominant class culture. Bourdieu felt that 'in schools working class culture is either not recognized and simply negated or is denigrated as an inferior form of culture, a kind of anti-knowledge' (Bartlett et al., 2001: 186). Although Bernstein was somewhat critical of the analytical depth to Foucault's work, he welcomed and acknowledged Foucault's work on power and knowledge, and particularly discourse, which links closely with language codes (Bernstein, 1990).

Bernstein's view that schools control the content and teaching of the curriculum, and as such manipulate knowledge in a way which suits the dominant class and culture, is similar to what Stenhouse was endeavouring to solve with his Humanities Curriculum Project (HCP – see Chapter 9). The HCP was concerned with enabling students to have access to knowledge so they could use it in innovative ways to solve problems, because, Stenhouse argued, the traditional (content) curriculum produced 'acceptance rather than speculation' (Stenhouse, 1975: 49). William Labov, an American linguist, like Bernstein discovered that social class and success in learning could be detected by the identification of language structures and codes. Although Labov and Bernstein used different approaches in their research, their findings demonstrate 'that language brought to and used in the classroom has a significant effect on what is learned and known to be learned' (Leighton, 2012: 62). However, Labov was to become one of Bernstein's critics; it was Bernstein's approaches to his work and the generalisation of his findings which attracted most criticism.

🧠 CRITIQUING THE THEORY

Throughout his career Bernstein, was very open about the possible shortcomings of his work and here in his last book he suggests the reasons for, and examples of, the criticism of his work, which

> has caused strong controversy and has sometimes become the object of crude oversimplification, miscomprehension, as well as political and ideological misuse. The case of language codes, elaborated and restricted, constitutes a notorious example of all of the above. (Bernstein, 2000: 197)

It was indeed his work on elaborated and restricted language codes which caused a bitter debate in the 1960s and 1970s. Even though Bernstein suggested that it was the language and not the children who were, or were not, capable of abstract thought and reasoning, his viewpoint was seen by many as a deficit model. For his critics this deficit model blamed the working-class children instead of the linguistically biased educational system (Moore, 2000). His main critic regarding language codes was Harold Rosen, a colleague of Bernstein's. Rosen disputed the insinuation that working-class language was in any way subordinate to the standard English used in schools, and further censured Bernstein that it was unsafe and misguided to say that it was. This criticism was reinforced by Labov whose own research found that working-class language was more animated, reasoned and effective than middle-class language which he considered to be hesitant and overburdened by detail (Moore, 2000).

He was also criticised by the political parties of the day in the UK. The left wing saw his work on language codes as a condemnation and the stereotyping of the working classes. On the other hand the right wing thought he had given some justification to the curious idea that 'high culture' was not for the working class (Bernstein, 1971: 18). It appears that he took the criticism of his language codes to heart, when his work was denounced by linguists and educators alike at a classroom level. These criticisms indicated that his work on language codes had lowered the expectations that teachers had of some of their children, and that the notion of the elaborated code had reinforced the teachers' middle-class perception of appropriate language. The code definitions themselves, Bernstein acknowledges, 'are said to have given rise to mechanical grammar and vocabulary drills' (Bernstein, 1971: 19).

Bernstein's writing was also unconventional in style, structure and content. Halsey, writing Bernstein's obituary, thought

> The prose is extremely difficult because being an autodidact and not a traditionally learned man, and being an innovator rather than one who seeks to maintain an established conversation, Basil developed his own, if I may borrow one of his own inventions, 'elaborate code'... He never hesitated to write down an incomplete argument. (Halsey, 2000)

Comments regarding his writing were plentiful, Atkinson thought a lot of readers 'find his ideas difficult, obscure and elusive ... leaving the reader to grapple with some rather abstruse and slippery notions' (Atkinson, 1985: 6). With typical honesty Bernstein responds to such criticism of his writing in his first book by stating towards the beginning 'the papers are obscure, lack precision and probably abound with ambiguities' (Bernstein, 1971: 19). In spite of these criticisms, there are a number of aspects of Bernstein's work such as the drive for equality and democracy which can, even within the constraints of a national curriculum, be used in practice.

APPLYING BERNSTEIN'S IDEAS IN PRACTICE

Applying some of Bernstein's theoretical ideas in practice could appear at first glance to be quite problematic. But perhaps somewhat surprisingly his ideas generate feasible opportunities for democratic practices in schools and universities. Before we consider these opportunities it is fitting that we reflect on a philosophical question, and response, regarding whether we change the school or the child, posed by Lawrence Stenhouse:

> To what extent is it the result of a gap between everyday culture and the culture of worthwhile learning which is greater in the case of working class than middle class children? Should we change the school or should we change the working class child?

> A bit of both I fancy, but I confess that I find it difficult to strike a balance. (Stenhouse, 1975: 31)

Stenhouse's response to his own question is interesting in that it implies a dilemma and a degree of uneasiness. It is intended to leave Stenhouse's response open to the reader's own way of thinking. What this section will do, however, is explore some progressive ideas which reflect Bernstein's thoughts.

Bernstein maintained that academic knowledge used in schools, particularly secondary schools, was different to everyday knowledge, because both forms of knowledge are rooted in different systems of meanings. Academic knowledge is arranged through subject discipline curricula which are strongly classified, and have clearly defined borders and their own language; all of which segregate them from other disciplines. The way in which each academic discipline is arranged affects the manner in which it is interpreted for teaching. Therefore, it is important that teachers enable students to be able to recognise the different types of knowledge, and their borders, so that they differentiate between subjects such as biology, physics and geography, for example. Teachers should ensure that the borders between academic subjects are made visible to the students. This is not only so that they are introduced to the forms of language that are specific to each subject, but more importantly so that they use that knowledge to make links between subjects and broaden their range of understanding. This can be best achieved by, firstly, during induction for studying a new subject, making students aware of the forms of language and knowledge types; and then during subsequent sessions ensuring that students know how the different subjects interlink (Wheelahan, 2009). In practice this has been, and still is, used with joint, or combined awards, in the sciences, for example.

Bernstein would likely propose that for the most part the student–teacher relationship in universities could be described as having a weak frame. The pedagogical relationship in higher education can offer both students and teachers an avenue with which they can open up. Some teachers who use a weak frame employ 'a wide range of human-being feelings, reflections and emotions, self-disclosure, hopes challenges and aspirations – to come into their exchanges' (Barnett, 2007: 133). On the other hand, some teachers in higher education preserve a tight relationship with their students keeping within the limits of the set curriculum. As such, these teachers do not allow the students to see them as a whole person, they view their task simply in rational and academic terms. There is no doubting that teachers who use a weak frame are engaging in a risky undertaking. Yet it is argued that the weak frame relationship will enhance the degree of criticality required by students at university. Such criticality is enabled by the willingness on behalf of the student, with the encouragement of the teacher, to access new experiences and new understandings which for many requires courage and curiosity. Therefore, teachers in universities who adopt a weak frame relationship are much more likely to foster a critical spirit in their students, than those teachers who adhere to the intellectual domain of the formal curriculum (Barnett, 2007).

In primary schools there is a greater scope for school staff to enhance children's vocabulary with the use of one-to-one teaching or small intervention groups led by teachers, teaching assistants, parents and carers, and by members of the community. Children are listened to while they read a selected text and then they discuss what they have read with an adult or with other children. This is done with a view to extending their vocabulary, and to increase their confidence in tackling what they may find to be difficult words and sentences. This in turn is supported by the use of word and grammar walls and the use of role play where children can model language acquired. Such activities are also aligned with the 'Narrowing the Gap' research findings by the National Foundation for Educational Research, which sought ways of breaching the gap in outcomes for vulnerable children (Waldman, 2009).

The involvement of parents and carers in schools, in the form of partnerships with teachers, is vital in closing the gap for disadvantaged children (McIntyre, 2003). Children's learning can be enriched if they have the assistance of parents' or carers' perceptions about their home lives; for example, what the children enjoy doing, their interests, attainments and ambitions. Parents and carers, rather than teachers, have more chances and usually more reasons to know their children. This is especially the case in secondary schools where teachers might only see their students once or twice a week. It is suggested that more use could be made of the parents' and carers' knowledge of their children not only in being involved in classroom learning activities, but also by greater sharing of information (McIntyre, 2003). Stenhouse (1975) likewise recommends that those who work in university teacher training and education departments could also be a resource that schools and teachers could utilise in classrooms to support children's language development.

Exploring the impact of policy and practice in further education, in line with Bernstein's notion of democratic pedagogy, Coffield et al. (2008) have analysed the individual stories of students who enter colleges. They found that students arrived at college 'with complex and multi-faceted needs that are not just educational, but social economic and personal; many have been scarred by their learning experiences in the school system' (Coffield et al., 2008: 67). From these student stories Coffield et al. have compiled a list of implications for policy and practice, which could be relevant and adopted across most sectors of education:

- Policy needs to refocus on supporting and sustaining the tutor–learner relationship.
- Success at lower levels depends upon a flexible, patient and informal approach that starts where the learners are, is tailored to their needs, and can gradually build their confidence through small group learning and one-to-one support.
- More needs to be done to support learner progression by, for example, providing step bridging courses.
- Provision for the most disadvantaged groups needs to be properly resourced.
- A truly effective lifelong learning strategy needs to pay greater attention to failures within the school system, to problems of transition and to the impact of poverty and deprivation on educational attainment.

(adapted from Coffield et al., 2008: 66)

It is appropriate at the end of this section on application that we briefly focus on Bernstein's own teaching. In a journal article written following Bernstein's death, a colleague, Julia Brannen, reflected on the nature of his teaching and learning:

> Basil's ability to engage in the discussion of ideas and their formulation and, in the moment of their realisation, to make it such fun! If this was a process of teaching and learning, which it clearly was, then the great art of the teacher and the magic of the learning that went on lay in the fact that neither of us noticed it nor even cared! (Brannen, 2001: 2)

REFLECTIVE TASK

Bernstein (2000) outlined the following three democratic rights for students that needed to be safeguarded:

enhancement;

inclusion;

participation.

Reflect upon your own experience from school or university and list, under each, your opportunities to access these rights.

SUMMARY

Basil Bernstein was a sociologist and educationalist whose ideas of linguistics, social class and education still have much to offer academics and practitioners today. Although his ideas evolved during his academic career their overall purpose was to discover the effects on social class in British schools and the associated repetitions of disadvantage inherent in the educational system. His works can be loosely categorised in three interrelated themes: language codes and social class; classification, framing and the construction of the curriculum; and the exploration of knowledge systems and pedagogies. The ethos of his work was shaped by his experiences as a youth worker and teacher in the East End of London. He had a distinguished academic career which was spent mainly, and latterly, at the London Institute of Education where he became the Karl Mannheim Chair of Sociology.

He was influenced by Emile Durkheim's analysis of the evolution of French education and his notion of showing how the structures of societies were separated into classifications and frames to demonstrate the division of power and norms of social control. Bernstein's ideas on democratic pedagogies are closely linked with John Dewey. His work on linguistics, as it is associated with different social classes and cultures, mirrors Bourdieu's notion of social reproduction and Foucault's work on discourse. Another whose work is closely related to Bernstein, particularly regarding pedagogies and the curriculum and social class, is Lawrence Stenhouse and his research and findings from his Humanities Curriculum Project, which is explored in Chapter 9 of this book.

Bernstein was the focus of considerable criticism regarding his elaborated and restricted language codes and how these related to the perceived disadvantage of working-class children. He also attracted censure because of his complex, ambiguous and unconventional writing style. Regardless of these criticisms and the theoretical nature of his ideas, there are opportunities for application of his work in all sectors of education. These opportunities include the breaking down of borders between subject disciplines and the fostering of student–teacher relationships. Practical ideas of small group work and one-to-one teaching and learning to close the gap, and the use of parents and carers in classrooms and in the sharing of information for children, are also linked to Bernstein's ideas. A final goal which would meet Bernstein's notion of democratic pedagogy would be to consider implementing policies which would improve the learning chances for disadvantaged groups.

FURTHER READING

Bernstein, B. (1997) 'Class and pedagogies: Visible and invisible'. In: Halsey, A., Lauder, H., Brown, P. and Stuart Wells, A. (Eds) *Education: Culture, Economy, Society*. Oxford: Oxford University Press.
A definitive account of visible and invisible pedagogies and the notion of social control, including how they relate to transitions between the different stages of education.

Coffield, F. and Williamson, B. (2011) *From Exam Factories to Communities of Discovery: The Democratic Route*. London: Bedford Way Papers.
A review of Bernstein's democratic pedagogies and democratic rights in education.

Davison, J. (2012) 'Social class and education'. In: Arthur, J. and Peterson, A. (Eds) *The Routledge Companion to Education*. London: Routledge.
An informative piece which demonstrates how social class and attainment levels in education in the UK are closely linked.

Goodson, I. (2005) *Learning, Curriculum and Life Politics: The Selected Works of Ivor F. Goodson*. London: Routledge.
Some interesting insights into Bernstein the person and his work by Ivor Goodson, a close associate and fellow educationalist.

REFERENCES

Atkinson, P. (1985) *Language, Structure and Reproduction: An Introduction to the Sociology of Basil Bernstein*. London: Methuen.

Ball, S. (2001) 'On first reading …' In: Power, S., Aggleton, P., Brannen, J., Brown, A., Chisholm, L. and Mace, J. (Eds) *A Tribute to Basil Bernstein 1924–2000*. London: Institute of Education, University of London.

Barnett, R. (2007) *A Will to Learn: Being a Student in an Age of Uncertainty*. Maidenhead: Open University Press.

Bartlett, S., Burton, D. and Peim, N. (2001) *Introduction to Education Studies*. London: Paul Chapman.

Bernstein, B. (1971) *Class, Codes and Control: Theoretical Studies towards a Sociology of Language*, Vol. 1. London: Routledge and Kegan Paul.

Bernstein, B. (Ed.) (1973) *Class, Codes and Control: Theoretical Studies towards a Sociology of Language*, Vol. 2. London: Routledge and Kegan Paul.

Bernstein, B. (1975) *Class, Codes and Control: Theoretical Studies towards a Theory of Educational Transmission*, Vol. 3. London: Routledge.

Bernstein, B. (1990) *Class, Codes and Control: The Structuring of Pedagogic Discourse*, Vol. 4. London: Routledge.

Bernstein, B. (2000) *Pedagogy, Symbolic Control, and Identity: Theory, Research, and Critique* (revised edition). London: Taylor & Francis.

Bernstein, B. (2006) 'Thoughts on the trivium and quadrivium: The divorce of knowledge from the knower'. In: Lauder, H., Brown, P., Dillabough, J.-A. and Halsey, A. (Eds) *Education, Globalization and Social Change*. Oxford: Oxford University Press.

Bernstein, B. and Solomon, J. (1999) '"Pedagogy, identity and the construction of a theory of symbolic control": Basil Bernstein questioned by Joseph Solomon'. *British Journal of Sociology of Education*, 20(2): 265–79.

Brannen, J. (2001) 'Basil Bernstein 1924–2000'. *International Journal of Social Research Methodology*, 4(1): 1–3.

Coffield, F., Edward, S., Finlay, I., Hodgson, A., Spours, K. and Steer, R. (2008) *Improving Learning, Skills and Inclusion: The Impact of Policy on Post-Compulsory Education*. London: Routledge.

Giglioli, P. (Ed.) (1972) *Language and Social Context*. Harmondsworth: Penguin.

Goodson, I. (2001) 'Basil Bernstein, 1925–2000'. In: Palmer, J. (Ed.) *Fifty Modern Thinkers on Education: From Piaget to the Present*. Abingdon: Routledge.

Halliday, M. (1973) Foreword. In: Bernstein, B. (Ed.) *Class, Codes and Control: Theoretical Studies towards a Sociology of Language*, Vol. 2. London: Routledge and Kegan Paul.

Halsey, A.H. (2000) Basil Bernstein's Obituary in *The Guardian*. www.guardian.co.uk/obituaries. 27 Sept.

Inglis, F. (2001) 'Elaborating Bernstein: The great sociologist and his pedagogic devices'. In: Power, S., Aggleton, P., Brannen, J., Brown, A., Chisholm, L. and Mace, J. (Eds) *A Tribute to Basil Bernstein 1924–2000*. London: Institute of Education, University of London.

Kelly, A. (2004) *The Curriculum: Theory and Practice* (fifth edition). London: SAGE.

Leighton, R. (2012) 'Sociology of education'. In: Arthur, J. and Peterson, A. (Eds) *The Routledge Companion to Education*. London: Routledge

McIntyre, D. (2003) 'Has classroom teaching served its day?' In: Nind, M., Rix, J., Sheehy, K. and Simmons, K. *Inclusive Education: Diverse Perspectives*. London: David Fulton.

McLaren, P. (2003) 'Critical pedagogy: A look at the major concepts'. In: Darder, A., Baltodano, M. and Torres, R. (Eds) *The Critical Pedagogy Reader*. London: RoutledgeFalmer.

Moore, A. (2000) *Teaching and Learning: Pedagogy, Curriculum and Culture*. London: RoutledgeFalmer.

Moore, R. (2006) 'The structure of pedagogic discourse'. In: Lauder, H., Brown, P., Dillabough, J.-A. and Halsey, A. (Eds) *Education, Globalization and Social Change*. Oxford: Oxford University Press.

Robertson, S. (2000) *A Class Act: Changing Teachers Work, the State, and Globalisation*. London: Falmer Press.

Sadovnik, A., Cookson, P. and Semel, S. (Eds) (2013) *Exploring Education: An Introduction to the Foundations of Education* (fourth edition). London: Routledge.

Scott, D. (2008) *Critical Essays on Major Curriculum Theorists*. London: Routledge.

Stenhouse, L. (1975) *An Introduction to Curriculum Research and Development*. London: Heinemann.

Waldman, J. (2009) *Narrowing the Gap in Outcomes for Vulnerable Groups – The Messages that Matter … To Narrow the Gaps*. Slough: National Foundation for Educational Research.

Wheelahan, L. (2009) 'The limits of competency-based training and the implications for work'. In: Field, J., Gallacher, J. and Ingram, R. (Eds) *Researching Transitions in Lifelong Learning*. London: Routledge.

6

PIERRE BOURDIEU

THEORY OF SOCIETY

LEARNING OUTCOMES

Having read this chapter you should be able to:

- Appreciate the life and works of Pierre Bourdieu
- Understand the contribution made by Bourdieu in the field of sociology
- Recognise the concept of cultural reproduction and how this is applied to the education system
- Critically evaluate Bourdieu's theories in the current education climate

KEY WORDS

Habitus; social capital; cultural capital; economic capital; symbolic capital; cultural reproduction; deficit discourse; field; symbolic violence; reflexivity

INTRODUCTION

Pierre Bourdieu was a French social philosopher who is renowned for his work which saw him engaged in the fight against social oppression and injustice. Bourdieu developed a methodology from the fields of sociology, anthropology, philosophy and literary theory in his attempts to uncover those mechanisms which resulted in the separation and inequalities that existed amongst different social groups (*New World Encyclopedia*, 2013). For Bourdieu, his aim was to create a fairer, more equitable society, for all.

Born into a peasant family, Bourdieu was an outstanding student who excelled academically and was able to attend some of the most prestigious schools in France. However, while Bourdieu showed a natural aptitude towards his studies he was acutely aware of the social differences between himself and his peers, which is undoubtedly one of the reasons why he chose sociology, particularly social inequality, as an area of study. Bourdieu was interested in the objective structure of social class, and studied how class relations conditioned everyday culture and social interactions (Dillon, 2014).

Bourdieu is perhaps best known for his work on capital, to conceptualise inequality and social stratification, and while this work reflects that of Karl Marx, Marx himself was predominantly interested in economic capital as the source of inequality in society. For Bourdieu the issue was more complex than this, leading him to identify economic, social and cultural capital, all of which he believed illustrated inequalities within society. Bourdieu believed that social class was distributed according to the ownership and use of the different types of capital held by the individual, and those lacking the economic and social capital of the dominant class were seen as the most deprived in society.

Further key terms popularised by Bourdieu were those of 'habitus', 'fields' and 'symbolic violence', which are further reflections on the position an individual takes in society. For Bourdieu, habitus related to the 'structured and structuring mental structure through which individuals acquire their views and behaviour as a second nature' (Johannesson and Popkewitz, 2001: 230). Habitus, then, is created from social processes, in which behaviour learned in one context can be transferred to another. Since it is those in upper-class society who would set the accepted rules and norms, this creates a further tension between the classes, in which those from the lower classes are already at a disadvantage due to poor understanding of the rules of expected behaviour.

Bourdieu was a prolific writer and some of his most well-known texts include: *The Inheritors* (1964 [1979]) (co-written with Jean-Claude Passeron), *Distinction* (1979 [1984]), *Homo Academicus* (1988) and *The State Nobility* (1989); he also wrote over 300 articles. Bourdieu referred to his work as reflexive sociology (Johannesson and Popkewitz, 2001), a phrase which refers to his desire not just to reflect on the individual in society, but to look at both the objective and subjective status of those individuals within a social and discursive framework (Johannesson and Popkewitz, 2001). For Bourdieu the aim was to see the world in an entirely different way, and to facilitate social change, thereby promoting a more equitable society.

PIERRE BOURDIEU, THE PERSON

Pierre Bourdieu was born on 1 August 1930, in Denguin, a rural area in south-western France. An only child, Bourdieu came from a typical rural peasant family (Grenfell, 2008), his father was a peasant sharecropper turned postman who had failed to complete his education, and while his mother had completed her education to the age of sixteen the family had moderate economic means. Bourdieu was educated at the local elementary school, before boarding at the *lycée* in Pau. While at the *lycée* Bourdieu gained his first insight into the impact of cultural difference on attitudes, since as a rural boarder he was made to wear a grey smock while his classmates wore the latest attire; he was also made fun of because of his accent. Bourdieu began to see education as a double-edged sword, one which highlighted idiosyncrasies, while at the same time offering a means by which to escape, and which Grenfell (2008) suggests may well be the reason why Bourdieu ultimately chose education and culture as the principal focus for his research.

Despite the challenges Bourdieu experienced at the *lycée* he showed academic talent (Grenfell, 2008), and was encouraged by one of his high school teachers to 'pursue an elite academic curriculum in Paris' (Ollion, 2012). Bourdieu passed the entrance examination to the elite Lycée Louis-le-Grand in Paris and then went on to attend the École Normale Supérieure, also in Paris, which was at the time at the apex of French academic life, and was seen as the 'incubator of the French intelligentsia' (Grenfell, 2008: 12). Bourdieu had then set out on an academic career for himself which was very much in contrast to his humble beginnings, and which set him alongside past graduates of the École including Jean-Paul Sartre and Simone de Beauvoir.

Bourdieu graduated from the École with a degree in philosophy, having studied epistemology and the history of science, which Ollion (2012) observes set him against the dominant discourse of existentialism, popularised by Sartre. However, his focus on philosophy shifted towards an interest in the social sciences following his involvement in the Algerian War, into which he was drafted in 1955. His time in Algiers saw him involved in administrative duties at the height of what was a cruel and bloody war of independence. His experiences both challenged and inspired Bourdieu (Grenfell, 2008), and resulted in him becoming more heavily involved in enquiry of a more empirical nature, involving ethnographical and statistical studies of colonial transformation (Ollion, 2012).

Bourdieu returned to France in 1960, where he documented his experiences of the Algerian war in some of his principal publications, including *Sociologie de l'Algerie*

(1958), *Travail et travailleurs en Algerie* (Bourdieu et al., 1963) and *Le déracinement: La crise de l'agriculture traditionnelle en Algérie* (Bourdieu and Sayad, 1964). Once back in France he also continued the transition to sociology, being offered a job as assistant to the French intellectual Raymond Aron, this was followed by his appointment as Director of Studies at the École Pratique des Hautes Études, which later became the School for Advanced Studies in the Social Sciences. While in position as Director, Bourdieu also founded his own research centre in 1968, followed by the launch of a journal, *Actes de la recherche en sciences sociales*, in 1975. In this journal Bourdieu sought to blend analysis, raw data, field documents and pictorial illustrations to make social science more accessible and explicable, the motto for the journal being 'to display and demonstrate' (Crossman, n.d.). Alongside this Bourdieu also assembled a research team with which he began to look more closely at symbolic power and social inequalities in their broadest manifestations (Ollion, 2012).

Ollion (2012) observes that throughout the 1980s and beyond Bourdieu began to tackle 'an increasingly diverse set of empirical topics' and also began to develop the conceptual framework for which he is perhaps best known, which includes his theory of habitus, capital and fields. During this time he was also elected to the Collège de France in 1982, which according to Grenfell 'marked a period of prolific output with major book publications' (2008: 14), reflecting his growing interest in topics including cultural life, academia and state training schools, methodological and philosophical statements, and language. During this time he also expanded his research interests to include the state, gender domination, the social foundations of the economy and the experiences of social suffering in contemporary society (Ollion, 2012). Bourdieu also joined political committees set up by François Mitterrand's socialist government in order to review the structure and curriculum of the French education system. Interestingly, Bourdieu seemed somewhat at odds with the socialist government at the time, since in his publication *La misère du monde* (*The Weight of the World*) (1993), he recorded the personal accounts of social suffering brought about by the neoliberal policies of the socialist government.

Prior to his untimely death in 2002, Bourdieu began to increase his public profile through appearances on television and radio, a surprising move since prior to this period he had eschewed public life (Grenfell, 2008). This period saw him increase his involvement in the global mobilisation against neoliberalism (Ollion, 2012), and he used meetings at social assemblies, strikes and pressure groups to further this cause; as a result Bourdieu became a leading figure, and gained international status in the fields of the social sciences and the humanities.

Over the course of his life Bourdieu published thirty books and over 300 articles, which spanned a wide range of disciplines including philosophy, literary theory, sociology and anthropology. Most notable was his development of methodologies, in which he combined theory and empirical data in an attempt to dissolve some of the most troublesome problems in theory and research, in order to increase accessibility of his subject matter to a wider audience.

CAPITAL, HABITUS AND FIELDS

As we have seen from the previous section Bourdieu's work was complex, covering a wide range of themes and ideas. It would be impossible to cover all of these in one short chapter so for the purpose of this book the focus will be on Bourdieu's work on capital, habitus and fields, which are most closely aligned with education.

It should be noted that Bourdieu himself rejected the use of the term 'theories' and did not refer to himself as a theorist despite the fact that his theoretical terminology, such as capital, fields, habitus and distinction, are used widely in a number of disciplines (Webb et al., 2002). For Bourdieu it was more important that his theories were able to be applied as tools to understand real situations. Bourdieu states,

> these tools are only visible through the results they yield, and they are not built as such. The ground for these tools … lies in research, in the practical problems and puzzles encountered and generated in the effort to construct a phenomenally diverse set of objects in such a way that they can be treated, thought of, comparatively. (Bourdieu and Wacquant, 1992: 160)

Nevertheless, given the wide-ranging applicability of the theoretical notions of capital, habitus, fields and distinction, this would seem to be an appropriate place to start when considering his 'theories'.

A key focus for Bourdieu was social inequality (Dillon, 2014), asserting that everyday culture and social interaction was, to a great extent, dictated by social class and class relations. Bourdieu also believed that social order was maintained through a complex hierarchy by which those in the higher classes were able to retain their position through their social and cultural capital (Gauntlett, 2011; Sullivan, 2002). Bourdieu identified that within any social space there were many different classes and class subcomponents, which would be distinguished by the different types of capital they held. For Bourdieu, capital and power amounted to the same thing, and he saw that there was a vast chasm between those who were best provided with economic and cultural capital and those who were the most deprived (Bourdieu, 1979 [1984]).

Dillon (2014) observes that economic capital is a fairly straightforward concept to understand, measurable by way of money in the bank, home ownership, investments and so on, and suggests that it is easy to see how the volume of economic capital can be measured between different groups and individuals. Bourdieu, however, believed that even within homogeneous groups, subcultures can be seen, creating competition within groups which he referred to as class fractions. This too applied to the cultural capital which a person held, a concept which Dillon (2014) suggests is more difficult to define and measure, but which Bourdieu saw as being equally important as economic capital.

Bourdieu used his observations of French society when defining cultural capital, referring to it as a 'familiarity with prestigious aesthetic culture' (Ritzer, 2002: 3), such 'high culture' encompassed the high arts, literary culture and linguistic ability, and Bourdieu believed these to be the trappings of the upper classes, used by people as cultural signifiers. In his book *Distinction* (1979 [1984]) Bourdieu outlines the way in which people seek to identify themselves with those above them on the social ladder while at the same time demonstrating their differences from those below (Gauntlett, 2011). Cultural capital is then very much linked to social class with each class having its own specific cultural capital, be that, for example, through listening to classical or hip hop music, and through this an individual will gain *cultural competence*, the ease with which an individual carries himself within the cultural capital of the group they are in. However, according to Bourdieu, within society it is inevitable that some cultures and competences will be more highly valued than others, and for Bourdieu this is the higher class culture which he referred to as the *legitimate culture*.

Bourdieu did not suggest that the dispositions of the higher classes had more value in themselves, rather it is the strategies employed by the upper classes to exclude other classes through their privileged positions which creates such distinctions between cultural capital. It is a perception, then, reinforced by the upper classes through their privileged positions, that their cultural capital is the dominant capital, often reinforced by economic capital, since those with greater economic capital can afford the trappings of the dominant culture, thereby buying cultural capital. This too leads to *cultural reproduction*, in which the status quo for social class is maintained, since parents will expose their children to the right cultural capital, and as we shall see later this is frequently reproduced through the education system.

Inevitably, the cultural capital possessed by an individual will have a direct correlation with their social capital, this being the social connections, social networks and alliances which an individual has access to (Dillon, 2014). In essence this refers to 'who you know, rather than what you know' and those who possess the dominant cultural capital will most likely move in the circles which allow them to retain that capital, a further example of social reproduction, and one which further reflects Bourdieu's observation of social inequality. For those who are outside of the legitimate culture it becomes increasingly difficult to gain the appropriate cultural and social capital to access the benefits apportioned to the dominant culture.

Sullivan (2002) suggests that a further way in which culture is reinforced is through the attitudes and values first learned through the home, an idea which reflects another central theme of Bourdieu, that of *habitus*. As with cultural capital, the set of dominant values and attitudes would then be those held by the dominant class. Bourdieu (1990: 53) defines habitus as,

> A system of durable, transposable dispositions, structured structures predisposed to function as structuring structures, that is, as principles which generate and organise practices and representations that can be objectively adapted to their outcomes without presupposing a conscious aiming at ends or an express mastery of the operations necessary to attain them.

Habitus is, therefore, an internalised set of schema and dispositions, first learned through early socialisations, and according to Sullivan (2002) is what gives the individual competence in certain social settings. For Bourdieu (1977: 506) it is 'the manners and tastes resulting from good breeding'. In unpacking these dispositions Sullivan (2002: 150) refers to definitions provided by Bourdieu, including a 'tendency', 'propensity' or 'inclination', but here again we see a strong illustration of a class divide in which children of the dominant culture learn from an early age how to behave accordingly in certain social situations, thereby setting them apart from their lower-class peers.

The final area of focus in this section is another central theme of Bourdieu's work which is that of *cultural fields*, or, put simply, the context in which cultural life and production is situated. Webb et al. (2002: 21) define cultural fields as 'a series of institutions, rules, rituals, conventions, categories, designations, appointments and titles which constitute an objective hierarchy, and which produce and authorise certain discourses and activities'. A cultural field might include an educational setting, a museum or a theatre. The challenge here is defining the rules and rituals for a particular field, and here again we can see how the dominant culture might be influential in the instigation of this, which too reinforces the dominance of that culture. Nevertheless, Bourdieu saw cultural fields as being fluid and dynamic, and anticipated that these would be subject to change dependent upon the group influence and the point of reference. The cultural field is then important in terms of contextualising a subject, thereby increasing the depth of understanding.

We can see then that through the combined lenses of capital, habitus and fields Bourdieu demonstrated the impact of class on an individual's social mobility, and later in this chapter parallels will be drawn with the education system, and how this might reinforce social reproduction. It should be pointed out, however, that this is a mere snapshot of Bourdieu's work and the further reading listed at the end of this chapter is highly recommended.

LINKS WITH OTHER THEORISTS

Bourdieu's work has parallels with Marxism, particularly in respect of the some of the terminology he uses such as capital and class; however, Wolfreys (2000) states that Bourdieu steadfastly refused to associate himself with Marxism, dismissing it as a 'religious alternative'. Despite this, there are aspects of Bourdieu's work which certainly support a Marxist philosophy, particularly when we consider his views on cultural reproduction and the role of education in perpetuating cultural domination. Bourdieu concurs with the Marxist philosophy that proposes the idea that the dominant class 'ensures its hold over the means of ideological production, not simply because of the fact of its control, but because it is able to legitimise its privileged status by disguising it as the result of meritocratic triumph through sheer talent' (Wolfreys, 2000).

Both Marx and Bourdieu dealt with the concept of class in their work; however, for Marx the main focus was that of class struggle as a catalyst for social change with economic capital being the main driver for distinguishing between the classes. Bourdieu, however, identified three fundamental types of capital: social, cultural and economic, with the two former able to convert to the latter.

As a social reformer Bourdieu was heavily influenced by founders of sociology including Max Weber and Emile Durkheim, along with the theories of phenomenologists Maurice Merleau-Ponty and Edmund Husserl. Brubaker (1985) suggests that Bourdieu owes the substance of his theory outlined in *Distinction* to Max Weber, particularly in respect of his theory of symbolic power and the relationship with economic and political power. Likewise, Brubaker (1985) suggests that Bourdieu took much of his ideas of *collective representation* and *primitive classifications* from the work of Durkheim.

Bourdieu was a contemporary of Michael Foucault and similarities can be seen across their work as they both engaged in social anthropology. Both Bourdieu and Foucault believed human beings to be historically structured agents, and both agreed that by living in the world human beings are structuring the world back (Jensen, 2014). However, Jensen (2014) also observes that there were inherent differences in their work, since while Foucault believed that thinking was determined as the result of historical processes, for Bourdieu it was social context which influenced thought.

Bourdieu believed that practical knowledge was informed by habitus, that is the knowledge gained from first-hand experiences related to the environment in which the individual is brought up. This too has parallels with Foucault's work since he also believed that it was through relationships with others that rules and boundaries were formed, and language developed.

CRITIQUING THE THEORY

Interestingly, when critiquing Bourdieu we need only look at his own experience to show where flaws might exist when considering how cultural capital and habitus might impact on the educational experience of children. According to Bourdieu's theory, those children who do not have the right cultural capital will be disadvantaged in an education system which is influenced predominantly by those from the dominant class. However, while Bourdieu himself would have lacked the cultural capital required to succeed in education, coming from a peasant family, he was clearly an exception to his own rule, succeeding as he did with an academic career. Nevertheless, Webb et al. (2002) observe that Bourdieu had always been conscious of how different he was to his colleagues, and suggest that as an academic and sociologist he was always more interested in observing the actions of others, than reflecting on his own experience. Bourdieu accepts that there will be exceptions to the rule; however, he sees this as strengthening the position of the dominant culture, since it legitimises a flawed system by giving the appearance of a meritocracy (Sullivan, 2002).

Of course, the first-hand experiences which Bourdieu was observing took place within the French education system, which in essence was a tiered system of education with elite *lycées* which focused on academic excellence, alongside the more vocational colleges and elementary schools. Webb et al. (2002) observe that the education system in France was heavily centralised with an emphasis on standardising the curriculum, rather than accounting for the needs of different social groups. It could, then, be argued that this lacks applicability to the current system of education in England which has seen a drive to promoting a system which caters for, and actively promotes, widening participation in education. Research undertaken by Halsey et al. (1980) showed that expansion of secondary education in 1970s Britain, designed to encourage social mobility was

> doing far more than 'reproducing' cultural capital; they were creating it, too... They were not merely maintaining a 'cycle of privilege' in which cultural capital is acquired by those from educated homes. They were at least offering an opportunity to acquire cultural capital to those homes that had not secured it in the past.

Thus, we can see that far from perpetuating a class system, as Bourdieu suggests, education can indeed be seen as a vehicle for social change, and a trend which began in secondary education can now be seen continuing in the field of tertiary education, with increasing numbers of students now entering the higher education system.

CULTURAL CAPITAL AND THE EDUCATION SYSTEM

Webb et al. (2002) acknowledge that Bourdieu's views on the education system will have certainly been influenced by the closed, elitist and openly competitive French education system he studied; however, they also suggest that his ideas have resonance with other Western education systems which should be more open and democratic. The field of education for Bourdieu is closely tied to his theory of cultural reproduction in as much as it perpetuates a link between original class membership and ultimate class membership (Sullivan, 2002).

It could be argued that success in the field of education has a correlation with the possession of cultural capital and higher class habitus, thereby advantaging those in the dominant culture. As we have seen previously, cultural capital is how far a person has a familiarity with the dominant culture of society, and in respect of the education system this would relate to how far the individual can access and use the language of education. For those lacking in the cultural capital of the dominant education system the use of educational language can create a barrier which will directly impact their ability to fully engage with the system; an issue which is intensified the further up the education ladder one climbs. Bourdieu states that,

> By doing away with giving explicitly to everyone what it implicitly demands of everyone,
> the education system demands of everyone alike that they have what it does not give.
> This consists mainly of linguistic and cultural competence and that relationship of famil-
> iarity with culture which can only be produced by family upbringing when it transmits
> the dominant culture. (1977: 494)

For Bourdieu, then, the education system is not a fair one, since those who have
already had access to the dominant culture in the home environment will already have
an advantage over those who do not. In this respect Bourdieu argues that the education system has inefficient pedagogic transmissions (Sullivan, 2002), in which teaching
automatically favours those in the dominant culture since the teachers themselves are
in possession of cultural capital. In this case those lacking in linguistic and cultural
capability will simply not understand what it is their teachers are telling them, leading
to disengagement with the school system, poor attainment and ultimately a failure to
continue with education beyond compulsory schooling.

While the education system could then be an agent of social change, presenting
young people with the tools with which to combat social inequality, Bourdieu argues
that what actually happens is that 'schools tend to reproduce existing social relationships and inequalities' (Webb et al., 2002: 113). He also notes that children from
working-class families are more likely to drop out of education, a factor which he
relates to the habitus of the working-class family, suggesting that preconceptions of
their chances in the education system might lead to a self-fulfilling prophecy,

> the negative predispositions towards the school which result in the self-elimination of
> most children from the most culturally unfavoured classes and sections of a class ... must
> be understood as an anticipation, based upon the unconscious estimation of the objective
> probabilities of success possessed by the whole category, of the sanctions objectively
> reserved by the school for those classes or sections of a class deprived of cultural capital.
> (Bourdieu, 1977: 495)

It would seem then that failure of lower-class students in the field of education is
inevitable, since the schools system automatically targets those in possession of cultural capital. For Bourdieu, this then serves to reproduce and legitimise social
inequalities, maintaining the status quo, and ensuring that the upper classes maintain
their position in society (Sullivan, 2002). Webb et al. (2002) suggest that the ruling
classes maintain their domination through ensuring that those members of less powerful groups have limited access to educational resources, thereby supposing that
education is fundamental to gaining economic, social and cultural capital.

This would seem to paint a rather bleak picture of the education system, reflecting
a system of control rather than one which presents opportunities for those who most
need it. It could be argued that changes to the education system in England, over the
past thirty years, have redressed the balance in terms of accessibility of the education
system, creating a fairer system of education. Government education policies have

reiterated the importance of a fair education for all (e.g., *Educational Excellence Every-where* (Department for Education, 2016); *Supporting the Attainment of Disadvantaged Pupils* (Department for Education, 2015); *2010 to 2015 Government Policy: Education of Disadvantaged Children* (Department for Education, 2010)), with an emphasis on those schools in the most deprived areas of the country providing a parity of provision. Likewise, in the higher education sector the drive to widen participation to include those who would not traditionally have entered higher education was outlined in the 1997 Dearing Report. In this report Dearing set out a vision which included widening participation to include those students who would not normally access a university education, including those with alternative qualifications to the standard A levels, mature students, students with disabilities, working-class students and those from minority ethnic groups. Individuals from these groups would certainly seem in direct contrast to Bourdieu's definition of those in possession of the dominant cultural capital required to attend university.

However, while such steps would appear to be encouraging a fairer system of education, in which the cultural capital of an individual would not adversely impact on their access to the education system, it must be questioned just how fair this is in reality. Webb et al. (2002) express the view that the child from the upper-class family will still be able to afford the best possible resources, so for a child who is struggling with their education, tutors can be employed, and access to elite schools will be made possible where classes are much smaller and the most up-to-date technology used. Regardless of the good intentions of the education policies, practically speaking these things are just not possible in systems of mass education. Likewise, the language used in schools is embedded in the culture of those delivering it, making it challenging for both teacher and student to make the necessary adjustments required to make this universally accessible.

In the field of higher education it could be argued that the illusion of fairness and accessibility is even more complex than in compulsory education. While the widening participation agenda and subsequent government policies have certainly expanded access to higher education, how open this is to all is an area of some discussion. When considering higher education choice in respect of Bourdieu's work it is conceivable that subconsciously an individual might choose an institution which best reflects their own cultural capital, and in which habitus does not become a barrier to success. Therefore, some young people will automatically discount applying to some of the more prestigious Russell Group universities due to the perception that they will not fit in, thereby reinforcing the theory of social reproduction. While selecting a higher education institution on the basis of how comfortable they feel with it would seem acceptable on the face of it, this may not provide graduates with the best chance of economic success since research also suggests that 'graduates from Oxford and Cambridge enjoy starting salaries approximately £7,600 (42%) higher per year, on average, than graduates from post-1992 universities' (de Vries, 2014: 5).

Baker and Brown (2007: 388) observed that even when students did choose a more prestigious institution they still maintained 'a realistic if sometimes allegorically framed grasp of the material differences in status and cultural capital between themselves as applicants and the prestige of the institutions to which they had applied', in which case choice of higher education becomes a form of social reproduction with students from lower-class backgrounds often opting for the less prestigious post-1992 universities since these better reflected their own cultural capital.

REFLECTIVE TASK

Potentially education can be a powerful catalyst for social change, yet we can see from Bourdieu's work that all too often this becomes a tool for social reproduction, where those in the dominant culture get access to the best and most prestigious education systems – how far do you agree that this is the case in the education system in your country – and how far does this reflect your own experience of education?

SUMMARY

Despite the fact that Bourdieu's work was positioned in French society there is much about his observations on social inequality that resonates across a range of different cultures and societies, making his work eminently applicable today. Bourdieu was interested in the way that inequality gets reproduced, creating a vicious circle in which those with the greatest cultural capital retain their position in society by means of symbolic violence, defined by Bourdieu and Wacquant (1992: 167) 'as the violence which is exercised upon a social agent with his or her complicity'. For Bourdieu, the lower classes allowed social reproduction to happen because they believed themselves to be inferior to the upper classes, lacking as they are the cultural capital of the dominant culture. Bourdieu asserts that people play the game of culture (Dillon, 2014), suggesting that despite recognising the power struggle that exists between different social classes, people are unwilling to change, accepting instead their place in society. This would seem a somewhat disheartening conclusion, and while he acknowledges that the social order can be changed, he suggests that this is a long slow process (Dillon 2014).

The Guardian (2002), in their obituary following Bourdieu's death, referred to him as being, for many, the leading intellectual of present-day France, and it is a testament to his position as a leader in the field of sociology, that his work has been translated into over two dozen languages. Bourdieu's work has influenced a number of fields in the social sciences, and has straddled sociology, education, anthropology and cultural studies, reflecting the wide appeal of his work.

In the final years of his life Bourdieu increased his standing in the political field, turning his attention from the development of methodological frameworks, and instead made numerous television appearances, writing in the press and delivering speeches. However, fundamentally the message remained the same: that of sympathy for the oppressed, anger for their life conditions and a scepticism for conventional wisdom (Ritzer, 2002).

FURTHER READING

Bourdieu, P., Passeron, J.C., Nice, R. and Burton Bottomore, T. (1990) *Reproduction in Education, Society and Culture*. London: SAGE.
An analysis of education in which the authors show how education carries an essentially arbitrary cultural scheme based on power, in which reproduction of culture through education plays a key part in social reproduction.

Bourdieu, P. (1979 [1984]) *Distinction*. Abingdon: Routledge.
One of Bourdieu's best-known works in which he illuminates the social pretensions of the French middle class.

Fowler, B. (1997) *Pierre Bourdieu and Cultural Theory: Critical Investigations*. London: SAGE.
A comprehensive and systematic study of Bourdieu's theory of culture and habitus. The book examines the role of cultural capital as set out by Bourdieu and outlines some of the key critical debates that inform his work.

Grenfell, M. and James, D. (1998) *Bourdieu and Education: Acts of Practical Theory*. London: Falmer Press.
An examination of some of Bourdieu's theoretical assumptions and how these relate to education, with some practical suggestions for those wishing to use Bourdieu's work when undertaking research in the field of education.

Savage, M. (2015) *Social Class in the 21st Century*. London: Pelican Books.
An introduction to Bourdieu's work through an examination of social class in modern-day society.

REFERENCES

Baker, S. and Brown, B. (2007) 'Images of excellence: Constructions of institutional prestige and reflections in the university choice process'. *British Journal of Sociology of Education*, 28(3): 377–91.
Bourdieu, P. (1958) *Sociologie de l'Algerie*. Paris: P.U.F.
Bourdieu, P., Darbel, A., Rivet, J.-P. and Seibel, C. (1963) *Travail et travailleurs en Algerie*. Haye: Mouton.
Bourdieu, P. and Sayad, A. (1964) *Le déracinement: La crise de l'agriculture traditionnelle en Algérie*. Editions de Minuit Chateau-Gontier: Print of el'Indépendante.

Bourdieu, P. and Passeron, J.-C. (1964 [1979]) *The Inheritors: French Students and Their Relation to Culture*. Chicago: University of Chicago Press.

Bourdieu, P. (1977) 'Cultural reproduction and social reproduction'. In: Karabel, J. and Halsey, A.H. (Eds) *Power and Ideology in Education*. Oxford: Oxford University Press.

Bourdieu, P. (1979 [1984]) *Distinction*. Abingdon: Routledge.

Bourdieu, P. (1988) *Homo Academicvs*. Stanford: Stanford University Press.

Bourdieu, P. (1989) *The State Nobility: Elite schools in the field of power*. Stanford: Stanford University Press.

Bourdieu, P. (1990) *In Other Words*. Cambridge: Polity Press.

Bourdieu, P. (1993) *La misère du monde (The Weight of the World)*. Paris: Seuil.

Bourdieu, P. and Wacquant, L. (1992) *An Invitation to Reflexive Sociology*. Cambridge: Polity Press.

Brubaker, R. (1985) 'Rethinking classical theory: The sociological theory of Pierre Bourdieu'. *Theory and Society*, 14: 745–75.

Crossman, A. (n.d.) *Pierre Bourdieu: A Biography in Brief*. http://sociology.about.com/od/Profiles/p/Pierre-Bourdieu.htm.

Dearing, R. (1997) National Committee of Inquiry into Higher Education. https://bei.leeds.ac.uk/Partners/NCIHE.

Department for Education (2010) *2010–2015 Government Policy: Education of Disadvantaged Children*. London: DfE.

Department for Education (2015) *Supporting the Attainment of Disadvantaged Pupils*. London: DfE.

Department for Education (2016) *Education Excellence Everywhere*. London: DfE.

de Vries, R. (2014) *Earning by Degrees: Differences in the Career Outcomes of UK Graduates*. The Sutton Trust. www.suttontrust.com/wp-content/uploads/2014/12/Earnings-by-Degrees-REPORT.pdf.

Dillon, M. (2014) *Introduction to Sociological Theory: Theorists, Concepts and Their Applicability to the Twenty-first Century*. West Sussex: Blackwell Publishing.

Gauntlett, D. (2011) *Three Approaches to Social Capital*. www.makingisconnecting.org.

Grenfell, M. (2008) *Pierre Bourdieu: Key Concepts*. Durham: Acumen.

Halsey, A.H., Heath, A.F. and Ridge, J.M. (1980) *Origins and Destinations*. Oxford: Clarendon Press.

Jensen, M.L. (2014) 'Structure, agency and power: A comparison of Bourdieu and Foucault'. *AU: Central Debates in Anthropology*. www.academia.edu/10258956/Structure_Agency_and_Power_A_Comparison_of_Bourdieu_and_Foucault.

Johannesson, I.A. and Popkewitz, T. (2001) 'Pierre Bourdieu, 1930–' In: Palmer, J. (Ed) *Fifty Modern Thinkers on Education: From Piaget to the Present*. London: Routledge.

New World Encyclopedia (2013) *Pierre Bourdieu*. www.newworldencyclopedia.org/entry/Pierre_Bourdieu.

Ollion, E. (2012) *Pierre Bourdieu*. www.oxfordbibliographies.com/view/document/obo-9780199756384/obo-9780199756384-0083.xml₁

Ritzer, G. (2002) *Encyclopedia of Social Theory*. Thousand Oaks: SAGE.

Sullivan, A. (2002) 'Bourdieu and education: How useful is Bourdieu for educators?' *The Netherlands Journal of Social Science*, 38(2): 144–66.

The Guardian (2002) *Obituary: Pierre Bourdieu*. www.theguardian.com/news/2002/jan/28/guardianobituaries.books.

Webb, J., Schirato, T. and Danaher, G. (2002) *Understanding Bourdieu*. London: SAGE.

Wolfreys, J. (2000) 'In perspective: Pierre Bourdieu'. *International Socialism Journal*. http://pubs.socialistreviewindex.org.uk/isj87/wolfreys.htm.

7

MICHEL FOUCAULT

POWER, SURVEILLANCE, DISCIPLINE AND CONTROL IN EDUCATION

LEARNING OUTCOMES

Having read this chapter you should be able to:

- Appreciate the life and works of Michel Foucault
- Identify and understand Foucault's concepts of discourse, hierarchical observation, normalisation of judgements, the examination and panopticism
- Appraise how Foucault's philosophy is related to education
- Critically evaluate Foucault's philosophy from an educational point of view

KEY WORDS

Poststructuralism; discourse; power-knowledge; discipline; docile bodies; hierarchical observation; normalising judgement; the examination; surveillance; panopticon

INTRODUCTION

Michel Foucault is considered by many to be one of the most influential French philosophers since the Second World War. Known primarily as a social historian, his main ideas revolve around the reciprocally empowering connection between knowledge and power, and the employment of these two in influencing social control (Schwan and Shapiro, 2011). The range and complexity of Foucault's philosophy spans a number of branches of learning which include sociology, history, literary theory and education (McNay, 1994). As such, it is difficult to classify his work, or compartmentalise him into a particular academic or philosophical category as he changed the focus of his interests so often. The purpose of philosophy for Foucault was to challenge the conventional 'ways we think, live and relate to other people and to ourselves in order to show how that-which-is could be otherwise' (Oksala, 2007: 10). It is this challenging of the taken-for-granted way of thinking which has fascinated educators, particularly as they try to understand the numerous politically driven policy initiatives, and the increased culture of performativity and surveillance (Murphy, 2013).

Foucault offers educators a radical concept of how children develop and learn, which centres on how we communicate with each other. He argues that the manner in which we communicate is governed by a set of regimes which are not primarily formed within our personal consciousness. For Foucault, the way in which we communicate develops from the historical perspectives in which we mature; they are not set but change as time passes. These perspectives are reflected in the language we use to make sense of the world. This concept, according to MacBlain (2014), has important consequences for how we converse and how we understand ideas which were previously considered to be firmly established as knowledge. As such, MacBlain (2014) suggests that educators should challenge the understanding that child development and learning are static in nature and never change. This in turn implies that educators should also query the approach to comprehending how children learn and how they are taught (MacBlain, 2014). Communication and the use of language are central to Foucault's philosophy as part of his notion of discourse, which will be considered later in the chapter.

Oksala (2007) suggests that Foucault's works (first published in French) have usually been grouped into three distinguishing stages. Firstly, in the 1960s were his historical studies which he termed his 'archaeology phase', which include *Madness and Civilization: A History of Insanity* (1961), *The Birth of the Clinic: An Archaeology of Medical Perception* (1963), *The Order of Things* (1966) and finally in this first stage *The Archaeology of Knowledge* (1969). The second stage in the 1970s he termed the 'genealogical phase', which focused on the study of power. It is this stage which attracted most attention and which is most relevant to education. His major works during this stage were *The History of Sexuality. Vol. 1: The Will to Knowledge* (1976), and *Discipline and Punish: The Birth of the Prison* (1979). In the third stage Foucault was concerned with works of the ancient ethical scholars. In this final stage he produced, in 1984, the last two volumes of *The History of Sexuality* – *Vol. 2: The Use of Pleasure* (1984a) and *Vol. 3: The Care of the Self* (1984b) (Oksala, 2007).

The importance of Foucault's work to education is that he presents conceptual and original approaches to examining education within the evolving field of human sciences by 'focussing on the power/knowledge relations and conditions under which subjects are constituted objects of knowledge' (Peters, 2001: 174). His work with power and knowledge relationships explored and evaluated the extent to which power and control were employed by different establishments and institutions (Cole, 2008). All of which provide fresh insight for viewing the field of education, and how we talk about education, in relation to policy and its implementation in places of learning. To acquire a deeper understanding of the aspects which underpinned his philosophical ideas we need to explore Foucault's upbringing and his career as a scholar.

FOUCAULT, THE PERSON AND THE SCHOLAR

Foucault was born in Poitiers, France in 1926 and died of an AIDS-associated illness in 1984 when he was fifty-seven years old. Despite his relatively short life he was recognised as one of the leading intellectuals in Europe and the Western world (Peters, 2001). During his formative years he must have been affected by a number of experiences, one of these being the advent of the Second World War. Following the German invasion of France in 1940, Poitiers firstly became part of the unoccupied area of Vichy France. Then in the latter stages of the war the city came under the direct control of the German Third Reich – a time of suspicion and anxiety for the population. Foucault grew up in comparative comfort; his father, Paul, was a successful surgeon. However, his father exerted firm control over his family and he expected his eldest son to follow in his footsteps and pursue a career in medicine – an idea which Michel rebelled against. This rebellious streak was also evident during Foucault's adult life where his refusal to acknowledge accepted norms and establishment authority was renowned (Oliver, 2010).

Foucault attended local state schools and gained his *baccalaureate* at a Roman Catholic school. From there he gained his *licence de philosophie* at the prestigious École Normale Supérieure. Then in 1950 he achieved his *licence de psychology* and also worked as a practitioner in a psychiatric in-patient institute, an experience he utilised to research his interest in mental illness. He became increasingly influential as a philosopher and historian and took up his first chair as Professor of Philosophy at the University of Clermont-Ferrand. From there he went on to the newly founded experimental University of Vincennes, and finally on to the esteemed Collège de France where he became Professor of the History of Thought (Peters, 2001). During his academic career Foucault held a number of international university teaching posts, which, it is argued, helped to develop his ever-shifting philosophy. These international posts were numerous: in Sweden, Germany, Poland, Brazil, Tunisia, Japan and Canada, and in his later years numerous visits to the United States (Oksala, 2007).

During his academic career he was also a political and human rights activist who challenged the established order. As a new graduate he briefly, like many French intellectuals of the time, joined the Communist Party and became increasingly engaged as an activist who supported the marginalised and oppressed of society. The late 1960s and early 1970s were a time of massive social protest, including demonstrations against the war in Vietnam and the university student riots in Paris, and both these causes were actively supported by Foucault. In 1970, with his partner Daniel Defert a fellow professor, he established the Group d'information sur les prisons (GIP), which was set up to publicise the degrading conditions of French prisons. GIP gained quick success and demonstrated how Foucault was able to sway the French government regarding the formation of prison policy (Oliver, 2010). This experience also stimulated his interest in the power used by authorities and their use of incarceration and surveillance to ensure compliance, and led to the publication of *Discipline and Punish: The Birth of the Prison* (1979).

Before we explore Foucault's concepts and philosophy, particularly how these relate to education, it is fitting to reflect that he considered his ideas and his works to be closely connected with events in his own life (Oksala, 2007). To take this personal association with his work further, Ball states:

> He regarded his intellectual endeavours as a way of working on himself; he was always work in progress, always unfinished, restless and angry. (Ball, 2013: 7)

FOUCAULT AND HIS IDEAS

Some of Foucault's works can be quite complex and convoluted to decipher but the meanings, once uncovered, are profound. Ball found 'reading Foucault was a struggle and a shock but also a revelation' (Ball, 2013: 2). With this in mind, and before we address his ideas which directly relate to education, this section will firstly explore some of the terms and key ideas associated with Foucault. These terms and key ideas are: poststructuralism, power–knowledge and discourse. This section will then consider those aspects of Foucault's ideas, mainly from *Discipline and Punish: The Birth of the Prison* (1979), such as discipline, docile bodies, hierarchical observation, normalising judgement, the examination and panopticism – all of which have resonance with education.

It is difficult to categorise Foucault's philosophy because of his disparate thoughts and the shifting of his ideas over time. For some he was at different times a Marxist and/or postmodernist. Nevertheless, it is commonly agreed that much of his philosophy emanates from poststructuralism, although Foucault would discount any attempt to be labelled as a poststructuralist (Oksala, 2007). The word poststructuralism is a contested and complicated term which has originated from European scepticism (Peters and Besley, 2012). Poststructuralist thinkers, such as Foucault, particularly challenged the established ways of thinking and the acceptance of knowledge that were formed during the Age of Enlightenment, which began at the time of the French Revolution. These poststructuralist ways of thinking encompassed a wide range of ideas and mind-sets

> concerning reason, justice, equality, progress and rationality and a series of political events ... [and for Foucault were] ... based on an interrogation of how and what things are, and as a particular self-referential attitude to one's time. (Danaher et al., 2000: xi)

Furthermore, poststructuralism can also be understood as a theoretical counter to the use of scientific approaches in the human sciences (Peters and Besley, 2012). The poststructuralist viewpoint is vital to understanding Foucault's notion of power–knowledge where the conventional idea of knowledge is powerful as 'it makes us its subjects, because we make sense of ourselves by referring back to various bodies of knowledge' (Danaher et al., 2000). However, power, for Foucault, is not only 'prohibitive it is productive ... [it] ... is sometimes an opportunity to be successful or loved. It is not always harmful' (Ball, 2013: 30).

The meanings which are created by the notion of the power–knowledge relationship, Foucault argues, are rooted in different political and social institutions; these meanings are communicated by way of what he calls discourses (MacLure, 2003). Discourse usually indicates the style of language used by different institutions or professions which reflects their particular beliefs and principles (Danaher et al., 2000). For example, the type of discourse used in an educational sense frequently encompasses notions of assessment, achievement, standards and qualifications (Oliver, 2010). Discourse can be firmly aligned with the use of power. There are some modes of discourse, especially those used by the more powerful and established professions like law and medicine, which are typified by complicated terminology. This allows those of the same profession to talk with each other with ease and understanding. However, it has the effect of excluding those outside the profession from participating in the communication, which in turn allows the professional to have power over those who are outsiders (Oliver, 2010).

These key ideas of Foucault are interwoven throughout his writing and are relevant in gaining a holistic understanding of his philosophy in connection with education. It is *Discipline and Punish: The Birth of the Prison* (1979) which 'charts how the eighteenth century saw a transition from public execution to penal retention as a technique of social control' (Fisher et al., 2010: 109). This book is particularly associated with schools because it examines notions of discipline and power, and of 'educational processes as being concerned with the construction of an obedient and governable subject' (Fisher et al., 2010: 109). Foucault organises the book about the history of prisons into four chronological phases. Part one is entitled

'Torture', part two 'Punishment', part three 'Discipline' and part four 'Prison', which has three sections: complete and austere institutions, illegalities and delinquency, and the carceral. By the sequential unfolding of the history of prisons:

> The story Foucault tells is the move from excessive public, physical punishments to private, invisible discipline of our psychological sense of selfhood, as a middle-class tactic to control popular (mass) socialization and alternative political and economic outlooks. (Schwan and Shapiro, 2011: 12)

Because of its association with education, it is part three, Discipline, which will be explored further in this section. Discipline has three elements: 'docile bodies', 'the means of correct training' (which is further subdivided into 'hierarchical observation', 'normalising judgement' and 'the examination') and 'panopticism' (Foucault, 1979).

'Discipline' in *Discipline and Punish: The Birth of the Prison* (1979) is closely associated with Foucault's notion of power–knowledge. He emphasised that discipline is not only enforced from above, but imposed by people themselves so that they could prosper in the 'new social and economic conditions that were emerging in Europe during the eighteenth and nineteenth centuries' (Danaher et al., 2000: 51). A core concern of discipline for Foucault was creating healthy docile bodies who could be controlled. As such, he argued that the human body was entering a process of the

> 'mechanics of power' … [which] … defined how one may have a hold over others' bodies, not only so that they may do what one wishes, but so that they may operate as one wishes, with the techniques, the speed and the efficiency that one determines. Thus discipline produces subjected and practised bodies, 'docile' bodies. (Foucault, 1979: 138)

This idea of docile bodies is aligned with schools where the day is governed by the timetable. Students and to some extent teachers, conform to the needs of time and move between different classrooms as well as changing from one subject area to another (Danaher et al., 2000).

Within 'the means of correct training' element of *Discipline and Punish: The Birth of the Prison* (1979) Foucault explains how people were restricted and constrained through the use of three surveillance methods of discipline to guarantee 'individuals were sorted, regulated, normalised and made to behave in particular ways' (Allan, 2013b: 24). The first of these was hierarchical observation. Observation he stated was the ideal disciplinary method 'which would make it possible for a single gaze to see everything constantly' (Foucault, 1979: 173). Hierarchical observation then

> encompassed a form of supervision of supervisors, with everyone accountable to authority from above. The effectiveness of the supervision was guaranteed … and since it was impossible to know when one was being watched, it was necessary to behave as if that was the case. (Allan, 2013b: 25)

This form of observation is evident in the design of schools where the 'buildings took on some of the characteristics of the factory … [which] … facilitated supervision, hierarchy and reward' (Fisher et al., 2010: 109).

The second notion within this element was normalising judgment, which Foucault argued was employed to rationalise methods of oppression. Humans can be assessed for the degree in which they differ from set standards. Then, 'disciplinary techniques can be used to homogenise and normalise, and, of course, exclusion can be justified as a means to these ends' (Allan, 2013b: 25). As such, normalising judgement is closely associated with the idea of discourse through the categorisation of certain behaviours as 'normal', or by identifying a student as a 'troublemaker' as a way of shaping the way they think about themselves. Therefore, this induces students not only to partake in scrutinising their own behaviours, they also become engaged in the practice of normalisation. In doing this they begin to develop an acknowledgement of what forms of behaviour are acceptable or not acceptable. Through this normalisation students in schools could come to understand, and agree, that particular behaviours could lead themselves or other students to be labelled 'troublemaker', without even challenging the label (Hope, 2013).

The third notion, the examination, Foucault explains is 'a normalizing gaze, a surveillance that makes it possible to qualify, to classify and to punish' (Foucault, 1979: 184).

> The creation of hierarchy through observation and judgement about deviations from the norm becomes fused in the examination, in the dual sense of looking (to examine) and grading (by subjecting individuals to tests). The examination is discipline's ritual ceremony that establishes the 'truth' about the subject, a knowledge that will both give individuals a subjective identity through their ranked result and objectify them as things to be manoeuvred or exercised further. (Schwan and Shapiro, 2011: 121)

The examination allows for individuals to be moulded in certain ways by society. It also enables society to have knowledge about individuals, which not only has the effect of creating homogenous and powerful groups, but in addition creates people who would also engage in self-monitoring (Scott, 2008).

The final element, and much cited principle, of the Discipline section is panopticism. A principle which applies a process of surveillance that was founded on an architectural prison structure 'the panopticon' designed by the eighteenth-century English philosopher and radical thinker Jeremy Bentham. The panopticon functions by prison officials being able to continuously observe the prison inmates in their tiered and back-lit cells from a central position in the prison building. However, the prisoners would be not be aware whether they were being watched. Thus 'control' would be 'internalised' in the mind of the individual. The prisoner therefore 'is seen, but he does not see; he is the object of information, never a subject in communication' (Foucault, 1979: 200). The aim of the panopticon is 'to induce in the inmate a state of conscious and permanent visibility that assures the automatic functioning of power'

(Foucault, 1979: 201). The designs of even recently constructed schools and colleges have physical similarities with the panoptic principle, with their large and easily observable open spaces (Fisher et al., 2010). Furthermore, modern schools also adopt simulated surveillance systems with the use of imitation CCTV cameras to encourage students to behave as if the cameras were authentic (Hope, 2013).

Many of Foucault's ideas were shaped by early and contemporary philosophers. His own thoughts have since been adopted by thinkers from a variety of fields, not least in education. Many of these thinkers are those who wish to explore and challenge the taken-for-granted idea of knowledge and power.

 ## LINKS WITH OTHER THEORISTS

Many of Foucault's ideas can be traced to the thoughts of the German philosopher Immanuel Kant (1724–1804) 'who challenged us to ask not what the world is made of but rather why we view it in the way we do' (MacBlain, 2014: 5). Kant was absorbed with critiquing the idea of what was seen as accepted knowledge during the Age of Enlightenment. What Foucault took from Kant's thinking about the Enlightenment was not a concept or theory but the idea of critique. Foucault challenged the thinking that knowledge is set for eternity; for him knowledge may alter from one historical period to the next (Bartlett et al., 2001). This notion of critique is evident throughout Foucault's writing, he even completed a thesis on Kant's works as part of his doctorate (Oliver, 2010). It was another German philosopher, Friedrich Nietzsche, whose thoughts inspired Foucault to structure his work as a history and to see individuals as subjects (Peters, 2001). Nietzsche suggested that knowledge and truth are created by, and between, establishments and professional disciplines and are offered as if they are timeless and complete, similar to Foucault's notion of dominant discourse (Barry, 2002).

Although Foucault was briefly a member of the Communist Party he did not consider himself a Marxist, yet he often cites Marx in his writing, particularly in *Discipline and Punish: The Birth of the Prison* (1979). Foucault uses Marx to substantiate his writing, and not in a disproving manner (Schwan and Shapiro, 2011). There is also a clear connection between the Italian Marxist thinker Antonio Gramsci and Foucault, particularly regarding power and knowledge in the way in which the state operated. Gramsci discussed how state institutions 'work to "win" popular consent for their authority through a variety of processes which disguise their position of dominance' (Barry, 2002: xii). Furthermore, Foucault's multi-faceted notion of power is linked with Gramsci's concept of 'hegemony' as a combination of 'coercion and consent to any organisation of society' (Schwan and Shapiro, 2011: 43).

Foucault's notion that power centres on certain sections of society, and that power is driven by his idea of dominant discourse, is similar to the English educational thinker Basil Bernstein's linguistic codes. A contemporary of Foucault, Bernstein, offered two codes of language: a restricted code and an elaborate code. The elaborate code, which was used by the middle classes, had the capacity for reasoning and had a wider vocabulary which gave learners an advantage in their schooling. On the other hand the restricted language code used by the working-class students was a hindrance to their learning (Moore, 2000). Foucault's challenge to the way society thought about knowledge was reflected also, to differing degrees, by his fellow philosophers in France. Jean-Francois Lyotard questioned the way in which knowledge is understood and how this process changes as time passes (MacBlain, 2014). Jacques Derrida, challenged us to think differently in the way in which we read and interpret the written word (MacBlain, 2014). The thoughts of Foucault and his contemporaries attracted considerable criticism.

CRITIQUING THE IDEAS

Today Foucault is considered one of the great philosophers whose ideas have formed the ways in which we think and understand. However, when his and the other contemporary French philosophers' works were first published they drew a great deal of condemnation. This was because their ideas were considered as 'posing threats and challenges to established fields and disciplines such as history, political economy, philosophy, sociology, literature, geography and psychology' (Danaher et al., 2000). Foucault and his colleagues were engrossed in the French academic debates of the time within the prestigious Paris universities. Each was conversant with the others' theoretical opinions and as such they developed a 'writing style that signalled their own position with a few casual words' (Schwan and Shapiro, 2011: 5). Foucault's writing in particular could be 'elliptical and obscure ... he is always trying out ideas and going off on tangents' (Ball, 2013: 12).

Foucault's convoluted and poetic style of writing has been seen by some of his critics as being a mask intended to perplex readers and cover the historical errors he made. Oksala (2007) states that there were a number of faults in his periodisation particularly in relation to the confinement of the mad, and the medicalisation of madness. Criticism also came from different intellectual fields, 'historians have rejected Foucault's work for being too philosophical, philosophers for the lack of rigour and sociologists for its literary or poetic quality' (McNay, 1994: 1). Perhaps the reason for such criticism is that his ideas can be employed in so many different fields of study even though they do not offer a definitive theory. Furthermore, Foucault's engagement in political action appears not to have been based upon any obvious theoretical standpoint. On the other hand his position as a philosopher was considered to be naïve and politically hollow because it lacked specific political evaluations (Oksala, 2007).

He received widespread condemnation from feminist and cultural thinkers because 'of gender blindness and ethnocentrism' (McNay, 1994: 10). Even though there is a scarcity of gender issues in his writing many of his ideas, such as discourse and power, have appealed to some feminist thinkers (Ball, 2013). Hope (2013) infers that Foucault could have paid more attention to the technologies of surveillance that were available during the 1960s and 1970s instead of the eighteenth and nineteenth centuries. This deficit of attention to the current technologies of the time, Hope argues, has weakened Foucault's analysis regarding surveillance. Furthermore, the rise in technologies since the 1960s and 1970s with the increasing use of CCTV, databases, social media and mobile communications should lead to a reappraisal of the panopticon principle (Hope, 2013). Notwithstanding these criticisms, Foucault's ideas have a profound relevance for education.

FOUCAULT'S IDEAS IN RELATION TO EDUCATION

The application of Foucault's ideas to education can be difficult for the practitioner working in classrooms. This is not surprising when his ideas are mainly conceptual and located within the intellectual milieu of continental philosophical circles which must seem detached from the realities of teaching practice (Murphy, 2013). However, the aim of Foucault's work was that as human beings we should 'work towards transformation, and, to a small degree, be agents of it … [and] … to change the way we perceive the people we judge' (Oksala, 2007: 24). These sentiments are core to caring and student-centred teaching, and many of Foucault's ideas have much to offer the education practitioner and researcher. This section will firstly explore his thoughts as they are specifically linked with education. Secondly, it will outline where his ideas can be related to practice.

Ball describes the state education system in England towards the end of the nineteenth century as 'ramshackle, ugly and smelly' (Ball, 2013: 39). However, it was a start of the state control of education which would shape and prepare children to be the docile bodies required to serve society and contribute to the nation's workforce. In line with Foucault's hierarchical observation, schools were being built to create an architectural 'space in ways that allow for total supervision' (Schwan and Shapiro, 2011: 115). It was not only buildings which allowed such classified observations, school inspectors observed teachers, who in turn observed students. Normalising of judgement and the examination were also evident:

> The judgements of the inspectors were also embedded in the classificatory practices of the classroom as new types of learner, 'bright' boys and their 'failing' counterparts, were identified within the newly evolving techniques of pedagogy and assessment. (Ball, 2013: 42)

School students and staff were being drawn into processes of discipline which normalise and standardise through observation and modification. This was done by breaking multi-faceted aspects of the school down into small components, so each part can be seen. Ball explains:

Schools are broken down into houses, the school day into a timetable and a curriculum (a serial space of serial knowledges) and into specialist locations; pupil movements are broken down within and into lessons, they are allocated to seats, organized onto tables or in rows, labelled, tested, measured and calculated by the techniques of examination. (Ball, 2013: 46)

These processes of discipline are evident in schools and other educational settings today. They are processes which are sustained and advanced by 'reforms' in education policy. Policy plays a significant role because it 'is about power to determine what gets done, or not done. These are profoundly political issues' (Bell and Stevenson, 2006: 23). Bell and Stevenson also stress the importance of taking into account 'the wider socio-political environment in shaping the discourse in which policy debate is conducted' (2006: 23).

When the Coalition Government in the UK came to power in 2010 they felt that there was a need to return to a more traditional approach to education in England which included deregulation; and the discourse from government certainly reflected that. This deregulation took the form of giving schools more autonomy in how they spent their funds; it also sought to expand the freedom of choice by increasing the number of academies and free schools. But schools were also required to improve examination results and comply with ever-more-stringent Ofsted inspections. Foucault was attracted to the idea of the power which emerges from changes in government and the resultant discourse that emerges. Both the Coalition Government and, from May 2015, the Conservative Government espoused the discourse of deregulation and freedom of choice in schools. This, however, it is argued, relates more to Foucault's idea of self-regulation rather than deregulation where the 'individual watches over his or her own behaviours, one that increases control while preserving the illusion of freedom' (Allan, 2013a: 219).

The education reforms in England since 2010 have centred on, as we have seen, the expansion of academies and free schools, a review of the curriculum, assessment (with an increasing level of importance of examinations over coursework) and qualifications. The new government also sought to revamp initial teacher education as they considered that not enough training took place in classrooms. The major skill set required for teachers was predominantly concerned with 'good behaviour management and the maintenance of effective classroom discipline' (Chitty, 2014: 96). The link between Foucault's notions of discipline and control was also evident in the Coalition's 'Troops to Teachers' initiative led by the then Education Secretary Michael Gove. This is a scheme to create a new and efficient teaching cadre from service personnel who are about to leave the Armed Forces, even though they may not have the standard qualifications to enter teacher training (Chitty, 2014).

There are a number of Foucault's ideas which can be related to work in classrooms. There are also some ideas which challenge the dominant discourse relating to what is perceived as good teaching. Moore uses the term discourse in the sense that Foucault does; he briefly outlines on the cover of his book *The Good Teacher:*

Dominant Discourses in Teaching and Teacher Education (2004) what he feels are the three dominant discourses of good teaching, which are:

- The competent craftsperson, currently favoured by central governments.
- The reflective practitioner, which continues to get widespread support among teacher trainers and educators.
- The charismatic subject, whose popular appeal is evidenced in filmic and other media representations of teaching.

He explores the idea that the two discourses of the competent teacher and the reflective practitioner are the 'dominant "official" discourses in teacher education, but have the capacity – if not the intention – both to weaken one another and to marginalise alternative teacher-education discourses' (Moore, 2004: 7). This then can create a dilemma for practitioners. However, for Foucault this dilemma presents teachers with an opportunity to question perceived notions of knowledge and truth about what is a good teacher, and make their own individual judgements.

The concept of reflective practice, from Foucault's point of view, is also problematic. Reflective practice has been heralded as a way of solving problems with the aim of improving future practice. The process of reflective practice involves the practitioner sharing problems or writing journals which contain personal feelings related to practice, as such

> This writing then is similar to autobiographical writing in the sense that one writes the self in connection with the presence of a virtual other. In this case, the virtual other takes the role of the master or the priest to compel us to speak (reflect on) the truth about ourselves and to interpret and assess this truth in relation to the norm… By confessing the true self to virtual others, a modification of behaviour is expected. (Fejes, 2013: 64)

It should be emphasised here that this represents Foucault's notion of reflective practice as being a process of self-monitoring, and is offered as an academic challenge with the aim of providing a critically analytic viewpoint. The role of reflective practice with its goal of personal development can be, and is, very actively emancipatory (Fejes, 2013).

As a university lecturer Foucault was suspicious of the value of teaching his students what they should think. He much preferred to urge the students to work things through themselves, which is similar to Socratic dialogue, where

> Instead of students being 'told' that something was true, they were invited to consider the logical consequences of certain forms of evidence. Students were thus invited to observe the empirical world, to record their observations, and then to draw systematic conclusions. (Oliver, 2010: 37)

During the late 1960s there was a movement, supported and practised by Foucault, to make education more student-centred. Students were given more liberty in their studies and teachers and students enjoyed more equitable relationships. This new movement also saw a rise in more diverse forms of assessment. The traditional examinations where students could be individually ranked and classified were being slowly replaced by group assignments and project work. These new forms of assessment made it difficult to contrast between students and as such there was a trend to keep clear of the system of categorising and ranking student outcomes. Foucault was a key influence in the advancement of student-centred teaching, and particularly assessment. The advances in student-centred education have 'helped make possible the transmission to the mass system of university education we know today' (Oliver, 2010: 37).

Foucault's philosophy has been instrumental in providing practical and theoretical depth to educational research. Silverman points out that Foucault had recognised that the effectiveness of observation had been core to prison development, and how interviewing had been key to the Catholic confessional (Silverman, 2006). Where Foucault's ideas have particularly influenced educational research is in the field of discourse analysis, which explores the nature and structure of data gathered from speech, text and images in association with power and hierarchies (Punch, 2009). The foundation of discourse analysis is that the data 'should never be taken "at face value" but, instead, should be investigated to reveal the hidden messages' (Denscombe, 2007: 308). This sceptical approach to research is closely connected to Foucault's ideas regarding education as a whole. His philosophy questions the ways of thinking rather than offering specific methods to apply. However, it is argued that educators should take a questioning approach to practice in their attempts at providing a transformational learning experience for students, and for themselves.

REFLECTIVE TASK

In *Discipline and Punish: The Birth of the Prison* (1979), Foucault explains the notion of the examination as 'a normalizing gaze, a surveillance that makes it possible to qualify, to classify and to punish' (Foucault, 1979: 184).
From your own experience of education:

1. List the mechanisms that support the notion of the examination.
2. Consider ways in which these mechanisms could be transformed to alleviate any undue pressure on those being examined.

SUMMARY

Foucault's profound and radical philosophy remains influential for educators and educational researchers. His ideas were contentious because they challenged long-held beliefs about truth, knowledge and the nature of power. Furthermore, he emphasised the ways in which knowledge and power were used to influence social control. His most important text for educators is *Discipline and Punish: The Birth of the Prison* (1979). From a practitioner and educational researcher's point of view there are two major aspects which are highly significant. Firstly, his ideas regarding discourse, which usually involve matters such as assessment, achievement, standards and qualifications. Secondly, his notion of surveillance, which includes the physical way we observe and are observed, but also the ways in which we self-monitor and self-regulate ourselves.

His philosophy emerged from his personal experiences and his involvement with other influential French philosophers of the time. He was actively involved in the protest movement during the 1960s and 1970s, a time of great social unrest. It is difficult to categorise Foucault as a follower of any particular movement. However, he is considered by many as being associated with poststructuralism because he contested conventional ways of thinking and the taken-for-granted forms of knowledge. Foucault's ideas were guided by Kant, Nietzsche and to some extent by Marx. There are strong links with Gramsci regarding power and knowledge. Furthermore, Basil Bernstein's work with language codes has resonance with Foucault's notion of discourse; there are also close associations with his fellow French philosophers Lyotard and Derrida.

Foucault attracted considerable criticism for a number of reasons. Much of his philosophy was considered a threat to the establishment and society because it challenged conventional thought and order. He was also censured due to his confusing writing style, and for the lack of rigour in his recording of history. Some commentators argued that Foucault could have addressed the more conventional modes of surveillance, rather than those used in a historical context. There are many aspects of his thoughts and ideas which are directly linked with education, and the way we think about education. These aspects include the formation of policy, the questioning of what is considered good practice, his student-centred approach to teaching, and the use of his ideas as practical and theoretical instruments for educational research. Although not all of these aspects have direct application to practice, they are all important because they enable practitioners to think critically about education.

 ## FURTHER READING

Deleuze, G. (1999) *Foucault*. London: The Athlone Press.
Written by a contemporary philosopher this is an insightful analysis of Foucault's major ideas such as knowledge, power and subjectivity.

Gutting, G. (2005) *Foucault: A Very Short Introduction*. Oxford: Oxford University Press.
A brief illustrated introduction to Foucault which is biographical and clarifies his key themes and the development of his philosophy.

Mills, S. (2003) *Michel Foucault*. Abingdon: Routledge.
An introductory text which not only explores Foucault's main ideas but offers some practical guidance for application in practice.

Rainbow, P. (Ed.) (1984) *The Foucault Reader: An Introduction to Foucault's Thoughts*. London: Penguin.
This book is an authoritative review of Foucault's works, with many extracts from his writings and material from interviews he gave.

REFERENCES

Allan, K. (2013a) *Contemporary Social and Sociological Theory* (third edition). London: SAGE.
Allan, J. (2013b) 'Foucault and his acolytes: Discourse, power and ethics'. In: Murphy, M. (Ed.) *Social Theory and Education Research*. London: Routledge.
Ball, S. (2013) *Foucault, Power, and Education*. London: Routledge.
Barry, P. (2002) *Beginning Theory: An Introduction to Literary and Cultural Theory*. (second edition). Manchester: Manchester University Press.
Bartlett, S., Burton, D. and Peim, N. (2001) *Introduction to Education Studies*. London: Paul Chapman.
Bell, L. and Stevenson, H. (2006) *Education Policy: Process, Themes and Impact*. London: Routledge.
Chitty, C. (2014) *Education Policy in Britain* (third edition). Basingstoke: Palgrave Macmillan.
Cole, M. (2008) *Marxism and Educational Theory: Origins and Issues*. London: Routledge.
Danaher, G., Schirato, T. and Webb, J. (2000) *Understanding Foucault*. London: SAGE.
Denscombe, M. (2007) *The Good Research Guide* (third edition). Maidenhead. Open University Press.
Fejes, A. (2013) 'Foucault, confession and reflective practices'. In: Murphy, M. (Ed.) *Social Theory and Education Research*. London: Routledge.
Fisher, R., Fulford, A., McNichols, B. and Thompson, R. (2010) 'The curriculum in the lifelong learning sector'. In: Avis, J., Fisher, R. and Thompson, R. (Eds) *Teaching in Lifelong Learning: A Guide to Theory and Practice*. Maidenhead: Open University Press.
Foucault, M. (1961) *Madness and Civilization: A History of Insanity*. London: Routledge.
Foucault, M. (1963) *The Birth of the Clinic: An Archaeology of Medical Perception*. London: Routledge.
Foucault, M. (1966) *The Order of Things*. London: Routledge.
Foucault, M. (1969) *The Archaeology of Knowledge*. London: Routledge.
Foucault, M. (1976) *The History of Sexuality. Vol. 1: The Will to Knowledge*. London: Penguin.
Foucault, M. (1979) *Discipline and Punish: The Birth of the Prison*. London: Penguin.
Foucault, M. (1984a) *The History of Sexuality. Vol. 2: The Use of Pleasure*. London: Penguin.
Foucault, M. (1984b) *The History of Sexuality. Vol. 3: The Care of the Self*. London: Penguin.
Hope, A. (2013) 'Foucault, panopticism and school surveillance research'. In: Murphy, M. (Ed.) *Social Theory and Education Research*. London: Routledge.
MacBlain, S. (2014) *How Children Learn*. London: SAGE.
MacLure, M. (2003) *Discourse in Education and Social Research*. Buckingham: Open University Press.

McNay, L. (1994) *Foucault: A Critical Introduction*. Cambridge: Polity Press.

Moore, A. (2000) *Teaching and Learning: Pedagogy, Curriculum and Culture*. London: RoutledgeFalmer.

Moore, A. (2004) *The Good Teacher: Dominant Discourses in Teaching and Teacher Education*. London: Routledge.

Murphy, M. (Ed.) (2013) *Social Theory and Education Research*. London: Routledge.

Oksala, J. (2007) *How to Read Foucault*. London: Granta.

Oliver, P. (2010) *Foucault – The Key Ideas*. London: Hodder Education.

Peters, M. (2001) 'Michel Foucault, 1926–84'. In: Palmer, J. (Ed.) *Fifty Modern Thinkers on Education: From Piaget to the Present*. London: Routledge.

Peters, M. and Besley, T. (2012) 'Education and postmodernism'. In: Arthur, J. and Peterson, A. (Eds) *The Routledge Companion to Education*. London: Routledge.

Punch, K. (2009) *Introduction to Research Methods in Education*. London: SAGE.

Schwan, A. and Shapiro, S. (2011) *How to Read Foucault's Discipline and Punish*. London: Pluto Press.

Scott, D. (2008) *Critical Essays on Major Curriculum Theorists*. Abingdon: Routledge.

Silverman, D. (2006) *Interpreting Qualitative Data* (third edition). London: SAGE.

8

NEL NODDINGS

CARING IN EDUCATION

LEARNING OUTCOMES

Having read this chapter you should be able to:

- Understand the work of Nel Noddings
- Distinguish between natural and ethical caring
- Recognise the difference between cared-for and carer, caring-for and caring-about
- Understand how ethics of caring can be applied to education
- Critique Noddings' theory of ethical caring

KEY WORDS

Ethics of care; caring; cared-for; feminist; moral education; engrossment; motivational displacement; natural caring; modelling; dialogue; practice; confirmation

INTRODUCTION

Nel Noddings is a well-known philosopher of education and feminist ethics who currently holds the role of Jacks Professor Emerita of Child Education at Stanford University. She is perhaps best known for her work around the ethics of caring, which she has applied to education, seeking a means by which to apply the ethics of care to schooling. In so doing, Noddings has demonstrated how caring in education can be seen as an educational goal, particularly for those wishing to apply a more ethical and moral foundation to their teaching.

Despite her early training as a mathematics teacher, Noddings' doctoral studies saw her exploring philosophy and the study of ethics, and her early work centred on moral action and the basis for this. Noddings sought to reconceptualise evil from the perspective of women, and began to consider how 'natural caring', that is the care of the mother for a child, could be seen as a moral attitude. In this respect Noddings began to see how 'care' was transferable as individuals attempted to replicate their own memories of caring. From this Noddings developed the concept of ethical caring, this being the moral obligation to care, and something which is developed from the early experiences of natural caring. Noddings (1984) suggests that the human condition is one that wants to be seen as moral, and in this respect individuals will want to be seen as caring in order to remain in a caring relationship.

Noddings firmly believes in the home as the primary educator, and recommends that, 'schools should as far as possible, use the sorts of methods found in the best homes to educate' (Noddings, 2002: 289). Noddings also advises that schools should include education for home life as part of their curriculum, believing this to be important in the development of a good moral education.

Noddings has sought to transform education through her caring philosophy, and suggests that education should be more personalised, she argues that the current curriculum fails to take account of the individual needs and talents of pupils, and relies too heavily on standardised tests and attainment. In addition, Noddings proposes that more should be done to improve relations between students and teachers, suggesting that teachers who truly care are more interested in the individual needs of their students, rather than those whose caring only extends to coercing students into achieving at subjects they have little interest in.

Noddings draws from her own personal experiences in developing her philosophies. She has sought to develop student–teacher relationships because she recalls her own positive relationships with teachers when growing up (Flinders, 2001), and in reflecting on the importance of home she must surely draw from her first-hand experience of being married for over forty years (her husband died of cancer in 2012), and raising ten children.

NEL NODDINGS, THE PERSON

Nel Noddings has a long and illustrious career in the fields of education and philosophy, and it was her own positive experiences of being taught that motivated her to seek both a career in education, and also to focus on the place of care in education. Flinders (2001) observes that schooling played a central role in Noddings' life, most specifically her first-hand experience of caring teachers, which later led to an interest in the relationship between students and their teachers.

Noddings' career in education has spanned the full range of educational settings, from elementary through to secondary and post-secondary education. Noddings gained her bachelor's degree in mathematics and physical science from Montclair State College, New Jersey, followed by a masters degree in mathematics from Rutgers University in New Jersey (Smith, 2016). She taught in both elementary and high school following this, as well as working as an administrator in New Jersey public schools. Her first job as a mathematics teacher reflected Noddings' early positive experiences of education since she chose subjects taught by the teachers she most admired. Flinders (2001) notes that it was only afterwards that she turned her attention to the subject matter itself.

While Noddings maintained an interest in mathematics through undertaking research into mathematics education, she became increasingly interested in educational theory and philosophy, gaining a doctorate in educational philosophy from Stanford University in 1975. After being awarded her PhD, Noddings served on the faculties of both Pennsylvania State University and the University of Chicago. At the University of Chicago she directed the Universities Laboratory School, a role which Flinders (2001) suggests must have held particular appeal given the school's past associations with John Dewey, who has heavily influenced Noddings throughout her academic career.

In 1977 Noddings took a position in the education faculty at Stanford University, where Flinders (2001) observes she served in all ranks, 'including as director of Stanford's teacher education program and as acting Dean' (2001: 210). In 1992 Noddings was appointed as an endowed chair, and was named the Jacks Professor of Child Education. Following her retirement from Stanford she taught at Teachers College Columbia until 2000.

Despite officially retiring from Stanford in 1998 Noddings continued to hold a number of high-profile positions including the A. Lindsay O'Connor Professorship of American Institutions at Colgate University and the Libra Professorship at the University of South Maine (Smith, 2016). At the time of writing she is the Jacks Professor Emerita of Child Education at Stanford University and also holds the John W. Porter Chair in Urban Education at Eastern Michigan University. In addition, she is president of the Philosophy of Education Society, and president of the John Dewey Society (Coleman et al., 2011).

While Noddings' early research was in the field of mathematics, a field in which she continues to make contributions, she became increasingly focused on philosophy and the study of ethics. In her first book, *Caring: A Feminine Approach to Ethics and Moral Education* (1984), Noddings raises the question: what is the basis for moral action? This is a theme which she has maintained throughout her subsequent works, including thirteen published books, and over 200 articles.

It was through this book and ensuing texts that Noddings established herself as a leading feminist scholar, since she drew on a range of feminist theories to support analyses made. This was further reinforced in her second book *Women and Evil* (1989), which saw her drawing on the experiences of women in establishing the 'need for a morality that will help individuals understand and control their own tendencies towards evil' (Flinders, 2001: 212). Noddings suggests that courage is required as a defence against this evil, and believes it is through a caring approach that such courage is nurtured.

While it is without question that Noddings' work has made a 'significant contribution to ethics, phenomenology and feminist scholarship' (Flinders, 2001: 212), it should also be noted that Noddings' work has impacted on educational practice, an area which will be focused on in this chapter. Flinders (2001) suggests that this aspect of her work should be seen as transformational since she sought to transform the structures of teaching and schooling in order to encourage more caring relations and the growth of individuals. Noddings outlined her beliefs in her 1992 book, *The Challenge to Care in Schools*, in which she critiqued liberal education in schools, the traditions of which she saw as being the best education for students (Flinders, 2001).

Noddings has, then, made some remarkable contributions to the fields of education and philosophy, and has received a number of accolades as testament to the contributions made. However, Noddings herself reflects on only three categories of things that matter to her: domestic life, learning and writing, and living life as a moral quest (O'Toole, 1998). In respect of her domestic life O'Toole reports that she describes herself as 'incurably domestic' – she was married to the same man for forty-eight years, and raised ten children. Noddings admits to liking 'order in the kitchen, a fresh table-cloth, flowers on the table and food for waiting guests', something she recognises may well be out of keeping with her feminist principles (O'Toole, 1998). However, despite her love for her family she also acknowledges her love of learning and writing through the need to seek solitude in her study on a daily basis.

THE THEORY

Nel Noddings is perhaps best known for her writing on the ethics of care, setting out her philosophy in the aforementioned book *Caring* (1984), in which she identified the idea of care as a feminine ethic, applying it to the practice of moral education (Fieser and Dowden, n.d.). In defining caring Smith (2016) suggests that, as a concept, it is not easy to establish, but from Noddings' point of view the principle behind it is to consider the actual experience of caring from the perspective of those engaged in caring encounters. Noddings suggests that while engaging in such encounters individuals discover that they are receptive and attentive in a special way (Noddings, 2002). For Noddings, care is basic in human life – that all people wanted to be cared for (Noddings 2002: 11). Drawing largely from a feminist perspective she suggests that caring relationships are fundamental to human existence and consciousness (Fieser and Dowden, n.d.).

Within a caring relationship Noddings identifies two discrete parties, the 'cared-for' and the 'one-caring-for'. Noddings theorised that both parties are obliged to care reciprocally, meeting the other morally, but not in the same manner. Noddings' notion of caring was very much established on the basis of individuals being guided by an ethic of care – that is 'natural caring', in which individuals have a natural propensity to care, such as the care a mother gives to a child (Flinders, 2001). Noddings sees this as something that is inbuilt, suggesting that 'natural caring, thus is a moral attitude – a longing for goodness that arises out of the experience or memory of being cared for' (1984: 220). Individuals who remember being cared for in the past will be able to model that caring as they latterly become the one-caring-for.

Noddings talks of the caring encounter in respect of the individual's response to it, and suggests that caring is an act of engrossment (Fieser and Dowden, n.d.). For a successful caring encounter the one doing the caring must receive the cared-for on their own terms, and should resist the temptation to project the self onto the cared-for, that is they should be open to what the cared-for is saying, which Noddings refers to as *receptive attention*. The encounter should be without judgement, that is it should not be measured against some pre-established ideal (Noddings, 2005), and the motives to care should be inherently selfless, that is the act is performed solely for the benefit of the cared-for, and the one doing the caring should expect nothing in return other than the acknowledgement that an act of caring has occurred. The carer should respond to the cared-for in ways that are helpful with the 'carers motive energy flowing towards the cared-for' (Smith, 2016: 6), also known as *motivational displacement*. Noddings (2005) does acknowledge that in the case of motivational displacement the carer may not always approve of the wants of the cared-for and may ultimately lead the cared-for to a better set of values, but she emphasises the importance of taking account of the feelings and values evident at the time and responding as positively as possible.

In this respect then it would appear that the cared-for is benefiting the most from the caring encounter; however, Noddings also observes that there should be some connection between both parties with some degree of reciprocity. Both parties should gain from the encounter, but in different ways; for example, in a successful encounter the cared-for recognises the caring and will respond in some detectable manner such as an infant smiling and wriggling in response to a mother caregiving (Noddings, 2005: 2). The mother gains her satisfaction from the response of her child.

Noddings identifies three elements to the caring encounter:

(1) A cares for B, that is A's consciousness is characterised by attention and motiva-tional displacement, and
(2) A performs some act in accordance with (1), and
(3) B recognises that A cares for B.

(Noddings, 2002: 19)

Noddings views a caring person as one who is able to regularly establish caring relationships, maintained over a period of time when appropriate.

In addition to identifying the cared-for and the one-caring-for Noddings also distin-guishes between caring-for and caring-about, and locates this as a form of moral obligation. In the case of the cared-for, Noddings refers to first-hand, face-to-face encounters where one person cares directly for another (Smith, 2016). However, con-sideration must also be given to the caring-about, which Fieser and Dowden (n.d.) define as the nurturing of caring ideas or intentions. When caring-about something this tends to be in more general terms, and is of less personal concern. So, for exam-ple, we might care about poverty in a poorer countries, and as a result carry out some charitable works to show we care. In her earlier writings Noddings proposed that caring-about involves a certain benign neglect, suggesting that

> One is attentive just so far. One assents with just so much enthusiasm. One acknowledges. One affirms. One contributes five dollars and goes onto other things. (Noddings, 1984: 112)

Noddings believed that caring needed to be reciprocal, and in the case of caring-about the more remote the object of care then the less likely reciprocity was to occur, so the scope of caring is diminished. Noddings expressed that it was impossible to care for everyone, and while we might care for objects in our immediate environment which might respond to but not reciprocate the care, this was less likely to occur where objects were so remote that care is unlikely to be completed.

Noddings' views on caring-about proved controversial (Fieser and Dowden, n.d.) and she later revised them, arguing that caring-about did in fact deserve more atten-tion, and suggested that caring should encompass learning what it means to be cared-for, then learning to care for and then finally learning to care about others (Noddings, 2002). Noddings began to view caring-about as being an important stage for inspiring local and global justice, although she maintained the view that it was impossible to care for all, especially for more distant others (Fieser and Dowden, n.d.).

↻ LINKS WITH OTHER THEORISTS

When considering Noddings' views on developing a curriculum which takes account of the individual needs of all pupils, parallels can be drawn with the work of John Dewey, who himself favoured a curriculum tailored in such a way. Similarly, both Dewey and Noddings argue that the curriculum should not reflect social or occupational needs (Flinders, 2001) and Noddings has openly supported Dewey's argument that no subject is inherently more intellectual than another (Noddings, 2008). Dewey too talked of education as a vehicle for preparing students for 'public life' and firmly believed that a college degree should not be the means by which one earned respect (Dewey, 1927). Noddings' (2008) ideas reflect this notion, as she suggests that adolescents should be educated for life in a democratic society, regardless of their eventual occupation, stating 'not everyone needs to go to college, but everyone needs and deserves a genuine education' (Noddings, 2008: 37).

Noddings has also criticised an education system which relies heavily on standardised testing as a means of measuring pupils' progress, and suggests that pupils are being forced to take courses which are considered necessary to enter college education, rather than courses in which they have a genuine interest. She goes on to suggest that teachers are compromising the delivery of these courses in order to protect pupils from failure (Noddings, 2008). This is reminiscent of the work of John Holt, who argued that the testing regime in American schools was inhibiting pupils' learning, and suggested that the fear of failure prevented pupils from accessing the form of learning which best met their individual needs. Holt believed that the school system was responsible for turning children away from learning, and this is echoed by Noddings who observes that 'youngsters who fail repeatedly in their school years are likely to reject opportunities for further learning' (2008: 37).

Noddings' work on care and moral education has clear links with the work of humanist theorists such as Carl Rogers, Abraham Maslow and Urie Bronfenbrenner. Like Rogers, she expounded the idea of the development of the 'true self', and claimed that '[selves] … are under continual construction through encounters of all kinds, the effects these encounters produce and reflective evaluation of these efforts' (Bergman, 2004: 153). This would reflect Rogers' theory of self-actualisation, in which individuals strive towards the 'ideal self', in order to reach fulfilment. Like Rogers, Noddings firmly believes in the role of those closest to the child in supporting them through their journey to the ideal, or true, self.

Noddings sees the foundations of care theory as very much situated in the home, and firmly believes that children should 'live in a home that has at least adequate material resources and attentive love' (Noddings, 2002: 289). This reflects the work of Urie Bronfenbrenner who, in his ecological systems theory, placed the influence of the home and family firmly at the centre of his model. Noddings believes that caring is learned and observes that the memory of being cared for is strong, and most often learned as result of being cared for, she quotes Bronfenbrenner saying, 'if we are lucky someone will have been "crazy about that kid"' (Noddings, 1984: 61; 2002: 25).

CRITIQUING THE THEORY

Noddings wrote from a largely feminist perspective, and has been subject to some criticism from other feminist writers. When discussing 'natural caring' Noddings uses the maternal experience as a means of defining this as a concept. Noddings uses the physical and emotional experiences of women carrying and bringing a child into the world to explain the different roles of men and women in caring, and while she acknowledges that men can care, she suggests that this is a different kind of caring. This could be considered a somewhat controversial view in a time when the family unit is less traditional than it once was. Keller (1995) suggests that Noddings' work is reinforcing gender stereotypes of the woman as the homemaker, which goes against feminist principles. In addition, there is some conflict between women taking the role of carer and their own moral development since, as Carol Gilligan (1977) observes, a woman who sacrifices her needs for the needs of others would be at 'level two' of her own moral development model for women. Therefore, according to Gilligan, this woman would not yet be fully morally developed.

The notion of total engrossment, as outlined by Noddings, which sees the carer as supporting those cared for without question or prejudice has also been criticised. Davion (1993) warns that total engrossment in another individual could be dangerous, and might see the carer compromising their own morals as they support the cared-for. This is particularly concerning if the moral path chosen is one which is lacking in good moral standing. Furthermore, Davion (1993) also cautions against a one-sided caring relationship in which caring is not reciprocated – she suggests that this reflects an unhealthy relationship in which the carer is sacrificing their own development of self.

From an educational perspective, Noddings considered that teachers and students should form a trusting and caring relationship, offering a pedagogic vision of authentic caring. Noddings saw this as teachers embracing students as individuals in a nurturing and caring manner. In opposition to this is aesthetic caring, in which teachers are only interested in caring from the perspective of how well students do in tests and assessments. While it would be difficult to argue against seeing students as individuals and planning their education accordingly, it must also be questioned how realistic this is in a society which is so driven by results and achievements. Noddings makes the assumption that teachers who are striving for the best for their students reflected through test results show caring at a largely superficial level; however, it could be argued that these teachers care enough to want their students to be the best they can, and sometimes 'tough love' is necessary to accomplish this.

 ## NODDINGS AND CARING IN AN EDUCATIONAL CONTEXT

Noddings' early work on caring and evil saw her making 'significant contributions to ethics, phenomenology and feminist scholarship' (Flinders, 2001: 212); however,

Flinders (2001) also observes that equally important was her application of philosophy to inform educational practice. Noddings saw how her work on caring and relations might encourage the growth of individuals, and she thus set out to transform school structures and curricula in a manner which might promote caring and moral education.

In her book, *The Challenge to Care in Schools* (1992), Noddings criticised a curriculum which failed to acknowledge the individual interests and talents of its students, focusing instead on mathematics, science, languages and so on (Flinders, 2001), and suggested that by delivering the same curriculum for everyone teachers would be forced into coercion, which ultimately could undermine the positive relationships required for learning and growth. It is perhaps through her own experience as a mother of ten children that Noddings began to ask how parents would like to see a diverse group of children educated, and called for an education which is organised around the individual needs of its pupils.

Noddings believes that fundamental to providing a curriculum which serves the needs of individuals, a caring relationship needs to be forged between teachers and pupils. Noddings sees the challenge in this relationship as defining exactly what is meant by 'a caring teacher', and suggests that for some teachers 'caring' in the virtues sense of the word might well be achieved, but this does not assume a relation of care and trust, which, for Noddings, would be the ideal. Noddings (2005) states

> But even for the majority [of teachers] who do 'care' in the virtues sense – that is they profess to care and work hard at their teaching – there are many who do not adopt the relational sense of caring. They 'care' in the sense that they conscientiously pursue certain goals for their students, and they often work hard at coercing students to achieve these goals. (2005: 1)

Noddings asserts that in order for an effective relationship to be forged pupils need to know that they are cared for and suggests that the pupils themselves are able to distinguish between the teachers that care and those who care for them. Noddings observes that pupils might respect those teachers who care, but maintains that work is undertaken due to a sense of duty rather than through any love of learning. Noddings continues to look to the organisation of the school in seeking reasons for this apparent lack of care, suggesting that 'sometimes the conditions of schooling are so bad that teachers who want to care and students who want to be cared for cannot form the kind of relations we would properly label caring' (Noddings, 2005: 2). In this respect Noddings suggests that more needs to be done to provide the right conditions for a caring relationship to form, for example through smaller classes so more time can be spent for positive interaction, less standardised testing allowing for exploration of topics of mutual interest and the development of a curriculum which builds on pupils' interests. Noddings recognises the challenge of this task and acknowledges the importance of the need for time and encouragement in order for this to be achieved.

Noddings sets out her recommendations for educating from a care perspective through recommending the application of four key components: modelling, dialogue, practice and confirmation.

MODELLING

For Noddings, care is not something that can be learned from a book, nor can students be told to care, instead 'we have to show in our behaviour what it means to care' (Noddings, 2012: 237). Noddings also advocates that the care shown must be sincere, so that it is not just shown for the purpose of modelling, but is a by-product of genuine care.

DIALOGUE

It is not enough to show caring, Noddings advises that students should be engaged in dialogue about the care they are receiving, Noddings suggests that dialogue is inherent to caring, but acknowledges that care can manifest itself in different ways so, in order to understand it, students may need help with the interpretation of care. It should also be noted that dialogue can also support the carer in reflecting on the care they give, and in this respect dialogue can open up a two-way discussion, which Noddings believes is important in raising ethical questions; she sees it as a stimulus to reflection and a powerful tool for promoting the building of students' ethical ideals (Noddings, 2012).

PRACTISE

Where the teacher models and engages in dialogue about care, the role of the student is to practise caring for themselves, and for Noddings this should be through engagement in caring apprenticeships, and subsequent reflections on this. Initially, Noddings advises this may come through working with school custodians, or as classroom aides to younger children, but then this should be extended to the wider community through some form of community service, such as in nursing homes or animal shelters. Noddings states, 'children need to participate in caring with adult models who show them how to care, talk with them about the difficulties and rewards of such work, and demonstrate in their own work that caring is important' (2012: 239).

CONFIRMATION

Noddings observes that 'when we confirm someone, we identify a better self and encourage its development' (2012: 239); however, she is quick to point out that the aspiration is not a single ideal for all, but rather high expectations for all (Noddings, 2012). Through confirmation Noddings suggests that the aim should be to 'recognise something admirable, or at least acceptable, struggling to emerge in each person we encounter' (2012: 239). Additionally, confirmation requires trust and continuity, with each seeing the goal to be achieved as worthy and credible. Noddings advises that confirmation should not be given where ways are judged to be wrong.

While Noddings aspires for education to be seen as central to the development of a caring society, a tension does exist since, as Smith (2016) observes, the school system in capitalist societies is organised around a need to equip youngsters for business and the economy, and while some attention is paid to personal and social life, this is not sufficient to meet the demands of Noddings' vision of a system which promotes care theory. For Noddings, policy-makers should look to the home as a child's primary educator as a means of developing a model for a caring system, suggesting that 'schools should, as far as possible, use the sorts of methods found in best homes to educate' (Noddings, 2002: 289). Alongside this Noddings advocates that children should, 'live in a home that has at least adequate material resources and attentive love; and second, that schools should include education for home life in their curriculum' (2002: 289).

In considering education Noddings (2006) also recommends that schools should create an environment which promotes critical thinking, suggesting that the incorporation of critical thinking skills and critical lessons will assist students in their daily lives. Noddings sees critical lessons as those which allow free discussion on topics viewed as controversial, such as Adam and Eve, and the invasion of Iraq, to give but two diverse examples, topics which Noddings believes have been avoided in schools. By allowing free debate on such issues Noddings suggests that students are being prepared for many aspects of adulthood which would not necessarily be learned through the more traditional curriculum subjects.

Noddings has then promoted an educational philosophy in which care is embedded, but also one which places less emphasis on the knowledge and skills required of the capitalist society, and more on the personal growth of the individual. She argues against a system which focuses on the specification of what must be learned and on testing (Noddings, 2005), and advocates a system whereby teachers, working from the care perspective, focus on the individual needs of their students. She acknowledges the role of the family in the child's education, and suggests that where secure relationships are formed between parents and teachers, and teachers and students then there will be fewer calls for accountability. Finally, Noddings urges schools to tackle controversial issues through open debate and free speaking, giving students the confidence to voice their opinions in a safe and supportive environment.

REFLECTIVE TASK

Noddings believes that: 'Classrooms should be places in which students can legitimately act on a rich variety of purposes, in which wonder and curiosity are alive, in which students and teachers live together and grow' (Noddings, 1992: 12).

Thinking back to your own experience of schools, do you recall experiencing this? How might you ensure that this is something you might aspire to as a classroom practitioner?

SUMMARY

Nel Noddings is the author of thirteen books and over 200 articles, and despite retiring from Stanford in 1998, she has remained a prolific writer in the fields of philosophy and education, receiving a number of accolades which pay testament to the contributions she has made to both fields.

Noddings began her career as a teacher in both elementary and secondary school, and drew on her own positive experiences of school to help her develop a teaching philosophy. This was then followed by a doctorate in educational philosophy, which set the foundation for her subsequent work that saw her establish herself as a feminist writer. Noddings began to consider the question of moral education, and how the ethics of caring could be used to help develop a moral attitude. Noddings saw how natural caring could be used to set the foundation for ethical caring, and set about applying her vision to school systems with the aim of encouraging a more personalised curriculum, and improving relations between students and teachers.

Noddings has not been without her critics, ironically this has frequently come from feminist writers, the perspective from which her early work was written. Noddings has been accused of perpetuating the gender stereotype of caring as being a predominantly feminine role. It could also be considered that Noddings' ethic of caring encourages unequal relationships, in which the cared-for becomes dependent upon the carer, and the carer sacrifices their own true self in favour of carrying out the role of carer.

Nevertheless, as Smith writes, Noddings 'has made a significant contribution to deepening our understanding of what education entails' (2016: 17). She has brought to the fore the importance of caring, especially in respect of its place as a moral attitude, and has encouraged a more caring attitude between students and teachers. Noddings emphasises the importance of caring, and shows how by learning to care, we can, not only care for others, but also care about others, which, in essence, provides the basis for a caring society, in which both the carer and cared-for receive mutual gratification.

FURTHER READING

Charney, R.S. and Noddings, N. (2015) *Teaching Children to Care: Classroom Management for Ethical and Academic Growth K-8*. Turner Falls: Center for Responsive Schools.
A practical guide for teachers in adopting a classroom management style which encourages cooperation and the building of positive relationships.

Lake, R. (2012) *Dear Nel: Opening the Circles of Care (Letters to Nel Noddings)*. New York: Teachers College Press.
A series of open letters providing a moving tribute to Noddings.

Noddings, N. (2003) *Happiness and Education*. New York: Cambridge University Press.
A debate as to whether happiness and education can co-exist through a critique of the American education system, and a view of how the curriculum might look if happiness was included as part of it.

REFERENCES

Bergman, R. (2004) 'Caring for the ethical ideal: Nel Noddings on moral education'. *Journal of Moral Education*, 33(2): 149–62.

Coleman, K., Depp, L. and O'Rourke, K. (2011) *The Educational Theory of Nel Noddings*. www.newfoundations.com/GALLERY/Noddings.html.

Davion, V. (1993) 'Autonomy, integrity, and care'. *Social Theory and Practice*, 19: 161–82.

Dewey, J. (1927) *The Public and Its Problems*. New York: Henry Holt.

Fieser, J. and Dowden, B. (Eds) (n.d.) 'Care ethics'. *Internet Encyclopedia of Philosophy*. www.iep.utm.edu/care-eth/#SH1b.

Flinders, D.J. (2001) 'Nel Noddings, 1929–'. In: Palmer, J. (Ed.) *Fifty Modern Thinkers on Education. From Piaget to the Present*. London: Routledge.

Gilligan, C. (1977) 'In a different voice: Women's conceptions of self and morality'. *Harvard Educational Review*, 47: 481–517.

Keller, J. (1995) 'Autonomy, relationality, and feminist ethics'. *Hypatia*, 12: 128–33.

Noddings, N. (1984) *Caring: A Feminine Approach to Ethics and Moral Education*. Berkeley: University of California Press.

Noddings, N. (1989) *Women and Evil*. Berkeley: University of California Press.

Noddings, N. (1992) *The Challenge to Care in Schools*. New York: Teachers College Press.

Noddings, N. (2002) *Starting at Home: Caring and Social Policy*. Berkeley: University of California Press.

Noddings, N. (2005) 'Caring in education'. *The Encyclopaedia of Informal Education*. http://infed.org/mobi/caring-in-education.

Noddings, N. (2006) *Critical Lessons: What Our Schools Should Teach*. New York: Cambridge University Press.

Noddings, N. (2008) 'Schooling for democracy'. *Phi Delta Kappan*, 90: 1: 34–7. www.pdkmembers.org/members_online/publications/Archive/pdf/k0809nod.pdf.

Noddings, N. (2012) *Philosophy of Education*. Boulder: Westview Press.

O'Toole, K. (1998) *What Matters to Nel Noddings and Why*. http://news.stanford.edu/news/1998/february4/noddings.html.

Smith, M. (2016) 'Nel Noddings: The Ethics of Care and Education'. *The Encyclopaedia of Informal Education*. http://infed.org/mobi/nel-noddings-the-ethics-of-care-and-education.

9

LAWRENCE STENHOUSE

LINKING THE CURRICULUM WITH THEORY, RESEARCH AND PRACTICE

LEARNING OUTCOMES

Having read this chapter you should be able to:

- Appreciate Stenhouse's background and contribution to education
- Understand and identify his ideas regarding curriculum development and the teacher as a researcher
- Recognise the links between his work and other educational thinkers
- Critically evaluate Stenhouse's notions on curriculum development, classroom research and teacher professionalism
- Recognise how his ideas could be applied in practice

KEY WORDS

Humanities Curriculum Project; Centre for Applied Research in Education; process curriculum model; objectives curriculum model; action research; extended and restricted professionalism

INTRODUCTION

Even though Lawrence Stenhouse died prematurely in 1982 while still working as an academic, he bequeaths a wealth of profound educational ideas. He was arguably the most prominent person in the field of curriculum development in the two decades leading up to his death. His work is exemplified by the thought that teaching should be informed by evidence-based classroom research; he also upheld the notion of teacher professionalism (Rudduck and Hopkins, 1985). His overriding contribution to educational thinking and practice was to emphasise the significance of artistry and self-improvement in teaching:

> More than any other contemporary educational theorist, Stenhouse grasped the pedagogical significance of viewing education as a form of *praxis* rather than a technological process. He understood that good teaching was an art rather than the mastery of techniques. (Elliott, 2007: 19)

It was during his leadership of the controversial Humanities Curriculum Project (1967–1972) that he was able to reinforce his interests in curriculum development and advance his ideas on the teacher as a researcher. The Humanities Curriculum Project (HCP) was funded by the UK Schools Council and the Nuffield Foundation and was set up principally for pupils in secondary education to help them consider, and make their own judgements, regarding the contentious issues of the day such as race and international conflicts. It was controversial mainly because the project rejected the use of pre-set learning objectives and encouraged teachers to become impartial during classroom discussions (Rowntree, 1981). At the heart of the project was Stenhouse's quest to discover 'the relationship between knowledge, authority and emancipation' (Rudduck, 1995: 6). As the project was coming to a close Stenhouse, and a number of his fellow academics, set up the Centre for Applied Research in Education (CARE) at the University of East Anglia. CARE evolved into a world-renowned centre of teacher research and curriculum design thinking (Rudduck, 1995).

Stenhouse's ideas were innovative and revolutionary; they focused on developing curricula which stressed the right of pupils to access knowledge, the use of classroom research to enable teachers to make judgements and the significance of collaboration in learning (Rudduck, 1995). He argued the case that teachers should be at the core of curriculum development. However, for them to be effective and to improve their practice teachers needed to be reflective and communicate their experiences with others. He contested the notion of the 'objectives' curriculum model, which he felt took knowledge to be preordained and also dampened student inquiry; the teacher being the expert and the student a passive partner in the learning. Stenhouse championed the 'process' curriculum model in which there were no set objectives and which allowed pupils to make their own meaning of the world through questioning and discussion with the teacher. This process model advanced learning as research, which in turn becomes the foundation for teaching – therefore research and teaching become implicitly linked (Stenhouse, 1975; Burton and Bartlett, 2005).

Stenhouse's ideas on curriculum development and design, his views on teacher research, and his enthusiastic support for teacher improvement and professionalism are all valid even in today's competitive and assessment-dominated educational environment. These ideas, as well as the censures they have attracted, the links with other educational thinkers and suggestions on how his thoughts could be applied in practice will be covered later in this chapter.

STENHOUSE, THE PERSON

Although born in Scotland in 1926, Lawrence Stenhouse's secondary education took place at Manchester Grammar School. He returned to Scotland to study for his first degree at St Andrew's University and then on to Glasgow University for his MEd, which he completed in 1956. By this time he had begun to develop an idea that he wished to explore, the issue of student emancipation. It was Stenhouse's own secondary education which helped develop his ideas and he was very aware of how some of his own teachers had enabled him to realise his own potential. However, when he began his teaching career he soon came to grasp the fact that schools were inhibited by conventional ideas about access to knowledge. Unlike his own, perhaps advantaged, experience of secondary school, the pupils he taught were not so fortunate in having such an enlightened school environment.

Following his foray into teaching he took up a staff tutorship in psychology and secondary education at the Institute of Education of the University of Durham, an institute which was resolute in its purpose of developing teaching practice in schools (Stenhouse, 1983). Stenhouse's next move was a return to Scotland as a principal lecturer in education at Jordanhill College. In 1966 while at Jordanhill he visited the United States for a conference where he met Joslyn Owen from the new Schools Council for Curriculum and Examination, who suggested he apply for the leadership of the HCP. Stenhouse, as we have seen, became the leader of the HCP until its demise; he then set up and led CARE at the University of East Anglia (Rudduck, 1995).

During his time at the HCP and CARE he drew together a number of like-minded progressive educational thinkers on curriculum development and research, such as Jean Rudduck, David Hopkins and John Elliott. Stenhouse himself went on to write a number of texts which gathered international acclaim. These included firstly *Culture and Education* (1971), and in 1975 his seminal text *An Introduction to Curriculum Research and Development*, a book heralded by Kelly as 'the definitive statement of the notion of curriculum as process' (2004: 224). Then just before his untimely death he collated his major writings in *Authority, Education and Emancipation*, which was published in 1983. Up until his death Stenhouse continued with his research interests on the curriculum. He also advanced a further body of knowledge on the relationship between theory and practice to demonstrate how practitioner research can help teachers develop their understanding and practice in classrooms (Rudduck, 1995).

THE IDEAS OF LAWRENCE STENHOUSE

Any attempt at chronologically outlining Stenhouse's ideas would be meaningless because his ideas, by their very nature, complement each other. With this in mind this section will only offer a rudimentary structure, which in turn will hopefully illustrate the synergy between his thoughts and concepts. Therefore, we will explore Stenhouse's work with the HCP and CARE in a little more detail; examine his ideas regarding curriculum design and development; and consider his views on practitioner research and how this is linked with teacher professionalism.

Perhaps the pinnacle of innovative thinking about curriculum development, and the championing of teacher research, was during the 1970s and at the heart of this pioneering movement was the Schools Council, which part-funded the HCP. The HCP worked very closely with schools and teachers to improve the manner in which contentious topics were taught. We have already discovered that the HCP shunned the use of prescribed learning objectives. As it was trying to empower secondary age pupils to engage in discussion about controversial matters and to arrive at their own conclusions, the HCP team argued that using set objectives at the start would 'pre-empt the very questions they wanted to raise' (Kelly, 2004: 151). The project tried to create an environment where pupils felt comfortable in evolving a culture of their own during their group discussions; in doing so they would be more adept at making sense of other cultures and the more formal language styles they encountered (Stenhouse, 1975).

The HCP and Stenhouse were also at the centre of the advancement of action research. He argued that meaningful development of the curriculum could only come from teachers themselves as they were at the core of classroom practice.

> [For Stenhouse] it was essential that teachers reflected upon practice, shared experiences and evaluated their work if the education of pupils was to improve. For Stenhouse, each classroom could be seen as a laboratory and each teacher a member of a research community... Stenhouse believed in the professional desire of teachers to improve education for their pupils and so benefit society... In this way a social democratic ideology ran through the work of the Schools Council. Curriculum reform was visualised as happening at the grass-roots level and involving all those with a stake in education. (Bartlett and Burton, 2016: 59)

It is interesting to note that aversion to the ideas of teachers being active and innovative in curriculum development, and the notion of teachers as influential authorities in education, eventually convinced Margaret Thatcher's Conservative Government to close the Schools Council (Burton and Bartlett, 2005). However, much of the work of the HCP moved on to CARE with Stenhouse as its leader. The importance of CARE was indicative of the growth of applied research and action research at the time (Goodson, 2005). CARE at the University of East Anglia was, until its closure in 2015, at the forefront of taking research outside universities and the promotion of democratic evaluation, action research, case study and ethnography. The CARE team worked not only with schools but with other public bodies (CARE, 2015). Because of the work of Stenhouse and the work of CARE, it is argued, practitioner research is now supported by departments of education at numerous universities.

At the beginning of his book *An Introduction to Curriculum Research and Development* Stenhouse makes an exploratory attempt at defining 'curriculum' as:

> an attempt to communicate the essential principles and features of an educational pro-
> posal in such a form that it is open to critical scrutiny and capable of effective translation
> into practice. (Stenhouse, 1975: 4)

In other words, for Stenhouse, the curriculum is a way of offering an idea for a learning experience which is open to criticism and ongoing evaluation – a process curriculum model. This notion was at odds with the widespread objectives model used in specific subject curricula, which focused on prescribed lists of learning outcomes that students have to passively achieve. This objectives model focuses on the training of skills and changing behaviours as well as the testing of students' attainment; it is also more concerned with stipulated instructional methods rather than allowing the teachers the liberty to think for themselves. As Kelly points out the objectives model 'substitutes teacher accountability for teacher responsibility ... it gives teachers responsibility without freedom' (Kelly, 2004: 151). The process model, on the other hand, is a process where the teacher invites active student inquiry rather than students submissively accepting given knowledge; it is related to the distinctiveness of the individual classroom and school; it allows students and teachers to work in harmony and gives the students opportunities – all of which Stenhouse argues will enable 'the attention [to] shift[s] from teaching to learning' (Stenhouse, 1975: 13).

The process model concentrates on the learning experience, which focuses on the roles and activities of the teacher and the learner as well as the learning environment. In focusing on these factors rather than prescribed learning objectives the 'process model appears to emphasise means rather than ends' (Neary, 2002: 62). Stenhouse makes the point that the process model is far more challenging in practice, as it 'rests with teacher judgement rather than teacher direction ... but it offers a higher degree of personal and professional development' (Stenhouse, 1975: 96–7). Unlike the objectives model, the process model also has the advantage of presenting a theoretical basis which more truthfully mirrors what actually is involved in classroom practice. In contrast to the mainly subject-specific objectives model, it is more to do with the making of numerous decisions and the 'complex process of dynamic interaction between the teacher and taught' (Kelly, 2004: 96). Some of the benefits of the process model include the weight given to dynamic positions of both teachers and learners, and the stress given to learning skills which can be transferable to other subjects and for life in general (Neary, 2002). For Stenhouse the process model fostered learner empowerment and emancipation, and gave teachers the freedom to improve their professional practice through research and evaluation.

Stenhouse advocated a closer link between research and teaching practice, and called for this to be encouraged from an early stage in teachers' careers:

> Students in training often notice a gap between the educationalist and the school not unlike that between Haig's headquarters and the mud of Flanders. So many seem elated by the discussion of educational ideas: so few are encouraged by close critical scrutiny of their own classrooms. The gap between aspiration and practice is a real and frustrating one. (Stenhouse, 1975: 3)

He argued that more experienced teachers should also be supported in engaging with a research community through in-service education and links with university education departments. Teachers, he thought, would be ideal researchers as they were always trying to improve their practice by knowingly, through reflection, recognising features of their teaching which they needed to develop. Stenhouse considered that this notion of the teacher researcher could be further advanced by teachers engaging more closely with the research community so they could access and link with other research and hence aim to build upon education theory from a practical viewpoint. The type of research he was promoting to achieve this aim was one 'which disciplines curiosity and calls certainty into question' (Rudduck and Hopkins, 1985: 112). Action research was what Stenhouse believed could be employed by teachers in their classrooms to develop their professional practice and further augment educational theory. According to Punch and Oancea (2014: 375) action research employs 'empirical procedures, in iterative cycles of action and research, to solve practical problems'. Action research presented teachers with the opportunity to participate in aspects of their own professional practice which they considered to be either issues to address, or aspects in which they were particularly interested, to ultimately improve the quality of the learning experience (Markless, 2003).

Stenhouse argued that curriculum development and the role of the teacher as a researcher should be the foundation for teacher professionalism. He was critical of the perceived demise of teacher professionalism, especially in the form of the 'teacher proof curriculum package' presented in the form of the objectives model (Rudduck, 1995: 4). Stenhouse alluded to the idea of a teacher being either a restricted professional, or an extended professional. The restricted professional was competent, adept at working with children, engaged in short training courses and even evaluated their own classroom performance. The extended professional has all these attributes as well as skills and values which involve engagement with curriculum development and research. The extended professional considers the broader issues of school and community, participates in a wide range of professional activities, seeks synergy between theory and practice, and is aligned with the critical evaluation of classroom teaching (Stenhouse, 1975). What was paramount for Stenhouse's principle for teacher professionalism was that 'Professionalism is based upon understanding as a framework for action and knowledge is always provisional' (Stenhouse, 1983: 192).

LINKS WITH OTHER THEORISTS

Stenhouse was particularly inspired by the sociologist Richard Peters' views on the process curriculum and the role of the teacher. But prior to the influence from Peters on the curriculum, Stenhouse was also aware of the similarity between Bruner's 'Man: A Course of Study' and his own HCP, both of which were devised without the use of behavioural objectives. Bruner's study was similar to the HCP in that it focused on areas of the social sciences and the experiences of differing cultures. There are also parallels with Dewey, particularly in regard to the importance of reflective practice and democracy for teaching practice. Furthermore, like Stenhouse, Dewey believed that classrooms should be like laboratories where teachers tested out their ideas to improve their professional practice. Dewey even set up a laboratory school in Chicago as early as 1894 when he was Professor of Pedagogy (Pring, 2004). Both Dewey and Stenhouse viewed the school as a community of pupils and teachers, where teaching was grounded in classroom research and such research was not only recognised but encouraged (Pring, 2004).

Stenhouse's concepts of extended and restricted teacher professionalism, albeit with some specific criticism about child-centredness and autonomy, emerged from the work of Eric Hoyle, who tried to capture the impact of teachers who were actively involved in curriculum development (Stenhouse, 1975). The origins of action research are located in the 1940s in the work of Kurt Lewin, who undertook a range of social experiments with a view to improving the opportunities of underprivileged groups in society, Stenhouse drew upon Lewin's ideas and adapted them for improving teaching and learning (Punch and Oancea, 2014). Furthermore, Stenhouse's notion of the teacher as researcher endeavouring to continually improve professional practice aligns closely with Schön's concept of the reflective practitioner, which suggests that action research is valuable in the construction of professional knowledge and practice (Wilson, 2013).

Stenhouse was the trailblazer for educational research in the UK and in many other countries and, as we have discovered, the centres for action research were the HCP and CARE, where he worked closely with schools and teachers to encourage and foster the notion of the teacher as researcher and curriculum developer. He also worked very closely with colleagues, who, in turn, carried forward and further developed Stenhouse's ideas with zeal and success. For example, Rudduck, Elliott and Hopkins have advanced classroom research and practice; 'while Carr and Kemiss continue to promote emancipatory notions of action research, and Whitehead and McNiff publish living theories' (Wilson, 2013: 235). So the spirit of Stenhouse's ideas on curricula, research and teacher professionalism lives on; however, some of his work has attracted a degree of disapproval.

CRITIQUING THE THEORY

It is perhaps not surprising in view of Stenhouse's idea of professional critical scrutiny that many of the most pertinent censures came from himself. He has been criticised for his sexist language in his writings and in the introduction of his 1983 book *Authority, Education and Emancipation* he offered an apology 'to all readers who for "he" must read "she", and my regrets to readers of whichever sex'. He was also very aware of the difficulties which were inherent in his process curriculum, particularly when it came to assessing student achievement. Even though he argued that assessment and examination were not altogether impossible accomplishments with the process curriculum model, he did concede that it was a difficult undertaking for teachers and students alike. He particularly acknowledged that the process curriculum could not be used to help low-ability students to pass examinations, as he argued the process model was a 'critical model, not a marking model' (Stenhouse, 1975: 95). Furthermore, he recognised the importance of examinations in modern society and admitted that most teachers would shape their teaching towards giving their students a greater opportunity for success in their examinations (Stenhouse, 1975). Another problem with the process curriculum model is that it relies heavily on the teachers. If they do not have the flexible skills needed for classroom discussion and the student-centred approach called for they will not have the back-up of the direction and accompanying resources available with the prescribed objectives curriculum model (Smith, 2000).

Stenhouse additionally accepted that the notion of the teacher as researcher is not a realistic option for most teachers given the increasing demands on their time in schools. Practitioner research takes time and a great deal of effort to develop good quality research methodology skills as well as some awkward critical professional scrutiny and reflection. It was for this reason that he urged education departments at universities to support teachers in schools and to play a part in teacher professional development. There is further criticism of the use of Stenhouse's idea of teacher research. Kemmis (1995: 4) suggests that the purpose of Stenhouse's notion of teacher research is somewhat vague:

> It was not clear, for instance, whether teachers were to contribute to public knowledge by writing about their work or whether it was enough that they deepen their own understanding and enhance their own practice. Nor was it clear whether the role of the practitioner in relation to theory-building was merely to test in the laboratory of the classroom, the ideas of professional researchers.

It is suggested that these limitations of time and the possible vagueness of the purpose of practitioner research are genuine factors in hampering the notion of teachers becoming extended professionals. Stenhouse granted that for this notion to become a reality for the majority of teachers 'that the teacher's professional self-image and conditions of work will have to change' (Stenhouse, 1975: 142). Despite these criticisms there are many facets of Stenhouse's work which can be adopted in schools to advance his ideas of curriculum development, research and professionalism.

APPLYING STENHOUSE'S IDEAS IN PRACTICE

Stenhouse did not see the teachers' role as being the experts who deliver knowledge to students, but as people who are adept at teaching because of their education and teacher training. He saw the role of the teachers as providing access to a world of knowledge and skills to students. Indeed he argued that teachers should see themselves as learners alongside their students rather than experts; this mode he contested fosters mutual learning through 'teaching by discovery or inquiry methods rather than by instruction' (Stenhouse, 1975: 91). He further suggested that if there were a generally accepted professional notion that teachers are also learners, there would be less of a threatening element in colleagues observing each other in classrooms (Stenhouse, 1975). The importance of peer observation, reflection and peer discussion following observation is central to Stenhouse's concept of 'systematic self-critical enquiry' to enhance not only the teacher and observer's skills as researchers but also to appraise and evaluate their teaching (Scott and Morrison, 2007).

These ideas of teachers as learners and the quest for self-critical enquiry are evident in Stenhouse's three aspects of what a curriculum should offer:

A. In planning:

1. Principles for the selection of content – what is to be learned and taught.
2. Principles for the development of a teaching strategy – how it is to be learned and taught.
3. Principles for the making of decisions about sequence.
4. Principles on which to diagnose the strengths and weaknesses of individual students and differentiate the general principles 1, 2 and 3 above, to meet individual cases.

B. In empirical study:

1. Principles on which to study and evaluate the progress of students.
2. Principles on which to study and evaluate the progress of teachers.
3. Guidance as to the feasibility of implementing the curriculum in varying school contexts, pupil contexts, environments and peer-group situations.
4. Information about the variability of effects in differing contexts and on different pupils and an understanding of the causes of the variation.

C. In relation to justification:

A formation of the intention or aim of the curriculum which is accessible to critical scrutiny.

(Stenhouse, 1975: 5)

It is this idea of what a curriculum should offer which, Stenhouse felt, should be adopted when discussing controversial issues with adolescent students. Controversial issues are by their nature divisive, in that society as a whole will have differing opinions, and this will include teachers, students and their parents. Therefore, it is paramount that teachers do not use their own standing to promote their viewpoint in an attempt to influence the students' thinking (Scott, 2008). Rather the teacher should facilitate a discussion between the students, a discussion where the divergence of views is defended without trying to gain a compromise, with the teacher acting as a chairperson to ensure that learning is taking place (Stenhouse, 1975). The teacher's role also includes creating an environment which stimulates communication between all group members and promoting a spirit of cooperation. These points were the outcomes from Stenhouse's observations of discussion-based teaching while at the HCP. These observations also revealed firstly that group dynamics were enhanced by the placing of chairs in such a way that encouraged discussion across the group, and a slow-paced discussion usually widens the participation. Secondly, understanding of a controversial issue is gained by sensitive listening to opinions and then employing questioning for elaboration 'rather than arguing against opponents and attempting to resolve divergence' (Stenhouse, 1975: 94).

Stenhouse stressed the significance of active learning as opposed to the passive learning evident in instruction. According to Harkin et al. (2001) active learning involved the three elements of creating, solving and 'hands-on' experience. Learners create meaning for themselves and are encouraged to interpret information in novel ways. Teachers should also give students the opportunity to use their experiences to solve problems, which not only helps with developing the decision-making process but also empowers and emancipates student learning. Hands-on experiences help students to be proficient and assured when using new tools and processes. It is certainly the case that the process curriculum model is appropriate for the student-centred approach to teaching which promotes active enquiry. To facilitate this active learning Neary (2002) suggests the teacher must be someone who is willing to change and develop, and be open to the unpredictability of the classroom. Furthermore, they should have 'empathy – the ability to see someone else's problem through one's own eyes and to communicate that understanding' (Neary, 2002: 63) Active learning for Neary (2002: 63) requires the characteristics of a 'facilitator' rather than those she considered inherent in a traditional 'teacher'; below she highlights the contrasting characteristics of these two notions:

Teacher	Facilitator
Focuses on teaching	Focuses on learning
Teacher centred	Student centred
Control	Sharing
Superior–subordinate relationships	Partnership

Director	Participant
Knowledge given	Knowledge available
Treats all the same	Perceives individual learning needs
Focuses on groups	Focuses on individuals
Closed learning environment	Open learning
Controls parameters of learning	Lets learners set parameters
Narrow horizon	Wider horizon

With a call for teachers to be facilitators it is interesting to note that Stenhouse favoured a formal approach between student and teacher, not a formality which was impersonal but a relationship which was fundamentally 'contractual' in its nature. This contract was a two-way process which required teachers to extend ways of thinking, and chances to discuss alternative ways of learning and the making of judgements in the classroom. The contract entailed students being responsible for their learning and that instead of acting up when being taught by a teacher who is easily unsettled by unacceptable behaviour, they should make the most of what that teacher has to impart – 'otherwise they are wasting their time and the teacher's, and disadvantaging themselves in terms of their right to learn' (Rudduck, 1995: 9). Such a contract would, Stenhouse believed, negate any personal partiality felt between the teacher and the student. Learning contracts also have a part to play in the somewhat problematic area of assessment in the process curriculum model. Within the process model, assessment, instead of coming at the end of the learning, occurs in every aspect of the process. The outcomes of this ongoing assessment are used to give feedback to students on their progress as a diagnostic or formative tool. As Neary (2002: 64) explains, the teacher takes a position of a 'critical appraiser of the learners' work with the emphasis on developing self-appraisal and self-assessment in the learners'.

One final feature of Stenhouse's ideas which is offered for consideration for application in practice revolves around the links he made between the extended professional and the teacher as a researcher. As we have seen, central to his notion of the extended professional was that teachers should demonstrate a willingness and readiness to allow fellow teachers to observe them in the classroom, and then talk about the observation in an open and frank manner. It is argued that this was the basis of his notion of a teacher as a researcher, where teachers work systematically and honestly with others by analysing ideas identified through classroom research techniques in order to develop their professional practice (Stenhouse, 1975). While this critical enquiry into teachers' own practice can produce a new body of knowledge and indeed inform and develop practice, Stenhouse argues that this could be further enhanced by teachers engaging with the wider research community. Perhaps by collaborating with university education departments, similar to the work of CARE, teachers have the opportunity not only to develop themselves as researchers in their own classrooms but to be involved in larger collaborative projects. As Davies (2013: 218) summarises, teachers can then enter:

> A research culture, located within the university–school partnership and supported by seminars, conferences, web-based dialogue and publication, [which] can involve students, staff and schools researching together.

It is acknowledged that applying some of Stenhouse's ideas in practice could be somewhat difficult with the constraints of the National Curriculum and the time available. However, it is argued that many of his ideas are worth pursuing in the quest for a student-centred approach to learning as well as development of teacher professionalism through self-evaluation and research.

REFLECTIVE TASK

Consider the two aspects of a teacher as a facilitator, and a teacher as a learner. What opportunities are there currently available for you to pursue these two aspects within the confines of the learning processes in your setting or placement? Try to think of ways in which you could develop these opportunities in the future.

SUMMARY

Even though Stenhouse died possibly at the peak of his academic career he is recognised as having had a significant impact on education both in the UK and globally. His influence as an advocate for curriculum research and development, and the promotion of teacher professionalism has been an inspiration for embryonic classroom researchers. The focal point of his work was firstly the HCP and then CARE, where with like-minded colleagues he championed the process curriculum as opposed to the prescribed 'teacher proof' objectives curriculum model. It was also at the HCP and particularly CARE that he encouraged teachers to collaborate with practitioner research activities. For Stenhouse the process curriculum model was a way of providing a learning experience which involved honest criticism, and ongoing reflection and evaluation, which in turn resulted in student empowerment and emancipation.

Stenhouse's ideas had similarities with those of a number of educational thinkers, specifically Dewey's thoughts on the importance of reflection and of schools being democratic communities where teachers developed their practice through research. Links are also evident between Bruner and Stenhouse regarding the rejection of the behaviourist objectives curriculum model. Stenhouse drew upon Lewin's action research approach and adapted this for developing and improving classroom practice. Interestingly, Stenhouse himself was the originator of a number of criticisms of his own work. He acknowledged the difficulties encountered, especially in the demands and expectations for high examination results, in assessment using the process curriculum model. There is also a high dependency on the teacher's skills for the process curriculum model to succeed, as it relies on active learning and the non-controlling teacher role. Finally, many consider that the restrictions of time for an increasingly overburdened workforce hamper the efforts of teachers to become extended professionals and researchers in their own right.

Notwithstanding these criticisms there are many possibilities for using active approaches to learning which involve students and encourage them to air their beliefs and values without unnecessary judgement, through the process of discussion. There are also opportunities for teachers to research their own practice and to be self-critical by being open to peer observation. This could then lead on to becoming involved in wider research projects through collaboration with teachers from other schools and departments of education in universities. As a closing statement Stenhouse argues the case for, and the reason behind, practitioner research: 'A research tradition which is accessible to teachers and which feeds teaching must be created if education is to be significantly improved' (Stenhouse, 1975: 165).

FURTHER READING

Carr, D. (2000) *Professionalism and Ethics in Teaching*. London: Routledge.
A thoughtful analysis of ethical and professional issues in relation to education theory and the role of the teacher.

Elliott, J. and Norris, N. (Eds) (2012) *Curriculum, Pedagogy and Educational Research: The Work of Lawrence Stenhouse*. London: Routledge.
An informative and detailed text about Stenhouse's work, as well as a contemporary insight into the meaning and application of his ideas.

Rudduck, J. and McIntyre, D. (2007) *Improving Learning through Consulting Pupils*. Abingdon: Routledge.
A research-based text which explores the realities of using pupils' voices in classrooms and aligned to Stenhouse's notions of the roles of teachers and students.

Stenhouse, L. (Ed.) (1967) *Discipline in Schools: A Symposium*. Oxford: Pergamon Press.
A dated, yet useful, guide to classroom management for student, or newly qualified, teachers.

REFERENCES

Bartlett, S. and Burton, D. (2016) *Introduction to Education Studies* (fourth edition). London: SAGE.

Burton, D. and Bartlett, S. (2005) *Practitioner Research for Teachers*. London: Paul Chapman Publishing.

CARE (2015) Centre for Applied Research in Education - University of East Anglia (CARE). www.uea.ac.uk/education/research/care.

Davies, D. (2013) 'Education research: So what?' In: Ward, S. (Ed.) *A Student's Guide to Education Studies* (third edition). London: Routledge.

Elliott, J. (2007) *Reflecting Where the Action is: The Selected Works of John Elliott*. London: Routledge.

Goodson, I. (2005) *Learning, Curriculum and Life Politics: The Selected Works of Ivor F. Goodson*. Abingdon: Routledge.

Harkin, J., Turner, G. and Dawn, T. (2001) *Teaching Young Adults: A Handbook for Teachers in Post-compulsory Education*. London: RoutledgeFalmer.

Kelly, A.V. (2004) *The Curriculum: Theory and Practice* (fifth edition). London: SAGE.

Kemmis, S. (1995) 'Some ambiguities in Stenhouse's notion of "the teacher as researcher"'. In: Rudduck, J. (Ed.) *An Education that Empowers: A Collection of Lectures in Memory of Lawrence Stenhouse*. Clevedon: Multilingual Matters/BERA.

Markless, S. (2003) 'The case for action research'. In: Lea, J., Hayes, D., Armitage, A., Lomas, L. and Markless, S. (Eds) *Working in Post-Compulsory Education*. Maidenhead: Open University Press.

Neary, M. (2002) *Curriculum Studies in Post-compulsory and Adult Education*. Cheltenham: Nelson Thornes.

Pring, R. (2004) *Philosophy of Educational Research* (second edition). London: Continuum.

Punch, K. and Oancea, A. (2014) *Introduction to Research Methods in Education* (second edition). London: SAGE.

Rowntree, R. (1981) *A Dictionary of Education*. London: Harper & Row.

Rudduck, J. (Ed.) (1995) *An Education that Empowers: A Collection of Lectures in Memory of Lawrence Stenhouse*. Clevedon: Multilingual Matters/BERA.

Rudduck, J. and Hopkins, D. (1985) *Research as a Basis for Teaching: Readings from the Work of Lawrence Stenhouse*. London: Heinemann.

Scott, D. (2008) *Critical Essays on Major Curriculum Theorists*. London: Routledge.

Scott, D. and Morrison, M. (2007) *Key Ideas in Educational Research*. London: Continuum.

Smith, M. (2000) 'Curriculum theory and practice'. *The Encyclopaedia of Informal Education*. www.infed.org/biblio/b-curric.htm.

Stenhouse, L. (1971) *Culture and Education*. London: Nelson.

Stenhouse, L. (1975) *An Introduction to Curriculum Research and Development*. London: Heinemann.

Stenhouse, L. (1983) *Authority, Education and Emancipation: A Collection of Papers*. London: Heinemann.

Wilson, E. (2013) 'What is educational action research?' In: Wilson, E. (Ed.) *School-based Research: A Guide for Education Students*. London: SAGE.

10

HENRY GIROUX

CRITICAL PEDAGOGY

LEARNING OUTCOMES

Having read this chapter you should be able to:

- Appreciate Giroux's background and his impact on education
- Understand his theoretical perspectives, in particular critical pedagogy
- Recognise the links between Giroux's ideas and those of other key educational thinkers
- Critically appraise his works
- Identify which aspects of Giroux's theories could be applied in practice

KEY WORDS

Critical pedagogy; border pedagogy; critical cultural pedagogy; radical education; corporate public pedagogy; neoliberalism; postmodernism; feminism; critical citizenship; transformative intellectuals; hidden curriculum; praxis curriculum model

INTRODUCTION

Henry Giroux can be considered one of the most notable present-day thinkers and writers on education; in particular on critical pedagogy, the role of schools and universities, the effects of neoliberalism and the plight of young people. He argues that the neoliberal economy has been a major driving force in the neglect and oppression of the younger generation. His central themes call for an emphasis in an education which embraces the community, and focuses on democracy, fairness and social justice. For these themes to be realised he contends that teachers and others concerned with education should be politically active. It is only through democratic processes and the advance of a critical and progressive pedagogy that neoliberalism and what Giroux considers a society riven by class structures can be challenged. His writing is optimistic and promotes the idea of teachers developing the notions of human empowerment and participatory democracy, regardless of their specific subject field (Nicholls, 2010).

Giroux has striven to extend our understanding of the nexus between schools and politics. In doing so he has defied the conventional positions of teachers and students within the schools and universities where they encounter each other. At the heart of Giroux's teaching and writing is a moral responsibility towards encouraging all those involved in education to engage in democratic practices and shared governance. These practices, he argues, cannot be handed down from previous generations, they need to be continuously discovered and rediscovered. It was with these underpinning thoughts that Giroux became a prominent and vocal advocate of the critical pedagogy group of thinkers, which was a fusion of the progressive educational ideas initiated by the Brazilian philosopher Paulo Freire. Freire's actions led him to evaluate the roles of teachers and students in view of an oppressive political environment and then plan for new and revolutionary curricula (Giroux et al., 1988).

For Giroux, schools ought to be centres of cultural creativity and transformation but not reproduction. They should be the focus for critical and participatory democracy which welcomes diversity and a range of different cultural and social alliances. In this idea of democracy, schools accept and greet such diversity instead of 'serving the agenda of the elite, powerful minority or ideology' (Morrison, 2001: 280). Although his views developed and changed over the years, Giroux's radical stance together with his visions of humanitarianism and social justice are evident throughout his writing:

> Education is not only about issues of work and economics, but also about questions of justice, social freedom, and the capacity for democratic agency, action, and change as well as the related issues of power, exclusion, and citizenship. (Giroux, 2011: 121)

In the preface of Giroux's *Ideology, Culture and the Process of Schooling* (1981), Aronowitz emphasises how Giroux's work is an enduring 'exploration of how education may contribute to the emancipation of human beings' (Aronowitz, 1981: 3). Such longevity continues in Giroux's writing some thirty-five years later. Giroux's thoughts, as well as the criticisms he encountered, together with the connections he has with other educational thinkers, and some ways in which his thoughts could be applied in practice will be covered in this chapter.

GIROUX, THE PERSON

Henry Giroux was born into a working-class family in 1943, in Providence, Rhode Island. He entered academia almost by default, gaining a basketball scholarship which enabled him eventually to enrol in a teacher training college. He enjoyed the collective shared aims of student life and he became acutely aware of the unjust aspects of racism, sexism and class division (Nicholls, 2010). With the United States' involvement in the Vietnam War he also developed a strong sense of social justice, and the more he read about social theory the more he became attracted to teaching: 'Not only did I see [teaching] as a way to make an impact but I saw teaching as a wonderfully noble profession' (Giroux, 1992: 14). Giroux went on to complete a masters degree in history; after this he was employed as a high school social science teacher as well as being deeply involved as a community activist. He worked with the black community in Baltimore, which, at that time, was a highly segregated city. In the schools where he taught he was recognised for his radical approaches to the curriculum (Nicholls, 2010).

In 1977 Giroux received his doctorate from Carnegie Mellon University; his thesis was written on curriculum theory, sociology and sociology of education. He then relocated to Boston University where he taught from 1977 to 1983. It is interesting to note that while at Boston University Giroux originally had his academic contract rejected because senior university staff were at odds with the radical views in his two early books: *Ideology, Culture and the Process of Schooling* (1981) and *Theory and Resistance in Education: A Pedagogy for the Opposition* (1983) (Nicholls, 2010). His next post was as Professor of Education and Renowned Scholar in Residence at Miami University, Ohio from 1983 to 1992. Then from 1992 he became Waterbury Chair Professor of Secondary Education at Penn State University. Later he assumed the role of the Global Television Network Chair in English and Cultural Studies at McMaster University, Canada (Morrison, 2001).

Giroux is often regarded as a leading light for the concept of critical pedagogy. He has a gift of making even the most complicated concept clear and comprehensible. Furthermore, he writes with a conviction which has emanated from his past experience as a teacher. He has written numerous articles and books mostly within the field of education, but lately his writing has also encompassed issues of culture (Howlett, 2013). His ideas in relation to his advancement of critical pedagogy are best discovered in his seminal work *Border Crossings: Cultural Workers and the Politics of Education* (1992) where he lists nine characteristics required for critical pedagogy (Scott, 2008). However, it is likely that Giroux himself would assert that critical pedagogy has evolved from an amalgamation of previous notions about social thought and radical education movements that have endeavoured to connect teaching and schools 'to democratic principles of society and to transformative social action in the interests of oppressed communities' (Darder et al., 2003: 3). The next section will explore the theoretical aspects of Giroux's work.

THE BACKGROUND AND THEORY OF CRITICAL PEDAGOGY

Giroux is best known for his ideas on critical pedagogy. However, to fully appreciate the context it is appropriate to explore the notion of radical education and how politics, culture, postmodernism and feminism underpin his philosophy. This section will then consider Giroux's notion of critical pedagogy, before reflecting on his thoughts on border pedagogy, the curriculum and teacher professionalism.

Radical educators such as Giroux examined and interrogated the very foundations of teaching. As a group they contested the conventional socio-political and philosophical justifications for learning and teaching. The aim of the radical educator is to give power to the student by transforming the association between learners and teachers with the long-term goal of achieving social reformation and equality (Preece and Griffin, 2006). However, to achieve this goal, radical educators contend that the education systems themselves also need to be transformed:

> Educational systems and the people within them need to problematise what seems normal. Within that the notion of how knowledge is perceived at all needs to be re-examined. (Preece and Griffin, 2006: 68)

For Giroux radical education is not a standalone concept which relates to a specific subject or speciality, neither does it describe a form of knowledge. He argues that radical education has three features: 'it is interdisciplinary … it questions the fundamental categories of all disciplines, and it has a public mission of making society more democratic' (Giroux, 1992: 10).

Giroux was incensed by the increasing use of neoliberal and corporate strategies which he saw as encroaching on education in the United States, which contradicted his notion of education being an active agent for social justice. Giroux saw such neoliberalism as serving the needs of private advantage where economic advancement becomes more important than matters of social democracy. Neoliberalism came at the expense of the marginalised in society and caused the stripping down of the welfare state. Giroux termed this 'corporate public pedagogy', the purpose of which was to serve the individual in a competitive environment where material gain was to the fore. In the culture of corporate public pedagogy, matters of social injustice such as gender, race and social class issues are all undervalued and normalised for the sake of economic gain. Giroux described this as 'an all-encompassing cultural horizon for producing market identities, values and practices' (Giroux, 2011: 134).

Neither does the idea of corporate public pedagogy, Giroux would argue, take into account the rapidly changing and diverse multi-cultural society. Giroux felt that school culture served the needs of the privileged learners of the governing and middle classes at the expense of the aspirations of the disadvantaged, diverse and often neglected sections of society. Radical educators contested that the United States by way of its discriminatory policies, funding and legal powers 'shaped school practice in the interest of capitalist rationality' (Giroux, 1985: xv). What was needed was a culture which promoted an environment where learners could be critically active and develop into democratically spirited members of society (Giroux, 2003).

Postmodernism and feminism both underpin Giroux's notion of critical pedagogy. Like other similar postmodernist thinkers his stance opposes the established ways of understanding and the formation of knowledge (Bartlett et al., 2001). For Giroux education is far too complex and ever-changing, he is sceptical of the conventional importance placed upon histories, society and knowledge itself. The postmodernist ideas which are the basis for critical pedagogy value the notion that there are no right or wrong answers to problems. Indeed 'there are *many* sides to a problem, and often these sides are linked to certain class, race, and gender interests' (McLaren, 2003: 71). Postmodernists take into account the differences and complexities of educational settings and cultures with a view to empowering learners to prevail against social limitations. This view of postmodernism aligns itself with feminism; both emphasise that peoples' social and cultural circumstances affect their lives (Ormston et al., 2014). Giroux has argued for the feminist cause – a cause which called for women to have an equal say in pedagogical practice and in the formation of the curriculum as well as advancing feminist educational theoretical standpoints (Preece and Griffin, 2006).

The purpose of critical pedagogy, for Giroux, is to reveal the disparities which are often concealed in different educational establishments, this is achieved by firstly emancipating students in the classrooms (Howlett, 2013). To achieve student emancipation as part of the critical pedagogy process, teachers should endeavour to:

> Take young people beyond the world they are familiar with and [make] clear how classroom knowledge, values, desires, and social relations are always implicated in power … critical pedagogy becomes a project that stresses the need for teachers and students to actively transform knowledge rather than simply consume it. (Giroux, 2011: 6–7)

As such, the student becomes an integral element of the education process and in doing so strives to critically question society and its problems to look for fundamentally different solutions; thus the role of critical pedagogy 'is to transform teachers, schools, and ultimately society' (Sadovnik et al., 2013: 196). According to Morrison (2001) there are a number of principles which are required for Giroux's notion of critical pedagogy:

- Attention needs to be paid to pedagogy as much as to traditional scholarship, (re) constructing schools as democratic public spheres.
- Ethics are of central concern in critical pedagogy, questioning educative practices that perpetuate inequality, exploitation and human suffering.
- The political implications of celebration of difference in democratic societies must be addressed.
- A language that embraces several versions of solidarity and politics needs to be developed.
- There is no single script or grand narrative, but rather, several scripts, several curricula, several versions of education which need to be critically interrogated, just as there are several versions and areas of exploitation and oppression in society which mediate each other.
- Cultural representations in curricula have to be regarded as discourses of power and asymmetrical relations of power.
- The curriculum is a 'cultural script' whose messages should be susceptible to critique.
- The politics of voice require an affirmation of diversity and of the rights of oppressed groups for recognition in education.

(Morrison, 2001: 282)

Giroux amplified his notion of critical pedagogy to challenge current boundaries of knowledge, which he termed 'border pedagogy'. A key facet of border pedagogy is the acceptance of the connections between knowledge and power, and how in practice this is used to bolster certain forms of authority (Giroux, 1992). He felt that for equality to be truly achieved in society, the function of power should be unmasked and refigured (Morrison, 2001). For Giroux, border pedagogy, as a process, was meant to cultivate a 'democratic public philosophy that respects the notion of difference as part of a common struggle to extend the quality of public life' (Giroux, 1992: 28). For this to happen he argued that students and teachers alike should examine and confront conventional boundaries (or borders) 'of power ... decision-making, cultural and social representation in the curricula' (Morrison, 2001: 283). Border pedagogy then is an opportunity for educators and students to destroy the boundaries which exist in education that fortify authority. He contended that learners ought to 'engage knowledge as border-crossers, as people moving in and out of borders constructed around coordinates of difference and power' (Giroux, 1992: 29).

These aspects of power and difference are very noticeable in Giroux's thoughts on the curriculum. He contests what he called the 'hidden curriculum' as the way in which authority tacitly embeds sets of values and beliefs by way of ordered and structural school procedures and routines. The hidden curriculum is an intervention to promote 'social control, one that functions to provide differential forms of schooling for different classes of children' (Giroux, 1983: 47). Further to this, Giroux extended Stenhouse's model of the process curriculum (Stenhouse, 1975). He, like other critical pedagogy theorists, advanced the praxis curriculum model, which had at its core the idea of social transformation and the nexus between theory and practice. The praxis model perceives knowledge as provisional and accessible to criticism, the model confronts traditional notions of knowledge, and the opinion of authority and coercion. The praxis model is valuable because it has explicit application to students' everyday lives (Curtis and Pettigrew, 2010). The intention of the praxis model is to nurture 'critical consciousness: the cultivation of informed action as a foundation for hope in the future' (Curtis and Pettigrew, 2010: 38).

As a final point in this section, and very much in line with critical and border pedagogy, Giroux took an interest in teacher professionalism and in particular how this was shaped at an early stage during initial teacher education. He criticised teacher education programmes, which he thought reinforced traditional practice with its rules and ways of thinking about measures of achievement, the transmission of knowledge and teacher competence. These practices were, he considered, left unchallenged, which in turn resulted in a move away from the perception of a teacher as a professional to that of a teacher as a technician (Giroux, 1981). Teachers, he contested, were not educated or encouraged to apply the different cultural and personal aspirations of students in their teaching practice:

> The result is a form of pedagogical violence that prevents teachers establishing conditions which allow students to speak with an authentic voice. (Giroux, 1981: 155)

Such restricted and didactic methods he thought were opposite to the democratic, experimental and emancipatory approaches to teaching espoused by Dewey. The connections with Dewey, and other progressive and radical educators, are outlined in the next section.

LINKS WITH OTHER THEORISTS

There is a clear-cut affiliation with John Dewey's desire to create a democratic form of education, which also encourages citizenship (Aronowitz, 1981). Giroux considered that critical pedagogy with its contention of critical reflection, thoughtful reasoning and the fostering of community spirit is 'central to the cultivation of what John Dewey once called "democracy as a way of life"' (Giroux, 2011: 8). Giroux's notion of democracy is directly related to Dewey's ideas and his conviction in the positive power of education as a force for social justice; like Dewey, Giroux also criticised the traditional didactic methods of teaching and learning (Howlett, 2013).

There are also quite strong links between the Brazilian philosopher Paulo Freire and Giroux. Both considered that their work had a much wider application than in schools. They both sought to emancipate students and their communities, in doing this they both believed that organised oppression would be abolished (Morrison, 2001). Freire facilitated learners to create an awareness of freedom, to identify and understand oppressive leanings and language, 'and learn to read the word and the world as part of a broader struggle for justice and democracy' (Giroux, 2011: 152). For Freire, then, critical pedagogy was not just a matter of students learning specific skills in literacy, it was also an approach to learning about literacy as a way of actively engaging in the world. It was more than learning facts, rather it was a way of questioning and confronting conventions and beliefs and engaging in critical discussions with the past to look forward to a future that would not just be a replication of the present (Giroux, 2011). Freire, was a leading light for Giroux, and other radical educators. It is suggested that from Freire, Giroux was inspired to reconfigure 'some of the implicit utopianism of the romantic tradition through the addition of a healthy dose of urban and inter-cultural pedagogical experience' (Irwin, 2012: 5).

There are also some similarities, and differences, between the work of Giroux and Pierre Bourdieu. According to Giroux, schools are places of cultural and social reproduction that exemplify what Bourdieu terms 'cultural capital' (Aronowitz, 1981). Bourdieu argued that it is through cultural capital that the middle classes can retain their place in the 'process of social reproduction while making this inequality legitimate ... to keep social order and perpetuate the existing inequalities' (Bartlett et al., 2001: 9). Although the similarities between the two regarding inequalities of social reproduction are acknowledged, Giroux differed in that he considered any analysis of social reproduction should also take into consideration matters of race and gender as well as social class (Gewirtz and Cribb, 2009).

Giroux thought schools which take students from subgroups of class and race are typified by over-restrictive systems and regulations, which in turn results in a passive and powerless student body for the marginalised. Basil Bernstein argued that such a regulation-dominated oppressive school environment is detrimental to the learning and social relations for students; Bernstein termed this a visible pedagogy. This type of teaching is an anathema to critical and border pedagogy espoused by Giroux. Like Giroux, Bernstein felt that such a controlling and hierarchical teacher and student relationship was unjust and that it favoured the students who were from the dominant race and class of the school, these students were able to 'operate within a classroom experience where flexible and interpersonal relations (soft socialisation), replace overt rule conformity' (Giroux, 1981: 75).

⊛ CRITIQUING THE THEORY

Giroux's radical ideas have been criticised as being over-optimistic and unachievable in today's schools. The main criticisms are concerned with the impracticality of his ideas as well as their overtly political nature. Morrison questions whether Giroux's writings have any explicit effect on teaching practice, or whether his work is too idealistic and does nothing more than 'put fire into one's belly' (Morrison, 2001: 284). Furthermore, the central theme to critical pedagogy is that teachers encourage their students to question education practices. Gore, a teacher educator, found when she tried to do this with her students it resulted in some unpredicted and not so positive outcomes. A number of her students felt they could not tolerate working in such restrictive working environments and never started their teaching careers; some of those who did take up teaching did so for a short time before changing careers. Others who persevered with a critical and questioning approach to practice were sometimes shunned by their colleagues and jeopardised their salary as a result of doing so; some others just accepted the status quo (Gore, 2003: 339).

Other criticisms of Giroux's idea of critical pedagogy include that it has not been accepted or endorsed by any Western government as a structure for learning and teaching; neither did Giroux clarify how critical pedagogy could be of benefit to students in gaining transferable skills to enhance employability (Howlett, 2013). Moreover, an overtly politicised form of education, particularly one which is led by teachers themselves, in school systems which are increasingly being compelled to focus on results and standards, is a very contentious proposition (Howlett, 2013). Similar criticism is also levelled at Giroux's praxis curriculum model, which Curtis and Pettigrew suggest 'risks representing to learners a partial and overtly critical standpoint on the world' (2010: 380).

Much of Giroux's work criticises the traditional role of schools as being authoritative and retaining power over students. This, however, disregards the student-centred innovations that are evident in practice in schools; despite the highly regulated curriculum in an ever-increasingly managerial profession, teachers do strive for a democratic model of professionalism which values matters of reflection, collegiality, and collaboration between students and teachers and other stakeholders (Sachs, 2003). Such collaboration is explained by hooks as 'mapping-out terrains of commonality, connection, and shared concern with teaching practices' (1994: 130).

APPLYING GIROUX'S IDEAS IN PRACTICE

Even though Giroux's thinking has undoubtedly given progressive teachers food for thought to apply in their classrooms, Preece and Griffin contend that his ideas 'present ideological, rather than practitioner perspectives on pedagogy' (2006: 60). Most of Giroux's suggestions for practical applications for his ideas are found in *On Critical Pedagogy* (2011); however, he does question just how much teachers can influence the curriculum and the decisions made in classrooms in schools today (Giroux, 2011). Yet he maintains that teachers should cultivate a critical pedagogy which connects classroom practice with society as a whole: teachers need to become 'transformative intellectuals' (Morrison, 2001). Transformative intellectuals make learning and teaching political acts by fostering students' own life experiences and their consciousness about subjects of contention, hence enabling students themselves to become critics, in doing so the aim is:

to expose oppression, inequality and the constrictions of social identities within asymmetrical relations of power of different groups in society, with a view to transforming students' ways of looking at their lives, life situations and life chances, so that they experience empowerment and emancipation as members of diverse cultures and communities. They develop their 'voice' within participatory democracies. (Morrison, 2001: 282–3)

Being a transformational intellectual requires unconventional and progressive methods of teaching which need to be complemented by a form of student and teacher relationship that involves discussion, negotiation, questioning and communication; it also needs self-reflection to be embedded into teachers' practice (Giroux, 2011). Such self-reflection needs to be augmented by research and action so that they can, with other teachers, help influence aspects of school experiences in the name of social justice (Goodson, 2005). In doing so teachers begin to create their own classroom theories and reform their practices, which will hopefully go beyond the confines of the classroom with the promise of transforming society as a whole. Giroux thought that teachers could achieve this in their practice by actively questioning traditionally held beliefs about teaching methods, forms of knowledge and assessment techniques; by taking such a critical standpoint, together with a self-reflective and inquiry-based approach 'teachers can help to raise the political consciousness of themselves, their fellow teachers, and their students' (Giroux, 2011: 42).

What is of importance is the understanding and recognition of the different issues in education, and in their everyday lives, that students experience. The use of these different experiences in teaching gives a meaningful basis of learning and underlines notions of principles, power and politics – all of which Giroux suggests are essential for students and teachers to develop their communication and collaboration (Giroux, 2011). Furthermore, encouraging students to question and argue from the basis of their own experiences within a democratically enriched classroom helps develop a sense of resistance to oppression, it also enhances their progress in thinking critically about the broader issues of inequality and injustice in the world. Giroux laments the lack of self-reflection, critical thinking and imagination evident in public schools in the United States: schooling has become a 'dead zone' where teaching to assessment and seeking ways to exclude badly performing students have become priorities (Giroux, 2011: 153). To counter such passivity, where students because of their race or class are both voiceless and powerless, Giroux offers a practical example which is very much associated with Freirean pedagogy:

Students could be asked to write short papers that speculate on the meaning and the power of literacy and why it was so central to the civil rights movement. These may be read by the entire class with each student elaborating on his or her position and offering commentary as a way of entering into a critical discussion of the history of racial exclusion, reflecting on how its ideologies and formations still haunt American society in spite of the triumphal dawn of an allegedly post-racial Obama era. (Giroux, 2011: 155)

This teaching method is aligned to the seminar approach favoured by Giroux because it encourages student engagement with discussion. Giroux, although he prescribes the issues and topics for discussion, wishes to let students have the opportunity to take a position they believe in from their experience and their personal history, and then to defend that position. Although it does not matter what position is taken, the student should appreciate the effect that position has on others. In doing this Giroux is politicising his teaching and the subject being discussed. Students are then agents in their learning and as such become 'self-conscious about the social relationships that undergird the learning process' (Giroux, 1992: 16). What is central to Giroux, in the use of discussions and seminars, is the significance of the student voice in the stories of their experiences which help them justify their point of view, these stories he felt opened up even larger issues of education philosophy; for example, using the actual voices of young black people to 'talk about the hidden curriculum of racism, about what black kids have to give up to become academically successful' (Giroux, 1992: 16). Giroux would argue that all students have experiences and that these are influenced, for better or worse, by their personal feelings, religious beliefs, languages, culture and family ties (Giroux, 1992).

Once students feel comfortable in discussing their own histories and experiences in matters of social justice, they should be encouraged to put these into practice in the classroom so they actually act as if they are living and learning in a democracy. Striving for social justice and democracy in the world is an ongoing struggle, which Peterson (2003) suggests could begin in the classroom by emphasising that many marginalised people have gained from such struggles, and students should decide whether or not to be involved in the struggles. Like Giroux, Peterson argues that the specific subject content areas are not so important, as they can be intertwined around themes of democracy and social justice. Current national and international social issues can be raised with recourse to curricula resources and texts that empower students (Peterson, 2003). This form of teaching, as we have seen, should be a form of critical inquiry, and 'of building a social imagination that works within a language of hope' (McLaren, 2003: 92). It is this shared understanding of language that students can use not only as a debating tool with other students in classrooms but also as a means to help teachers and students to construct the foundations for democracy and justice in society as a whole (McLaren, 2003).

From a teacher's own developmental point of view within critical pedagogy, they also need to listen critically to the voice of their students during seminar discussions. This critical listening is of importance because it allows the teacher to adopt a more self-reflective understanding of the boundaries of their bias regarding their own political standpoint and personal and pedagogical values. In doing so teachers, while perhaps not agreeing with the views listened to, respect and acknowledge the student's history and experience. This critical listening enables teachers to become self-critical and reflective of their own experiences and stories, and reinforces the notion of teachers as intellectuals. This in turn keeps the discussions and seminars unfettered and subject to continuing criticality (Giroux, 1992).

It is recognised that it is somewhat troublesome to put into practice some of Giroux's ideas of critical pedagogy, particularly because of their ideological nature and the restrictions of a national curriculum. Nevertheless, his views on student voice and his altogether inclusive approach to teaching and learning are all embedded in the continuing struggles for social justice. Just having an awareness of the inequalities of oppression will help us develop our classroom practice and seek to address these issues. Finally, there are some areas, such as the celebration of student difference and the use of seminars and discussions, and self-reflection, which are indeed of a practical nature.

REFLECTIVE TASK

One of the principles of Giroux's notion of critical pedagogy is to encourage the student voice in education to confirm and celebrate diversity, and the rights of marginalised groups.

What procedures are there in your setting which enable the voice of difference to be heard?

What other processes could be put in place to develop this voice even further?

SUMMARY

Henry Giroux is arguably one of the most influential progressive and radical thinkers and writers on education today. He has railed against the effects that neoliberal ideology has had on public education, which he argues has had negative connotations for many young people, particularly those from oppressed groups by virtue of their race, culture, class or gender. He has been relentless in trying to demonstrate the need for a link between politics and schools, where schools and those who work and study in them take a moral responsibility to engage in democratic practices through his notion of critical pedagogy. For Giroux, education is more than just economic gain, it should be about issues of social justice, democracy, and being an agent for change and fairness for all. His ideas of critical pedagogy and border pedagogy are, to some extent, ideological stances but they also have very profound practical implications and applications for progressive teachers with the emphasis on self-reflection and self-criticism, the use of inquiry, and the striving for democratic teacher and student relationships.

He is one of a number of radical educators who took a revolutionary approach to teaching and learning which questioned traditional thoughts on education starting with John Dewey. He can also readily be associated with the anti-oppression position taken by Paulo Freire, and, to a certain degree, with Pierre Bourdieu and Basil Bernstein, who stressed the relevance of culture and social reproduction on the education aspirations and achievements of students. Despite the criticisms levelled at his ideas, Giroux's writings are filled with hope and visions of social justice, even within increasingly restrictive and market-driven educational systems. Finally, perhaps a fitting overview of the value of Giroux's work should come from Morrison:

> His work holds out hope for a better life for us all. His work is profoundly humanitarian; that is unsettling as it is optimistic. Education needs its visionaries. (Morrison, 2001: 284)

FURTHER READING

McLaren, P. (2006) *Life in Schools: An Introduction to Critical Pedagogy in the Foundations of Education*. Boston: Pearson.
An example of how teachers can practically apply critical pedagogy into their classrooms through the formation of communities of practice.

Giroux, H. (1988) *Teachers as Intellectuals: Towards a Critical Pedagogy of Learning?* South Hadley: Bergen and Garvey.
Giroux explores the matters of transformation and empowerment and the relationships between schools and society at large.

Giroux, H. (1997) 'Crossing the boundaries of education discourse: Modernism, postmodernism and feminism'. In: Halsey, A., Lauder, H., Brown, P. and Wells, A. (Eds) *Education: Culture, Economy and Society*. Oxford: Oxford University Press.
An analysis of the how modernism, postmodernism and feminism shape radical education.

Giroux, H. (2000) *Breaking in to the Movies: Film and the Culture of Politics*. New York: Routledge.
This book uncovers the role of films as powerful teaching methods when exploring issues of society and culture.

Giroux. H. (2009) *Youth in a Suspect Society: Democracy or Disposability?* New York: Palgrave-Macmillan.
Giroux reveals how public policy has forsaken the aspirations of young people.

REFERENCES

Aronowitz, S. (1981) Preface. In: Giroux, H. *Ideology Culture and the Process of Schooling*. London: Falmer Press.
Bartlett, S., Burton, D. and Peim, N. (2001) *Introduction to Education Studies*. London: Paul Chapman.
Curtis, W. and Pettigrew, A. (2010) *Education Studies Reflective Reader*. Exeter: Learning Matters.
Darder, A., Baltodano, M. and Torres, R. (Eds) (2003) *The Critical Pedagogy Reader*. London: RoutledgeFalmer.
Gewirtz S. and Cribb, A. (2009) *Understanding Education: A Sociological Perspective*. Cambridge: Polity Press.

Giroux, H. (1981) *Ideology, Culture and the Process of Schooling*. London: Falmer Press.

Giroux, H. (1983) *Theory and Resistance in Education: A Pedagogy for the Opposition*. London: Heinemann Educational.

Giroux, H. (1985) Introduction. In: Freire, P. *The Politics of Education: Culture, Power and Liberation*. Westport, CT: Bergin and Garvey.

Giroux, H. (1992) *Border Crossings: Cultural Workers and the Politics of Education*. New York: Routledge.

Giroux, H. (2003) 'Critical theory and educational practice'. In: Darder, A., Baltodano, M. and Torres, R. (Eds) *The Critical Pedagogy Reader*. London: RoutledgeFalmer.

Giroux, H. (2011) *On Critical Pedagogy*. New York: Continuum.

Giroux, H., Shumway, D., Smith, P. and Sosnoski, T. (1988) 'The need for cultural studies'. In: Giroux, H. *Teachers as Intellectuals: Towards a Critical Pedagogy of Learning?* South Hadley: Bergen and Garvey.

Goodson, I. (2005) *Learning, Curriculum and Life Politics: The Selected Works of Ivor F. Goodson*. London: Routledge.

Gore, J. (2003) 'What we can do for you! What can "we" do for "you"?: Struggling over empowerment in critical and feminist pedagogy'. In: Darder, A., Baltodano, M. and Torres, R. (Eds) *The Critical Pedagogy Reader*. London: RoutledgeFalmer.

hooks, b. (1994) *Teaching to Transgress: Education as the Practice of Freedom*. London: Routledge.

Howlett, J. (2013) *Progressive Education: A Critical Introduction*. London: Bloomsbury.

Irwin, J. (2012) *Paulo Freire's Philosophy of Education*. London: Continuum.

McLaren, P. (2003) 'Critical pedagogy: A look at the major concepts'. In: Darder, A., Baltodano, M. and Torres, R. (Eds) *The Critical Pedagogy Reader*. London: RoutledgeFalmer.

Morrison, K. (2001) 'Henry Giroux, 1943–'. In: Palmer, J. (Ed.) *Fifty Modern Thinkers on Education: From Piaget to the Present*. Abingdon: Routledge.

Nicholls, D. (2010) 'Henry Giroux: neoliberalism's nemesis'. *The Encyclopaedia of Informal Education*. http://infed.org/mobi/henry-a-giroux.

Ormston, R., Spencer, L., Barnard, M. and Snape, D. (2014) 'The foundations of qualitative research'. In: Richie, J., Lewis, J., McNaughton Nicholls, C. and Ormston, R. (Eds) *Qualitative Research Practice* (second edition). London: SAGE.

Peterson, R. (2003) 'Teaching how to read the world and change it: Critical pedagogy in the intermediate grades'. In: Darder, A., Baltodano, M. and Torres, R. (Eds) *The Critical Pedagogy Reader*. London: RoutledgeFalmer.

Preece, J. and Griffin, C. (2006) 'Radical and feminist pedagogies'. In: Jarvis, P. (Ed.) *The Theory and Practice of Teaching* (second edition). London: Routledge.

Sachs, J. (2003) *The Activist Teaching Profession*. Buckingham: Open University Press.

Sadovnik, A., Cookson, P. and Semel, S. (Eds) (2013) *Exploring Education* (fourth edition). London: Routledge.

Scott, D. (2008) *Critical Essays on Major Curriculum Theorists*. London: Routledge.

Stenhouse, L. (1975) *An Introduction to Curriculum Research and Development*. Oxford: Heinemann.

11

HOWARD GARDNER

MULTIPLE INTELLIGENCES AND EDUCATION

LEARNING OUTCOMES

Having read this chapter you should be able to:

- Understand the life and works of Howard Gardner
- Critically appraise the theory of multiple intelligences
- Compare and contrast the work of Gardner with other contemporary theorists
- Recognise how Gardner's work can be applied to the classroom

KEY WORDS

Multiple intelligence – linguistic, logical–mathematical, musical, bodily–kinaesthetic, spatial, interpersonal, intrapersonal, naturalistic, spiritual, existential; Project Zero

INTRODUCTION

Howard Gardner currently holds the position of John H. and Elisabeth A. Hobbs Professor of Cognition and Education at the Harvard Graduate School of Education. He has had an academic career spanning five decades, the majority of which has been spent at Harvard University. Gardner has published over thirty books, and several hundred articles, and is perhaps most well-known for his theory on multiple intelligences.

Gardner showed a passion for learning from the early days of his schooling, and, despite attending a mainstream preparatory school, he managed to secure a place at Harvard with the original intention of studying law or medicine. However, after meeting a number of influential people at Harvard, and with the support of some high-profile mentors including Jerome Bruner and Erik Erikson, Gardner changed his focus of study to that of developmental psychology, and later cognitive development. Gardner was heavily influenced by some of the key thinkers in the field of neurobiology, most significant of whom was renowned neurologist Norman Geschwind, who encouraged Gardner to work with brain-damaged patients in a local hospital (Winner, 2012). It was through this work that Gardner became interested in brain pathology, something which Gardner used when formulating his theory on multiple intelligence (MI) and identifying the characteristics of the initial seven intelligences.

While Gardner is most well-known for his MI theory he was also a founding member of Project Zero at Harvard University, and remains active in the project to this day. Originally led by Geschwind, Project Zero looks at the higher cognitive processes of individuals, with a specific focus on creativity and the arts (Winner, 2012). Project Zero has since resulted in further areas of focus for Gardner and his colleagues, including linking to the development of a personalised curriculum in respect of his work on MIs. Project Zero also led to Gardner's involvement in the Good Project, 'a group of initiatives that investigate work, collaboration, citizenship, digital life, and more' (Howard Gardner, online biography: https://howardgardner.com/biography); he has also sought to gain a greater understanding of good work among young people.

It would be fair to say that Howard Gardner has ensured currency in his work, with current foci on digital media and an examination of current college provision from a national and international perspective. Winner (2012) describes Gardner as an accomplished grant-getter who has been responsible for bringing significant funds into Harvard University. Gardner sees himself as an independent scholar and public intellectual. He describes himself as a happy workaholic, who enjoys spending his free time with his close-knit family (Winner, 2012).

HOWARD GARDNER, THE PERSON

Howard Gardner was born in 1943 in Scranton, a mid-sized former coal mining city, in north-east Pennsylvania (Winner, 2012). Gardner's parents, Ralph and Hilde Gardner, arrived in America as Jewish immigrants, on 9 November 1938, the day of the infamous

'Kristallnacht' (Night of Broken Glass) in Nazi Germany. Gardner comments that his parents had a traumatic history, they were forced out of Germany and the business they ran there by the Holocaust (Amrein-Beardsley, 2013). Gardner explains that, prior to their arrival in America, his mother and his brother Eric were held hostage in Germany for three years while his father tried to find someone who would sign an affidavit so they could leave for the United States. The family arrived in America with very few material possessions, in stark contrast to the life they had lived in Germany, where they had lived reasonably comfortably. Gardner observes that his mother had never cooked a meal or made a bed before coming to America as this had always been done by the people who worked for the family (Amrein-Beardsley, 2013). Tragedy hit Gardner's family just prior to his birth when his brother Eric was killed in a sleighing accident. Nevertheless, Gardner recalls having a fairly uneventful upbringing, asserting that he was largely unaware of the trauma experienced by his family prior to his birth, and stating that, 'my parents did not talk about the Holocaust. They did not talk about my brother. In fact, I only discovered that he had died by finding some old clippings' (Gardner in Amrein-Beardsley, 2013).

Although his parents did not directly talk with Gardner about those events prior to his birth, Gardner does suggest that they indirectly impacted on his upbringing (Amrein-Beardsley, 2013): dangerous pastimes were understandably discouraged, and his parents were keen for him to get a good education, encouraging creative and intellectual pursuits. Gardner was, in fact, an excellent student, both academically and musically, being a gifted pianist. While his parents were keen for him to attend the renowned Phillips Academy in Andover, Massachusetts, Gardner refused and instead attended the nearby preparatory school in Kingston, Pennsylvania, where he proved himself to be a conscientious student, embracing opportunities and gaining the support and interest of his teachers.

Gardner was the first of his extended family to attend university, commencing study at Harvard in 1966, where he claims his education began in earnest (Winner, 2012). It was his time at Harvard which saw him developing a love of learning ultimately leading to him pursuing an academic career. Gardner states, '[on entering college] I immediately liked studying. I liked taking courses. I probably audited more courses than anybody in the history of Harvard – dozens and dozens of courses' (Amrein-Beardsley, 2013).

During his early days at Harvard Gardner was able to work with a number of eminent people, including David Reisman, and Jerome Bruner, with whom he worked on the 'Man: A Course of Study' (MACOS) programme, a social studies curriculum programme. As an undergraduate he also worked with renowned psychoanalyst Erik Erikson (Winner, 2012), after which he spent a postgraduate year as a Harvard Fellow at the London School of Economics, reading philosophy and sociology. Of his time in London Gardner states, 'I have to admit that I was rarely seen there [London School of Economics]. But I loved going to theatre and plays. I actually wrote a novel – it was terrible – concerts, and so on' (Amrein-Beardsley, 2013). However, he also explains that his time in London led to some reflection on the work of cognitive psychologists Piaget and Bruner. Gardner began to question the scientific focus which Piaget had emphasised in his theory of cognitive development, and began to examine how those who had an interest in the arts looked at works, acknowledging that they too had a mind, and a way in which to view the world. This ultimately led to Gardner's early work on style perception in the visual arts, and latterly to his involvement in Project Zero.

Following his year at the London School of Economics Gardner decided to continue graduate studies in developmental psychology at Harvard, where he had the opportunity to work with psycholinguist Roger Brown and epistemologist Nelson Goodman. Following the completion of his doctorate, Gardner worked with Norman Geschwind, a renowned and brilliant neurologist (Winner, 2012). Gardner was inspired by Geschwind to research into neuropsychology, and combined this with his interest in the arts, studying the, 'breakdown of artistic and other high level skills under various forms of brain pathology' (Winner, 2012: 2). His interest in the higher cognitive processes and the arts also resulted in the aforementioned Project Zero undertaken at Harvard University. This also inspired his work on MIs, for which he is probably most well-known, and which will be explored in more detail in this chapter.

Gardner has spent his entire academic career associated with Harvard University; as a doctoral student he held a tutoring position there and following his doctorate Gardner held a teaching positon at Clark University for a short period, while maintaining his contact with Harvard through Project Zero. Gardner recalls that despite teaching some well-received courses at Harvard, he failed to get tenure there. As a result Gardner was forced to live off grants, including a MacArthur Fellowship in 1981 that supported him for five years (Amrein-Beardsley, 2013), which was later followed by a fellowship from the John S. Guggenheim Memorial Foundation in 2000.

Gardner has had a phenomenally successful career as an academic and has received honorary degrees from twenty-nine colleges and universities across the world. He was also selected by *Foreign Policy* and *Prospect* magazines as one of the 100 most influential public intellectuals in the world in 2005 and 2008. In addition to holding the position of John H. and Elisabeth A. Hobbs Professor of Cognition and Education at the Harvard Graduate School of Education, he is also an adjunct professor of psychology at Harvard University.

THE THEORY OF MULTIPLE INTELLIGENCES

Gardner first began to develop his MI theory in the late 1970s and early 1980s (Davis et al., n.d.). In this theory Gardner challenges some of the early perceptions of intelligence which assume that it is a singular, inherited entity, measurable by a single IQ test. Instead Gardner proposed that humans have several, or multiple, intelligences, which the individual is able to draw upon 'individually and corporately, to create products and solve problems that are relevant to the societies in which they live' (Gardner, 1983, 1993a, 1999a, 2006). Gardner also observed that the only intelligences really valued and tested in schools related to linguistic and logical–mathematical intelligence, suggesting that this language–logic combination was seen as 'academic' or 'scholarly intelligence' (Davis et al., n.d.).

For Gardner there was much more to intelligence than those factors which were associated with more scholarly endeavours, and he postulated that there were in fact 'a multitude of intelligences, quite independent of each other; that each intelligence has its own strengths and constraints' (Gardner, 1993a: xxiii). Gardner set out his first full-length statement on the theory of MI in the text *Frames of Mind* (1983, 1993a), where he drew on his interest in the work of cognitive psychologists, and more recent developments in neurobiology. Gardner suggested that the brain had certain areas which roughly corresponded to specific forms of cognition, and which also proved 'hospitable to the notion of different forms of information processing' (Gardner 1993a: 59). In this respect the way an individual processed information was unique to them and their brain structure, and hence each individual would form knowledge in different ways. Ironically, Gardner also goes on to say that there will never be a 'single irrefutable and universally accepted list of human intelligences' (Gardner, 1993a: 60), suggesting that this could only really be achieved through the application of one level of analysis.

Nevertheless, in the early model of Gardner's MI theory he formulated a provisional list of seven intelligences, which were a combination of: the typical intelligences most valued in schools, intelligences more commonly associated with the arts and then, finally, intelligences which relate to the personal attributes of an individual. Gardner suggested that each form of intelligence could be subdivided and that the list could be rearranged (Gardner, 1993b). He also recognised that each individual had their own intelligence profile, which might be subject to change as the individual grew and developed, and in respect of the influence of environmental factors.

THE SEVEN INTELLIGENCES

We will now examine the seven intelligences that Gardner proposed in his early work:

Linguistic intelligence – this relates to the knowing which comes through the various forms of language transmission: spoken language, reading and writing. Gardner saw the gift of language as being universal, and consistent across all cultures and suggested that even in deaf populations, where manual sign languages may not be taught, children will devise their own forms of communication (Gardner, 1993b). Those with a mastery of language will understand the meaning and order of words – spoken and written – and will have an understanding of the sociocultural nuances of language, such as word play, idioms and humour in language. An individual showing linguistic intelligence is likely to have highly developed skills in reading, writing and speaking, and will have 'the capacity to use language to accomplish certain goals' (Gardner, 1999b: 41). Gardner (1999b) suggested that people likely to be high in linguistic intelligence would include lawyers, speakers, writers and poets.

Logical–mathematical intelligence – As the name suggests this intelligence relates to people who use numbers, mathematics and logic to make sense of the world. A person with a logical–mathematical intelligence 'is able to analyse problems logically, carry out mathematical operations and investigate issues scientifically' (Gardner, 1999b: 42). A person inclined towards logical–mathematical intelligence is likely to be able to think conceptually and abstractly, and can often see patterns and relationships which others may not. For Gardner the process for solving problems is rapid and often involves coping with many variables and creating multiple hypotheses (Gardner, 1999b).

Gardner identified that it was both linguistic and logical–mathematical intelligences which formed the basis for the traditional IQ test, and as such both types of intelligence had been heavily investigated by traditional psychologists. He also suggests that an individual blessed with both of these intelligences is at a significant advantage when it comes to traditional tests and examinations, since these invariably are the areas most commonly tested. Gardner also postulates that since most psychologists and academics exhibit a combination of linguistic and logical intelligence then it is inevitable that these faculties dominate tests of intelligence (Gardner, 1999b).

For Gardner, it was important, then, to acknowledge that for some people intelligence may not fall into these traditionally tested areas of intelligence, hence the following three intelligences had much more in common with the arts; an area which we have already seen was of particular interest to Gardner.

Musical intelligence – Gardner defined musical intelligence as 'entail[ing] skill in the performance, composition and appreciation of musical patterns' (Gardner, 1999b: 42). Knowledge is formulated through sounds and vibration, and captures sound, tones, beats and vibrational patterns; those high in musical intelligence are likely to be very sensitive to sounds around them in the environment. Gardner (1999b) saw a direct parallel between musical intelligence and linguistic intelligence, and indeed a person high in musical intelligence is likely to be particularly sensitive to voice tone and intonation and likely to be skilled in mimicking speech patterns and accents. Gardner (1999b) questioned then why one should be called an intelligence (linguistic) and the other a talent (musical) when the two were so very similar.

Bodily–kinaesthetic intelligence – Gardner linked bodily–kinaesthetic intelligence to both the control of one's bodily motions and the capacity to handle objects skilfully (Gardner, 1993b). Therefore, he identified individuals such as dancers and swimmers alongside artisans, ball players and instrumentalists as being high in bodily–kinaesthetic intelligence (Gardner, 1993b). For Gardner, bodily–kinaesthetic related to the capacity to use the body or parts of the body to solve problems or fashion products (Gardner, 1999b). People with this intelligence have a great sense of body awareness and can often communicate well through body language and physical expression.

Spatial intelligence – Like logical–mathematical intelligence, spatial intelligence relates to people who are able to see things through shapes, images, patterns, designs and textures. Patterns can be seen and manipulated in wide open spaces, but also in confined areas, so those with spatial intelligence might include navigators and pilots, but equally sculptors, surgeons and architects.

In the final two intelligences Gardner focused his attention on personal intelligences.

Interpersonal intelligence – Gardner saw this as being, 'a person's capacity to understand the intentions, motivations and desires of other people' (Gardner, 1999b: 43). A person strong in this intelligence works effectively with others as part of a team, having well-developed social skills to work person-to-person. Those most requiring good interpersonal intelligence unsurprisingly include salespeople, teachers, politicians and religious leaders.

Intrapersonal intelligence – In this final intelligence Gardner looked at the capacity for a person to understand themselves, 'to have an effective working model of oneself – including one's own desires, fears and capacities – and to use such information effectively in regulating one's own life' (Gardner, 1999b: 43). In this intelligence a person shows skills in self-reflection and is able to recognise emotions, values and beliefs as they apply to their self, they tend to be internally motivated and highly intuitive.

While Gardner initially identified seven intelligences he continued to research intelligences throughout his academic career, and in the mid-1990s identified an eighth intelligence, naturalistic intelligence, which, for him, met the criteria for identification as an intelligence (Davis et al., n.d.). As the name suggests someone high in naturalistic intelligence is able to develop knowledge through their encounters with the natural world, having a propensity towards plants, animals and environmental factors.

As we will see in the following section Gardner was influenced by many key thinkers in the field of psychology; however, his work also met with criticism from his contemporaries. It is testament to Gardner that he was able to respond to these critics in developing and adapting his theories in response to these observations.

LINKS WITH OTHER THEORISTS

As we have seen, Gardner worked with a number of eminent psychologists and neurobiologists. His critique of the work of cognitive psychologists was influential in the formation of his MI theory, and while he admits to being influenced by the cognitive psychologists Piaget and Bruner, he suggests that 'the bulk of my scholarly career has been a critique of the principal claims that Piaget put forth' (Gardner, 2008). It may well be that his work with neuropsychologist Norman Geschwind contributed to his questioning Piaget's work, since this resulted in Gardner working with brain-damaged patients, which raised questions regarding Piaget's views on intelligence. Where Piaget saw intelligence as 'a single general capacity that developed pretty much in the same way across individuals' (Gardner, 2008), Gardner came to believe that 'humans possess a number of relatively independent intelligences and these can function and interact in idiosyncratic ways' (Gardner, 2008).

Gardner was mentored by both Erik Erikson and David Reisman while at Harvard and he acknowledges their influence in setting him on the course to study how humans think. He also cites Jerome Bruner as being highly influential, and following a period of working with Bruner on the development of a curriculum in social studies, Gardner became interested in cognitive and developmental psychology. This is particularly noteworthy since prior to this Gardner was set to study clinical psychology, thus it could be argued that this marked a turning point in his life, setting him on the course to the academic career for which he is renowned.

While Gardner was influenced by a number of eminent thinkers in the field of psychology and neurobiology, he has continued to work with more-contemporary psychologists. As his field of study has widened so too has the range of people Gardner has worked with, each project seemingly presenting the opportunity to work with an increasingly diverse range of people. Winner (2012) outlines some of his more recent projects and accomplishments, including working with Dennie Wolf on tracing the development of young children in using symbols, and working with his then wife, Judy Gardner, demonstrating the imitative capacities in early infancy.

It has also been noted that Gardner has continued his association with Project Zero, which was first developed at Harvard University in the late 1960s. Alongside founding member and project leader Nelson Goodman, work focused on artistic knowledge and practice, with a view to examining how artistic skills and understanding can be enhanced through school- and museum-run projects. Gardner names Goodman as a further influence on him, suggesting that he encouraged scepticism in Gardner, leading him to search for evidence through asking questions. This is reflected throughout Gardner's work.

In a long and illustrious career Gardner has always sought to work with, and learn from, a wide range of people on a number of different projects. It is no surprise then that with such a wide range of influences and foci, Gardner's work has at times met with some criticism, which we shall look at in the next section.

CRITIQUING THE THEORY

Despite a successful academic career spanning five decades, and with over thirty books and hundreds of articles to his name, Gardner's work has been met with some criticism over the years. However, far from being distressed by this criticism Gardner appears to have relished the opportunity to respond to his critics, reflected, for example, in the text *Howard Gardner Under Fire* (Schaler, 2006), an edited volume to which Gardner has contributed a 'reply to my critics' for every chapter and through the article 'Reflections on multiple intelligences: Myths and messages' (1995). Gardner has also shown a willingness to amend and develop his theories in response to criticism or observations made.

White questions just how far Gardner's work on intelligence is either unique or new, suggesting that for centuries philosophers and psychologist have acknowledged the existence of intelligence, and furthermore have recognised it as something 'flexible in pursuit of one's goals' (2005: 2). White goes on to suggest that Gardner's identification of seven (later eight) intelligences is understating the range of intelligence, and states that, 'as there are as many types of human intelligence as there are types of human goal. Gardner has corralled this huge variety into a small number of categories' (White 2005: 2). Perhaps then Gardner has oversimplified the true nature of intelligence.

A further criticism of Gardner's work is the lack of empirical evidence available to support his claims, with the suggestion that Gardner's work is founded on his own intuition and reasoning rather than any research evidence. Gardner (1995) himself disputes this criticism however, stating that in the book *Frames of Mind* hundreds of empirical studies have been reviewed and the seven intelligences were identified and delineated through a review of this evidence.

The question of measuring the seven intelligences is also an area of interest when applying MI theory. In the same way that traditional intelligence is measurable through the conventional IQ test some of Gardner's critics suggest that the seven intelligences identified by Gardner should also be measurable. Again Gardner defends this by observing that, 'a battery of MI tests is inconsistent with the major tenets of the theory' (1995: 202). The principle of MI theory is in direct contrast to the measuring of intelligence through linguistic and numerical means, so for Gardner to attempt to measure intelligence in this way is in discord with the theory, additionally Gardner raises concerns regarding labelling and stigmatisation which inevitably comes with testing.

APPLYING GARDNER IN THE CLASSROOM

Gardner suggests that due to his criticism of the views on intelligence within the field of psychology his MI theory was not well-received by fellow psychologists; however, he also admits to being unprepared for the impact his work had in the field of education (Gardner, 1995). In fact MI theory potentially lends itself well to the classroom, and might offer educationalists a means by which to approach teaching and learning, alternative to the traditional mode of learning through predominantly academic subjects.

Gardner (1995) observes that he saw numerous approaches to the application of MI theory in the classroom, and given that he admits 'to having presented an "ensemble of ideas" (or "memes") to the outer world' he states that he was, 'inclined to let those "memes" fend for themselves' (Gardner, 1995: 200). Gardner does, however, question the purpose to which schools used ideas about the mind, suggesting that,

> MI ideas and practices cannot be an end in themselves; they cannot serve as a goal for a school or an educational system. Rather, every educational institution must reflect on its goals, mission, and purposes continuously, and, at least at times, explicitly. Only after such reflections can MI ideas be usefully implemented. (Gardner, 1999a: 143)

Gardener was keen then that MI theory should not be seen as a quick fix to teaching, something he saw frequently in American schools in which new practices were embraced for a short period until the next trend was adopted. For Gardner, MI theory saw a change in the way that intelligences were viewed and as such, in order for MI theory to work at an educational level, it is necessary for education systems to be responsive. If MI theory were to be adopted in schools then the ways in which children are tested and assessed must also change to reflect this.

We can see then, there is no fixed approach to the application of MI theory, and it was never Gardner's intention when he first introduced MI theory that it should be an educational approach. By its very nature, the application of MI theory should be responsive to the needs of the learners for whom it is being applied. Nevertheless, White (2005) proposes that in British schools MI theory was adopted as a basis for a more flexible approach to teaching and learning, a response to the recognition that children have different preferred learning styles. As Gardner himself identified, not all children have a propensity to learn through the more traditional literate and numerate means; as such, MI theory allows opportunities for children to bring to their learning other means, for example through music or movement, areas which they may show greater intelligence in.

When applying MI to the classroom, then, it is necessary for the practitioner to plan work which is outside of the traditional modes of learning, for example when writing about a historical event it may be the case that for those children who show high musical intelligence, the event could be written as a rap or performed as a song as an alternative to the more traditional essay. In this way, learning is presented in a way that is more accessible to the child, and is then more likely to be retained. White (2005) suggests that a further advantage of applying MI theory is that it raises a child's self-esteem, and a child who might have previously considered themselves not as clever as their peers, can be allowed to shine through, for example, their musical or bodily–kinaesthetic endeavours.

However, for MI theory to be fully capitalised on there is a need for a curriculum which embraces this mode of learning, since while knowledge is still tested in the manner of the more traditional examination, those children lacking in linguistic and logical–mathematical intelligence will still find themselves at a disadvantage compared with their more academic peers. White (2005) suggests that ideas linked to MI theory may well have been, inadvertently, responsible for educational policies and practices which led to 'selection, specialisation, individualisation of learning, and assessment' (2005: 16). Certainly the 1999 DfEE report *All Our Futures* called for a creative curriculum that 'develops young people's capacities for original ideas and action' (DfEE, 1999: 2). This was followed by further reports (Rose, 2009; Williams, 2008; Alexander, 2008) all of which called for a curriculum which placed less emphasis on the academic subjects, and instead allowed children to realise their creative potential.

Such measures would certainly have lent themselves well to MI theory, allowing teachers to teach in a way which actively promoted those subjects not deemed to be as academic as others, and therefore allowing those children with intelligences outside of linguistic and logical–mathematical to shine. Indeed, this would reflect Gardner's own liberal approach to education in which he suggests that,

> Education in our time should provide the basis for enhanced understanding of our several worlds – the physical world, the biological world, the world of human beings, the world of human artifacts, and the world of the self. (1999b: 158)

He also advocates a curriculum which favours, 'the pursuit of knowledge for its own sake over the obeisance to utility' (1999b: 39).

Unfortunately, a change in the UK government in 2010 meant that the creative curriculum was never fully realised. Instead government policy saw a return to a more formal curriculum, in which subjects were to be taught as disciplines in their own right, and in which there was a heavy emphasis on the core subjects of English, mathematics and science. Additionally, a heavy emphasis on the assessment of these core subjects saw a return to a more formal style of teaching, since a less traditional mode of learning could be seen as a risky business.

In many ways this reflects the fear which Gardner had that MI theory could be seen as a passing fad, a trend which lasts for only as long as government policy dictates. Certainly, while educational attainment is still to be tested by traditional means then some students will remain at a disadvantage. However, it could be argued that Gardner's MI theory did open the doors to a new way of thinking about how children learn. Gardner has always maintained that MI theory was never intended as an 'educational prescription' (Gardner, 1995: 206), but suggests instead that it should be down to educators to decide how MI theory should be applied in their settings if at all. This reflects previous observations that MI theory should always be about a best fit, and Gardner cautions against trying to force such a fit, arguing that some topics lend themselves well to MI theory, and others not so well, in which case a common sense approach should be applied. However, what Gardner does advocate, where MI theory is concerned, is that educators consider an alternative approach to education, approaching topics from a number of perspectives in the hope that more children will be reached.

REFLECTIVE TASK

Take a topic traditionally taught in schools (such as the Victorians, forces and energy, the water cycle) – how would you apply each of Gardner's intelligences to delivering this topic?

What do you see as the advantages to this method of delivery?

What are the challenges?

SUMMARY

Howard Gardner has had a long and illustrious academic career; from his own early experiences with education he showed a propensity for learning which he has capitalised on throughout his life. With the advantage of supportive and encouraging parents, and then later through working alongside a number of high-profile mentors, Gardner has made significant contributions to the fields of both psychology and education. Gardner is best known for his theory on multiple intelligences, which emerged from the two main themes of his work: looking at how the mind develops, particularly when developing abilities in the arts; and, as a result of his work with patients with brain trauma, looking at how the mind processes break down under special conditions.

Gardner challenged some of the traditional theories of cognitive development, and also some of the thinking on intelligence. He suggested that measurement of intelligence through the traditional IQ test did not fully reflect the extent of intelligences available to the individual, and proposed that there were seven key intelligences which should be taken account of when looking at learning. It was his MI theory which propelled him to the forefront of education, with educationalists adopting his theory to find an alternative means of content delivery.

Gardner's work has not been without its critics; however, it is testament to his conviction and tenacity that he has faced his critics head on, showing a willingness to adapt his theories, but also defending his work publicly.

In conclusion, it should be noted that while MI theory is the best-known area of Gardner's work this is only a part of an academic career which spans five decades. Gardner has been involved in numerous recent projects, and has been responsible for significant funding at Harvard University through research grants. He has worked, and continues to work, with a range of academics in the field, showing a diversity of ideas in a variety of projects.

FURTHER READING

Baum, S., Viens, J., Slatin, B. and Gardner, H. (2005) *Multiple Intelligences in the Elementary Classroom: A Teacher's Toolkit*. New York: Teachers College Press.
A practical guide to supporting teachers in meeting the needs of a diverse group of learners in the classroom through the application of pathways related to MI theory.

Craft, A., Gardner, H. and Claxton, G. (Eds) (2008) *Creativity, Wisdom and Trusteeship: Exploring the Role of Education*. Thousand Oaks: Corwin.
An examination of creativity and wisdom and how they relate to classroom practice. Contributions are made by scholars and educators in the fields of cognitive psychology and the neurosciences.

Gardner. H. (2006) *Five Minds for the Future*. Boston: Harvard Business School Publishing.
Some of Gardner's more recent work which looks at the 'five minds' that Gardner believes individuals will need to face a fast-paced future.

Komhaber, M., Fierros, E. and Veenema, S. (2003) *Multiple Intelligences: Best Ideas from Research and Practice*. Cambridge: Pearson.
Using original research from Project Zero this book shows how MI theory can be applied in schools and classrooms.

Schaler, J.A. (Ed.) (2006) *Howard Gardner under Fire: The Rebel Psychologist Faces His Critics*. Chicago: Carus Publishing Company.
In this text Gardner has the opportunity to respond to some of the fiercest critics of various aspects of his work.

REFERENCES

Alexander, R. (2008 [2010]) *Children, Their World, Their Education* (The Cambridge Primary Review). London: Routledge.

Amrein-Beardsley, A. (2013, March 16). *Inside the Academy,* video interviews with Dr Howard Gardner. http://insidetheacademy.asu.edu/howard-gardner.

Davis, K., Christodoulou, J., Seider, S. and Gardner, H. (n.d.) *The Theory of Multiple Intelligences*. www.pz.harvard.edu/sites/default/files/Theory%20of%20MI.pdf.

DfEE (1999) *All Our Futures*. Crown Copyright.

Gardner, H. (1983) *Frames of Mind: The Theory of Multiple Intelligences*. New York: Basic Books.

Gardner, H. (1993a) *Frames of Mind: The Theory of Multiple Intelligences* (tenth anniversary edition). New York: Basic Books.

Gardner, H. (1993b). *Multiple Intelligences: The Theory in Practice*. New York: Basic Books.

Gardner, H. (1995). 'Reflections on multiple intelligences: Myths and messages'. *Phi Delta Kappan*, 77: 200–9.

Gardner, H. (1999a) *The Disciplined Mind: What All Students Should Understand*. New York: Simon & Schuster.

Gardner. H. (1999b) *Intelligence Reframed*. New York: Basic Books.

Gardner, H. (2006) *Multiple Intelligences: New Horizons*. New York: Basic Books.

Gardner, H. (2008) *Wrestling with Jean Piaget, My Paragon*. www.edge.org/q2008/q08_1. html#gardner.

Rose, J, (2009) *Independent Review of the Primary Curriculum*. London: DfE.

Schaler, J.A. (Ed.) (2006) *Howard Gardner under Fire: The Rebel Psychologist Faces His Critics*. Chicago: Carus Publishing Company.

White, J. (2005) *Howard Gardner: The Myth of Multiple Intelligences*. http://eprints.ioe.ac. uk/1263/1/WhiteJ2005HowardGardner1.pdf.

Williams, P. (2008) *Independent Review of Mathematics Teaching in Early Years Settings and Primary Schools*. London: DCSFT.

Winner, E. (2012) *The History of Howard Gardner*. https://howardgardner01.files.wordpress. com/2012/06/ellenwinnerbio.pdf.

12

JOHN HOLT

UNSCHOOLING OR HOME SCHOOLING

LEARNING OUTCOMES

Having read this chapter you should be able to:

- Show an appreciation for the philosophy of John Holt
- Recognise Holt's notion of unschooling
- Critically evaluate Holt's work
- Reflect on your own views of the schooling system

KEY WORDS

Home schooling; unschooling; radical education reform; youth rights; child's voice; non-traditional

INTRODUCTION

John Holt was a key figure in American education during the 1960s and 1970s who was perhaps best known for his work with the home schooling movement in America. Holt coined the phrase 'unschooling' to explain a system of home schooling which did not rely on traditional teaching methods or a set curriculum, and which allowed children to learn at their own pace in a way which best responded to their individual needs.

Holt's work with the home schooling movement arose from his discontent with the American school system, which he believed to be flawed, and his frustration with policy-makers who seemed reluctant to change it. Holt appeared well placed to make these observations in his capacity as a classroom teacher, and despite having no formal teaching qualifications he spent fourteen years teaching grade school in America. During his time as a teacher Holt observed that his colleagues failed to make the best use of the pedagogical techniques available to them, and as result bright and competent children were becoming 'self-centred, self-protective students who aimed above all else to avoid trouble, embarrassment, punishment, disapproval or loss of status' (Lant, 1976–7: 329). Holt carried out a number of observations on his own classroom practice, and that of his co-teacher Bill Hunt, and used these observations, and his commentary on them, in his seminal texts *How Children Fail* (1964; revised 1982) and *How Children Learn* (1967; revised 1983). It was these texts which launched Holt's career as an education lecturer and consultant, and he was praised for his work, which seemed to show what really happened in schools.

Despite his contention that compulsory schooling was destroying children's natural curiosity (Gaither, 2015), Holt's work was well received by his contemporaries, and his books sold well (Lant, 1976–7). Released at a time when social reform was being welcomed, Holt continued to offer suggestions as to how classroom practices and school systems might be reformed to better meet the needs of their pupils through a further series of books. However, as Holt's ideas became increasingly radical he soon met with resistance from teachers and policy-makers, leading him to conclude that it was a waste of time trying to reform schools (Farenga, n.d.).

In turning his attention away from the school system and the classroom Holt became increasingly interested in the rights of the child and their position in society. In his books *Freedom and Beyond* (1972) and *Escape from Childhood* (1974) Holt challenged the notion of childhood and suggested that society was responsible for suppressing a child's rights until they reached the age of eighteen. At this time he also began to support those parents who were looking to extricate their children from compulsory education, he became an advocate for these parents, offering practical support through the bi-monthly newsletter *Growing without Schooling*, first published in 1977.

Holt's untimely death from cancer at the age of sixty-two meant he did not see the legacy of an ever-growing home schooling movement in America; however, his name remains synonymous with both home schooling and unschooling, and the periodical *Growing without Schooling*, which he founded, continues to be published today.

JOHN HOLT, THE PERSON

John Holt was born in New York in 1923 to parents Henry and Elizabeth Holt. He had a privileged upbringing and attended one of the more prestigious private schools in New England (Farenga, n.d.). He later went on to graduate from Yale University with a degree in industrial administration, although Farenga suggests that he was later somewhat scathing about this qualification, often adding 'whatever that means' after it. Indeed, as Holt's philosophies developed he became increasingly reticent in talking about his academic accomplishments, and despite having an excellent academic record he believed his experiences of formal education to be mostly worthless, Holt is often quoted as saying,

> I have come to believe that a person's schooling is as much a part of his private business as his politics or religion, and that no one should be required to answer questions about it. May I say instead that most of what I know I did not learn in school, and indeed was not even taught. (cited by Farenga, n.d.)

On graduating from Yale, Holt served in the navy as a lieutenant aboard the submarine *USS Barbero* (Lant, 1976–7), an experience which he later reflected on as being hugely significant in terms of the learning he gained from it. Holt expressed the notion that while no-one was talking or thinking about learning, the demanding work which was jointly accomplished, alongside the experience and skills gained, were far more powerful than any formal learning experience previously undertaken (Lant, 1976–7). Holt's three-year stint in the navy also led to him reflecting on war in the nuclear age, which he considered to be 'suicidal for mankind' (Farenga, n.d.); as a result, on leaving the navy he began to work for the World Federalist Movement, a group intent on bringing peace to the planet through the organisation of a one-world government.

Holt's work with the World Federalist Movement led him to the role of lay missionary, which saw him spending six years travelling the world promoting 'a visionary postwar program of international unity' (Lant, 1976–7: 328). Unfortunately, after six years Holt became disillusioned with the ineffective work of the movement and as a result he left the organisation.

It is the period following this that saw Holt direct his attention to the education system, encouraged by his sister, who suggested he visit the newly opened Colorado Rocky Mountain School. Holt was so impressed by what he saw that he began teaching there. It is perhaps fortuitous that this school was unconventional (being co-educational and maintained by faculty and students) since without a formal teaching qualification Holt was restricted in where he was allowed to teach. Holt related how he was unable to seek work in public schools without such qualifications, and was unable to gain the required degree having limited time or financial resources to do so.

Nevertheless, Holt spent four years at the Colorado Rocky Mountain School before moving to Boston 'to experience city life again' (Farenga, n.d.). Here he found work teaching fifth grade in a private school in Cambridge, Massachusetts, and it was during this time that he met 'his intellectual comrade and collaborator Bill Hunt' (Gaither, 2015). While working in this school Hunt and Holt began to observe one another's classes, making notes of their observations, and engaging in discussion around their shared interest in children's learning. Through their observations both Hunt and Holt began to reflect on their own teaching, particularly around seeking a means by which children could become better learners. They began to question what it was they wanted the children to achieve and how this could best be achieved (Farenga, n.d.).

It was the notes from his observations with Bill Hunt that provided Holt with the material for his first texts, and after eleven years of teaching and observing Holt published his first book, *How Children Fail* (1964; revised 1982), swiftly followed by his second, *How Children Learn* (1967, revised 1983). In these texts Holt is critical of an educational system which fails to make the best use of the pedagogical techniques available, and suggests that children's fear of the education system stifles their creativity and ability to learn effectively. Holt and Hunt had both begun to make changes to their own classroom practice in the light of their observations, and attempted to encourage other faculty members to do the same.

Despite believing the school to be supportive of his 'new ideas and new thinking about education' (Lant, 1976–7: 329), Holt was soon to find that this was to be his undoing since 'many of his fellow teachers were not happy about what the upstart Holt was doing' (Lant, 1976–7: 329), and in addition his application of classroom strategies which saw him downplaying grades, cutting back on tests and decreasing classroom stress and competition (Lant, 1976–7) ultimately led to him being fired; as Holt observed, 'I only found out later that they were interested in old "new ideas" not new "new ideas"' (Lant, 1976–7: 329).

Holt continued to attempt to pursue a career in teaching following his firing from Cambridge; however, his increasingly radical ideas led to him being fired from several more positions. Despite being unpopular with his colleagues and superiors Holt was rapidly becoming a mainstream figure in American education in the mid-1960s, and alongside his other commitments he frequently contributed to magazines such as *Life*, *The Saturday Evening Post* and *Redbook* (Gaither, 2015).

Holt left teaching in 1968 and became a lecturer at Harvard Graduate School of Education and the University of California, Berkeley. His experience as an academic spurred him on to write *The Underachieving School* (1969 [2005]), which saw him turn his attention away from his earlier classroom case studies to the school system itself. This book reflected Holt's increasing frustration at what he perceived to be a flawed system which appeared to show no signs of changing. He believed the school system to be self-serving and demeaning to its pupils (Farenga, n.d.).

Throughout, the 1970s Holt's ideas became increasingly radical, particularly as he became interested in the work of social critic Ivan Illich. Illich's work resonated with Holt since he too believed 'the concept of mass education was inherently self-defeating' (Gaither, 2015). Holt went on to publish further texts which showed his increasing frustration at the reluctance of policy-makers to change the education system, including *Freedom and Beyond* in 1972 and *Escape from Childhood* in 1974.

The more radical his ideas became the more marginalised Holt found himself, which resulted in him turning his attention to the American home schooling movement, and Holt's final work was very much centred on this. Despairing of the American education system Holt theorised that children would be better educated from home, proposing his ideas in the book, *Instead of Education: Ways to Help People Do Things Better* (1976), and latterly through the fortnightly newsletter *Growing without Schooling*. Thus, Holt spent his final years securing a legal framework for home schooling in America. Holt's untimely death from cancer in 1985 meant that this work was largely unfinished; however, the home schooling movement is Holt's enduring legacy, remaining as it does, an important part of the American education system today.

THE EDUCATION SYSTEM ACCORDING TO HOLT

As we have seen, Holt's work was based predominantly on his own first-hand experiences and observations of classroom practice and school systems, and along with his colleague and friend Bill Hunt he set out to address some of the perceived flaws identified through these observations. As such, what was developed from this work could be considered more of a philosophy than a theory, since Holt wanted teachers themselves to mirror the work that he and Bill Hunt were doing, by reflecting on their own classroom practices, and challenging the systems which he believed to be harming children's learning.

Lant (1976–7) suggests that it may well have been the lack of formal training as an educator which led Holt to view classroom practices in such a disparaging way, since he was entering the classroom without the insight of one who had been formally trained in the art of teaching. For the trained teacher there was already an awareness of the constraints which a curriculum and school system could place on the educator; however, for Holt who was entering the system oblivious to such restrictions there was a sudden realisation of 'the disjunction between what the school said it was doing and what was in fact going on in the classroom' (Lant, 1976–7: 328).

Through his observations Holt identified that the pedagogical techniques and methodological approaches applied in the classroom were actually resulting in potentially bright and competent children becoming increasingly self-centred and self-protective. He believed that the fear of failure inherent in the education system was leading children to avoid situations which might lead to 'trouble, embarrassment, punishment, disapproval or loss of status' (Lant, 1976–7: 329). In short, children were constrained in their educational endeavours, preferring to play safe to protect themselves.

Holt was frustrated by what he observed in classrooms since he recognised that children were indeed by their very nature curious, and showed a natural desire to learn. He observed 'babies are not blobs but true scientists' (Holt, 1982: xxv) and as such he believed that schools should be places where children should be allowed and encouraged to explore and make sense of the world around them, in the ways which most interested them (Holt, 1982). Holt recognised that human beings are learning animals, who don't need to be shown how to learn; however, he also believed that what killed the process was people interfering with or trying regulate or control it (Bumgarner, 1980).

Holt believed that the most powerful learning happened before the child entered the school system, and ideally learning in the classroom should be a natural progression from the learning already experienced. However, while he observed that children had a style of learning unique to their individual characteristics, he also believed that the educator trains them out of this natural desire to learn. In the preface to his book *How Children Learn*, Holt states,

> we like to say that we send children to school to teach them to think. What we do, all too often, is to teach them to think badly, to give up a natural and powerful way of thinking in favour of a method that does not work well for them and that we rarely use ourselves. (Holt, 1983: xi)

Holt believed that children developed their own coping mechanisms to deal with the challenges of the school system, often becoming distracted from the learning experience by trying to second guess what the teacher wanted from them. While he acknowledged that a few children did learn in school, for the majority he suggested that they used their minds, not to learn but to get out of the things teachers were trying to make them do to make them learn (Holt, 1983).

However, despite Holt's somewhat disparaging assessment of the education system, in his early observations he maintained that the school system could indeed be changed for the better. In both books *How Children Fail* (1964) and *How Children Learn* (1967), he used his own reflections on the observations he made to demonstrate what could be learned from the situation described, and also how classroom practice could be changed to better meet the needs of the pupils. His vision was that school should become the place where all children could grow, not just in size and knowledge but in 'curiosity, courage, confidence, independence, resourcefulness, resilience, patience, competence and understanding' (Holt, 1983: viii). He believed that this could best be achieved by developing a better understanding of 'the ways, conditions and spirit in which children do their best learning' (Holt, 1983: viii), schools should then become places where children could improve their own style of thinking and learning.

As we have noted, it was during the 1970s that Holt's vision of the school system became increasingly radical, and the more opposition he met the more frustrated he became by the lack of desire for schools to change. In the opening chapter of his book *Instead of Education* (1976) Holt's disillusionment is expressed as follows

> Do not waste your time trying to reform these schools. They cannot be reformed. It may be possible for a few of you, in a few places, to make a place called school which will be a humane and useful doing (as distinct from educating) place for the young. If so, by all means do it. In most places, not even this will be possible. (Holt, 1976: 8)

Holt turned his attention away from reforming the school system, which he now believed to be 'among the most authoritarian and destructive of all the inventions of man' (Farenga, n.d.), and instead looked to working around it. He explored the notion of free schools and learning exchanges, and offered practical support to parents who themselves sought to remove their children from the school system. It was at this time that Holt became interested in the idea of home schooling and, while parents had been schooling their children from home for some time, it was through Holt's work that a network of like-minded people was formed.

In order to offer support to these parents Holt began to publish the bi-monthly newsletter *Growing without Schooling*, in which he offered practical support to parents who preferred to educate their children from home. Holt's vision of home schooling, however, very much reflected his early ideas of how children should be educated, through taking their own interests and needs into account. So rather than simply replicate the school curriculum in the home environment, Holt advocated what he called *unschooling*, in that the learning experience developed should be directed solely by the child. For Holt, unschooling is the natural way to learn, and while it is conceivable that curriculum materials and traditional teaching materials could be used, this would be decided by the child and parent. Holt expressed that it was unnatural for learners to learn things in a particular way as decided by policy-makers, and postulated that leaners would learn what they need to learn when it made sense to them. In this way they are learning what others learn, but not necessarily in the same order. According to Holt and Farenga, 'it isn't unusual to find unschoolers who are barely eight-years-old studying astronomy or who are ten-years-old and just learning to read' (2003: 239).

Although in his later years Holt reverted back to the term home schooling, finding that unschooling led people to assume this meant being uneducated, Holt's name remains synonymous with unschooling, and his work is still closely tied to the home schooling movement in the United States. Regardless of the term used, Holt sought to support parents who wanted to present children with a more natural way to learn, in which the quest for knowledge seen in the preschool years could be continued, and in which learning was no longer impeded by a fear of failure, and in which natural curiosity was quashed because it wasn't on the curriculum.

LINKS WITH OTHER THEORISTS

Holt's work was celebrated throughout the 1960s and 1970s, a period which saw an abundance of new ideas about education emerging (Farenga, 1999). Holt himself was heavily influenced by the work of philosopher and social critic Ivan Illich, who himself believed that, 'the concept of mass education was inherently self-defeating' (Gaither, 2015). In his book *Deschooling Society* Illich wrote

> universal education through schooling is not feasible. It would be no more feasible if it were attempted by means of alternative institutions built on the style of present schools. (1970: 2)

Illich then goes on to discuss the negative impact of the school system on the child, particularly with regards to the relationship between teacher and student, which he believed impacted on the child's individual freedom. Illich argued that the function of education in society should be to provide information to the individual when and how they wanted it. He believed that individuals should have access to information, and should have a means by which to share their knowledge through distinct channels or learning exchanges. This was echoed in Holt's later work as he too sought to turn schools into resource centres and teachers into guides in his own vision to reform the education sector (Farenga, n.d.). Holt's vision of unschooling was undoubtedly influenced by Illich's *Deschooling Society* (1970), which encouraged people to become less dependent on institutions and therefore 'deschool' themselves.

Similarities with the work of A.S. Neill can also be seen in Holt's vision for education. Holt and Neill first met in 1965 (Allen, 1981) and Holt supported Neill's belief that children could be trusted to learn about the world without interference from adults (Allen, 1981). Both men shared a vision for an education system which sought an alternative to the more traditional school, and which encouraged pupils to take responsibility for their own learning. The difference between the two was that Neill was able to realise his dream of a more progressive school system, being the founder of the renowned Summerhill School, a school whose principles lay in the ideal that children learn best when free from coercion (see Chapter 3).

CRITIQUING THE THEORY

Despite being a mainstream figure in American education during the 1960s (Gaither, 2015), Holt's increasingly radical ideas about the American education system saw him rapidly falling out of favour with policy-makers. It could be argued that the more extreme his ideas became the less credible he became, which is unfortunate given that his aspiration was always that the education system should be responsive to the individual needs of the child.

Holt's philosophy was a result of his observations and discussions with his colleague Bill Hunt; however, as Lant observes these observations resulted in a series of 'explosive descriptive data about schools' (1976–7: 330) which Holt himself was unable to draw any significant conclusions from. It must also be considered that Holt's early observations were small in scale, being restricted to his own and Hunt's practice, which would call into question any generalisations formed. Alongside this, Holt's lack of formal qualifications meant he was restricted to teaching in private schools, which would also have a significant impact on the data he was collecting, since we must question how far what he was observing in the private school sector was reflective of the education system as a whole. Parents opting for a private school education for their children would surely have been expecting a formal education, resulting in the best academic performance, which would be underpinned by examinations and test results.

It must be questioned how realistic Holt's philosophy was, since leaving a child's education to chance must surely be a risky business. Holt believed that allowing a child to follow their own interests would ultimately lead to the child learning what needed to be learned, albeit not always in the order that a formal curriculum might dictate. However, without testing this philosophy on a wider scale it cannot be assumed that all children would be motivated to learn in this way, and it would surely not be ethical to risk a child's education based on this premise. Similarly, Holt spoke out about the use of testing and assessments in school; however, he himself acknowledged that this is a culture so heavily ingrained in schools that while pupils themselves complain and rebel against testing they also defend the system asking, 'if we're not tested and graded how can we tell whether we're learning anything, whether we're doing well or poorly?' (Holt, 1969 [2005]: 40).

In conclusion, when considering Holt's work we must question then how far his observations were simply based on his own preconceived ideas about the shortcomings of the education system. It could be argued that Holt had become so disillusioned by the system that he failed to see the positives in his observations, and perhaps what he assumed about children's feelings towards their education was not in reality an accurate assumption.

APPLYING HOLT IN AND OUT OF THE CLASSROOM

Although Holt was unsuccessful in persuading his contemporaries to adopt his ideas in their classrooms, it could be argued that the ideas which Holt was proposing can now be seen reflected in many of the curriculum developments in the UK, and to some extent in the changes to the English school system, which now encourages the development of free schools and academies.

Holt was a keen advocate for learning which began with the child, using their own interests as a starting point. He recounts an example of a fifth grader with a deep interest in snakes, and while snakes were not part of the curriculum Holt suggested that, 'any time he spent learning about snakes was better spent than in ways I could think to spend it' (1982: 292). Holt goes on to say that in the process of learning about snakes the child is learning about many other things which he would not otherwise be learning (Holt, 1982). Holt sums this up by suggesting that,

> It is not the subject matter that makes some learning more valuable than others, but the spirit in which the work is done. (Holt, 1982: 293)

This is a notion which can be seen reflected in the 2014 Statutory Framework for the Early Years Foundation Stage in England which states that,

> Practitioners must consider the individual needs, interests, and stages of development for experiences for each child in all of the areas of learning and development for each child in their care, and must use this information to plan challenging and enjoyable activities. (DfE, 2014: 8)

Of course, it could be argued that this is much easier to achieve in the formative stages, where there are far fewer pressures to meet standards and pass assessments. In this respect a more formal curriculum might well be considered a requirement to ensure that children meet the standards as set out by government policy. This notion of meeting set standards, measured through formal examinations and tests, was a further area of contention for Holt, who suggested that 'the test-examination-marks business is a gigantic racket' (1982: 232). Holt believed the sole purpose of assessments to be a joint pretence to show that 'students know everything they are supposed to know; when in fact they only know a small part of it' (1982: 232). He suggested that the very fact that tests are announced to the students in advance is to ensure that students prepare themselves in the best way possible, in order that the best results might be achieved.

Similar views were postulated by Black and Wiliam in 2001 with the publication of *Inside the Black Box* in which they proposed that rather than assessing children summatively at the end of a module or scheme of work, assessment should take more of a formative form. Through the formative assessment model teachers would carry out ongoing assessments of the learning process, allowing them to address any issues as they arise, rather than at the end when it is often too late to do anything about it. This way, teachers could adapt their teaching to meet the needs of each individual child. Black and Wiliam's work was reflective of Holt's in that they were more interested in the process than the product – understanding how an answer had been reached rather than the answer itself. For Holt, his interest was in how the mind worked, something he suggested was almost impossible to measure (Holt, 1969 [2005]).

Black and Wiliam's work had a significant impact on assessment in schools through the assessment for learning strategy, introduced in England by the Department for

Children, Schools and Families in 2008. Here, the then Minister of State for Schools and Learners, Jim Knight, set out his aims to personalise learning and teaching through embedding assessment for learning in all classrooms. Building on the work of Black and Wiliam the assessment reform group, responsible for the implementation of the strategy, highlighted the importance of assessment in the classroom which placed less emphasis on the more traditional formal assessments used in schools. Instead, they presented a vision which saw assessment as an ongoing system of continuous monitoring, central to classroom practice and designed to inform planning and teaching methods. More importantly, it saw pupils as at the heart of the process, involved in the assessment of their own work and that of their peers, a notion which Holt himself certainly embraced suggesting that, 'all serious practice can be seen as a way in which the learner tests his own skill and knowledge' (Holt, 1969 [2005]: 37). While a change in government in 2010 saw a return to a more traditional style of assessment in schools, it could be argued that the assessment for learning strategy has left a legacy in schools which sees teachers continuing to use ongoing formative assessment to help inform and personalise the learning experience for children, which Holt would surely have approved of.

By the late 1970s Holt had turned his attention away from classroom practice, and instead turned his attention to the school system as a whole. In his book *Instead of Education* (1976) he provided examples and methods for running free schools and learning exchanges as an alternative to compulsory schooling. Although not as radical as Holt's ideas, free schools came to the fore in British politics following the election of the Coalition Government in 2010. In their academies and free schools policy document the government set out their aim to reform the school system to prevent standards in England from falling behind those of other countries (DfE, 2010). Through the models of both academies and free schools more control was given to the setting to decide on their own curriculum, set their own term dates and school times, and control staffing and budgets in the best interests of the stakeholders. Of course, we cannot overlook the impetus for this policy change, since for the Coalition Government this was about raising standards, a concept which would have held no appeal for Holt unless it was in best interest of the child. However, arguably the sense of control, if in the right hands, could well appeal to Holt's ideal of an education system tailor-made for its intended audience.

It would be an oversight not to consider the home school movement when evaluating the impact of Holt's work on practice, since in abandoning all attempts to change the education system, it is in the American home school movement that Holt has perhaps had the most significant and lasting impact. Holt was keen, however, when encouraging parents to take their children out of compulsory schooling that they did not simply replicate the school system in their homes. Holt urged the parents of home schoolers to make the most of their natural environment in the learning process, taking education into the environment and creating a secure foundation for lifelong learning. Holt suggests:

Experience being the greatest of all teachers, homeschoolers can make their children part of their everyday adult lives. By being accepted into the continuum of their parents' lives, a child learns by doing, by seeing other people work and do things and wanting to do them themselves. (cited in Farenga, n.d.)

To this end, Holt believed that the home schooler should be allowed autonomy over their own learning, learning what they wanted when they wanted without the pressure of a set curriculum which showed no respect for a child's individual needs. This may well be seen reflected in the most recent government guidelines, which state that home schooling is a right for all parents and children, and there is no legal obligation to follow the National Curriculum in England (Gov.uk, 2015). However, we must question the reality of this notion set against a society which relies so heavily on the standards set by formal examinations.

REFLECTIVE TASK

What is most important and valuable about the home as a base for children's growth into the world is not that it is a better school than the schools but that it isn't a school at all. It is not an artificial place, set up to make 'learning' happen and in which nothing except 'learning' ever happens. (Holt and Farenga, 2003: 279)

Holt believed that children should be educated at home, following their own needs and interests. In this way he believed they would learn what they needed to learn when they needed to learn it.

How practical do you think this is in today's society? Make a list of advantages and disadvantages of this approach to schooling.

SUMMARY

It is testament to Holt's tenacity that, despite being met with resistance from both policy-makers and colleagues, he never gave up on his desire to promote a more positive learning experience for children. His attempts to reform education saw him turn his attention away from classroom practice, into policy and school reform, and latterly to the rights of the child and home schooling.

Aside from his influence on the home schooling movement in America, Holt is probably best known for his two seminal texts, *How Children Fail* and *How Children Learn*, in which he presents a somewhat disparaging view of the American education system. However, despite his initial contention that, 'school is a place where children learn to be stupid' (Holt, 1964, cited in Lant, 1976–7), Holt continued to offer practical suggestions to help parents and teachers improve matters for children, before eventually concluding that schools simply did not want to change.

Despite setting out neither as an educationalist, nor as writer, Holt made a significant impact in both fields at the height of his success in the 1960s and 1970s. His books sold well, and there continues to be a market for those seeking an alternative to traditional schooling even today. It is unfortunate that his ideals just became too radical even during the heady times of social reform.

FURTHER READING

Gatto, J.T. (2002) *Dumbing Us Down: The Hidden Curriculum of Contemporary Schooling*. Gabriola Island, Canada: New Society Publishers.
An account of the impact of compulsory schooling on children in America

Holt, J. and Scheffer, S. (1990) *A Life Worth Living: The Selected Letters of John Holt*. Athens: Ohio State University Press.
A selection of letters written by John Holt providing an insight into some of his thoughts on educational reform, schooling and politics.

Meighan, R. (2014) *John Holt*. London: Bloomsbury.
An account of John Holt's work with a critical exploration of some of his key publications, along with a discussion of the application of Holt's ideas in personalising the learning experience.

Miller. R.J. (2005) *Free Schools, Free People: Education and Democracy after the 1960s*. New York: State University of New York Press.
An account of the free school movement of the 1960s, charting the works of some of the key figures of the time including John Holt and A.S. Neill.

REFERENCES

Allen, M. (1981) *The Education of John Holt*. www.holtgws.com/educationofjh.html.
Black, P. and Wiliam, D. (2001) *Inside the Black Box: Raising Standards through Classroom Assessment*. British Educational Research Association. https://weaeducation.typepad.co.uk/files/blackbox-1.pdf.
Bumgarner, M. (1980) *A Conversation with John Holt*. The Natural Child Project. www.naturalchild.org/guest/marlene_bumgarner.html.
DfE (Department for Education) (2010) *2010–2015 Government Policy: Academies and Free Schools*. Crown Copyright.
DfE (Department for Education) (2014) *Statutory Framework for the Early Years Foundation Stage*. Crown Copyright.
Farenga. P. (1999) *John Holt and the Origins of Contemporary Homeschooling*. http://mhla.org/information/resourcesarticles/holtorigins.htm.

Farenga, P. (n.d.) *Homeschooling and John Holt's Vision*. http://spinninglobe.net/spinninglobe_html/hs%26jholt.htm.

Gaither, M. (2015) 'John Holt'. *Encyclopaedia Britannica Online*. http://www.britannica.com/biography/John-Holt.

Gov.uk (2015) *Home Education*. www.gov.uk/home-education.

Holt, J. (1964) *How Children Fail*. London: Penguin Books.

Holt, J. (1967) *How Children Learn*. London: Penguin Books.

Holt, J. (1969 [2005]) *The Underachieving School*. USA: Sentient Publications.

Holt, J. (1972) *Freedom and Beyond*. New York: E.P. Dutton.

Holt, J. (1974) *Escape from Childhood*. USA: Holt Associates.

Holt, J. (1976) *Instead of Education: Ways to Help People Do Things Better*. New York: E.P. Dutton.

Holt, J. (1982) *How Children Fail* (revised edition). London: Penguin Books.

Holt, J. (1983) *How Children Learn* (revised edition). London: Penguin Books.

Holt, J. and Farenga, P. (2003) *Teach Your Own: The John Holt Book of Homeschooling*. USA: Perseus Books Group.

Illich. I. (1970) *Deschooling Society*. London: Marion Boyars Publishers.

Lant, J.L. (1976–7) 'Considering John Holt'. *Educational Studies*, 7: 327–35.

13

BELL HOOKS

EDUCATION AS THE PRACTICE OF FREEDOM

LEARNING OUTCOMES

Having read this chapter you should be able to:

- Understand how hooks' upbringing has influenced her teaching and writing
- Appreciate the impact of hooks' notion of education as the practice of freedom
- Identify and understand hooks' concern with issues of race, gender and class as they relate to education
- Apply the principles of engaged pedagogy to your practice
- Critically evaluate hooks' writing and her views on educational practice

KEY WORDS

Engaged pedagogy; critical thinking; democratic education; spirituality; learning community; practical wisdom

INTRODUCTION

bell hooks is an American scholar, author, feminist, progressive educator and social activist born in 1952 in Hopkinsville, Kentucky, USA. Her actual name is Gloria Watkins, she adopted the pen name bell hooks, written in lower case, from her great-grandmother Bell Blair Hooks (Burke, 2004). Although she is probably more renowned for her writings on the black female in US culture, this chapter will mainly focus on her significant contributions to the practice of progressive and democratic higher education. These significant contributions to education have emerged and are embedded in her convictions of the inequality that is still evident where matters of race, gender and social class are concerned. From these convictions hooks has campaigned for a powerful and active form of engaged pedagogy with which to defy how conventional education is practised and has called for 'education as the practice of freedom' (hooks, 1994; Thomas, 1997) – a notion of education which is both influenced by, and closely related to, Freire's antipathy to a 'banking' system of education (Freire, 1970 [1996]).

The motivation for her writing on education came from her own experiences of how she was influenced by teachers from her time at school and as an undergraduate and postgraduate student at university. Her writing also stemmed from her positive, and not so positive, experiences as a teacher:

> Nurturing the self-development and self-actualization of students in the classroom I soon learned to love teaching. I loved the students. I loved the classroom. I also found it profoundly disturbing that many of the abuses of power that I had experienced during my education were still commonplace, and I wanted to write about it. (hooks, 2010: 3)

She was furthermore moved to write because of what she saw as a widespread lack of black women writers in present-day scholarly works which tackled the inequities of gender, race and class issues (hooks, 1994). Writing in 2010, hooks comments 'although our nation has made significant strides in the area of civil rights, the United States remains a society where segregation is the norm', this she feels was particularly the case in education and on university campuses (hooks, 2010: 95).

hooks has written a trilogy of influential, and radical, educational books: *Teaching to Transgress: Education as the Practice of Freedom* (1994), *Teaching Community: A Pedagogy of Hope* (2003a) and *Teaching Critical Thinking: Practical Wisdom* (2010). All are written in the autobiographical memoire style of the storyteller, which uses a combination of reflection and narrative (Cole and Knowles, 2001). Each book is a collection of critical essays where she shares some quite personal issues, particularly about her family; this style is not written to disturb but rather to confront honestly those issues which normally go unspoken (Cheng, 1997; hooks, 2003a).

The first of the trilogy, *Teaching to Transgress* (1994), is a set of fourteen essays which endeavour to consider the associations between engaged pedagogy and matters of gender, race and class. In addition, it reflects on the influence that Freire's philosophy has had on hooks' writing. In this work she also urges teachers to move on from traditional practices to surmount the *ennui* of what is currently experienced in the classroom (Thomas, 1997). The second book of sixteen essays, *Teaching Community* (2003a), enabled hooks to build on the success of the first in that the broad and diverse essays were drawn from a wide section of society not just those directly involved in teaching; as such, she was able to reach out and promote her ideas and the importance of a more progressive education to a wider community. In the final part of the trilogy, *Teaching Critical Thinking* (2010), hooks again covers a diverse range of issues, nevertheless with the same focus on gender, race and class. In this work the thirty-two essays (or 'teachings' as she calls them in this book) have arisen from conversations with teachers and students in a 'collected desire to understand how to make the classroom a place of fierce engagement and intense learning' (hooks, 2010: 5).

To gain a full insight into what shaped hooks' notions of education as the practice of freedom and engaged pedagogy we need to consider the culture of her upbringing as a black female child in the 1950s and 1960s in the South of the United States, and to examine her experiences during her academic career in higher education.

BELL HOOKS, THE PERSON

hooks was brought up in a black working-class neighbourhood and her rise to become a distinguished scholar is a phenomenon. She appreciated the meaning of gender inequity as a young girl growing up in a patriarchal family where 'our daily life was full of patriarchal drama – the use of coercion, violent punishment, verbal harassment to maintain male domination' (hooks, 1994: 119). She, like her siblings, realised that her father's authority held more weight than her mother's. These early experiences, together with what she felt as a student, regarding the effect of racism and sexism for black women, were explored in her first feminist book *Ain't I a Woman: Black Women and Feminism* (1982). These early experiences have shaped her current thinking, and today she is an anti-racist and committed feminist; however, the core theme to her work stresses that issues of 'gender, race and class distinctions are not viewed as being more than the other' but they are all interlocked (Burke, 2004: 2).

Because of the racial apartheid at the time, hooks' early education took place in segregated schools, it was in these black schools, with black teachers:

> where I experienced learning as a revolution ... black children who were deemed exceptional, gifted, were given special care. Teachers worked with us to ensure that we would fulfil our intellectual destiny and by doing so uplift the race. My teachers were on a mission. (hooks, 1994: 2)

At this stage school, for hooks, was a place of happiness and discovery, 'where I could forget ... and, through ideas, reinvent myself' (hooks, 1994: 3). Teachers knew their students' family backgrounds and, as such, teaching was culturally meaningful. However, this changed dramatically with racial integration in the 1960s, the enthusiasm of her teachers to strive to improve students' learning was gone. Now knowledge was concerned with gathering information and it had no links with black culture. Black children were now 'bussed to white schools, we soon learned that obedience, and not a zealous will to learn, was what was expected of us' (hooks, 1994: 3). She is very critical about her teachers when she attended her new white school, who she said considered themselves racially superior and thought that black students were unable to learn. Her comments about this period of her education are thought provoking and quite disturbing; for example, she states 'Imagine what it is like to be taught by a teacher who does not believe you are fully human' (hooks, 2010: 2). These feelings about race domination stayed with her through her time at university both as an undergraduate and postgraduate student. She was, in the main, not impressed by her lecturers, but 'learned a lot about the kind of teacher I did not want to become' (hooks, 1994: 5).

Despite her unhappiness as a university student within a dominant culture, hooks progressed well in her academic studies. She was awarded a scholarship to study at Stanford University where she gained a BA in 1973, then in 1976 she achieved an MA from the University of Wisconsin before her PhD in 1983 at the University of Santa Cruz (Burke, 2004). She went on to become a prolific writer of many books and journal articles on race, feminism, film and class, as well as education. She has taught for many years in a variety of higher education institutions in the United States, becoming Distinguished Professor of English at the City College of New York (Burke, 2004). In 2014 she founded the bell hooks Institute in Berea, Kentucky, which endeavours to encourage the ending of domination and discrimination through critical thinking and teaching (bell hooks Institute, 2015). Her ideas on education and teaching were shaped by the anti-racist civil rights movement, feminism and her wish to become an active cultural critic (hooks, 2010).

HOOKS AND HER NOTIONS OF LEARNING

Before exploring the specific notions held by hooks, such as engaged pedagogy, critical thinking, learning communities and practical wisdom, it is appropriate at this stage to consider her overall rationale for changes in teaching practice and her untiring quest for education as a practice of freedom. hooks feels that democratic education in the United States has been weakened because 'business and corporate capitalism encourage students to see education solely as a means to material success' (hooks, 2010: 16). This materialistic notion of education values the gathering of information. Whereas the democratic model of education values the process of attaining knowledge and critical thinking. She laments that progressive university lecturers who strive for a democratic education are often ostracised or urged to leave academia. Yet she calls for lecturers to continue the struggle to create a democratic environment in their classrooms where learning and thinking critically are appreciated and esteemed, where student voice and dissent are not just allowed but also promoted (hooks, 2010). Such a democratic learning environment needs to be 'a place that is life-sustaining and mind-expanding, a place of liberating mutuality where teacher and student together work in partnership' (hooks, 2003a: xv).

Drawing upon events from her own education where teachers in her segregated schools acknowledged and valued individual student's experiences as part of the learning process, hooks explains how this was certainly not the case when she later attended desegregated schools where black children were 'regarded as objects and not subjects' (hooks, 1994: 37). For her, student experiences are explicitly linked with the politics of gender, race and issues of class. As such, teachers should not submissively consent to use pedagogies which mirror the prejudices of the dominant standpoint of education by the 'imperialist white-supremacist capitalist patriarchy' (hooks, 2003a: 166). Her aim of creating education as the practice of freedom is focused on hope for the future, a future away from segregation towards a radical vision which endeavours to salvage the full potential of anti-racist and democratic integration (hooks, 2003a). Central to this aim is her notion of engaged pedagogy (hooks, 1994).

Engaged pedagogy, hooks argues, should embrace and celebrate student experiences; it is a way of defining a process of interactive learning and teaching where everyone's existence and voice in the classroom is acknowledged (Collins et al., 2002). But engaged pedagogy has a more all-inclusive advantage.

> When education is the practice of freedom, students are not the only ones asked to share, to confess. Engaged pedagogy does not seek simply to empower students. As any classroom that employs a holistic model of learning will also be a place where teachers grow, and are empowered by the process. (hooks, 1994: 21)

hooks concedes that engaged pedagogy is a demanding practice, which involves both teachers and students taking risks, and stresses that 'teachers must be actively committed to a process of self-actualization that promotes their own well-being' in order to empower students (hooks, 1994: 15). For hooks engaged pedagogy involves 'a flexible agenda, spontaneity, interaction and critical reflection' (Collins et al., 2002: 106).

Engaged pedagogy challenges the traditional and dominant way of thinking that all classrooms are the same, even when there are differences in students' gender, race and class. hooks argues that with engaged pedagogy the classroom is in a constant state of flux, 'It's dynamic. It's fluid. It's *always* changing' (hooks, 1994: 158). As such, engaged practice fosters discussion and interpersonal associations that enable critical reflection to flourish between students and teachers; 'it allows students to recognize their own and others' humanity and assists them in becoming critical citizens' (Carolissen et al., 2011: 158). Engaged pedagogy is a teaching approach which strives to re-establish students' motivation to think critically as part of the learning process. This, she argues, is not an easy process as the majority of students are more secure with passive learning (hooks, 2010).

For hooks, critical thinking is a process that insists on students and teachers openly and honestly participating together to deconstruct and delve below the surface in their search for knowledge, and together building what she terms as learning communities (hooks, 2010). She sees critical thinking as a perceptive way to uncover knowledge that can be shared and valued despite differences. According to hooks, what is crucial for successful critical thinking practice is not so much the analysis of the debate, but rather the capabilities of students to 'transcend race, class, and gender biases to transform their lives, moving beyond these into places of power and possibility' (Lim, 2011: 5). Key to the success of critical thinking is the building of trusting classroom relationships in a safe environment for students to openly discuss topics of contention and sensitivity. Engaged pedagogy which involves critical thinking enables students and teachers to face their feelings and rebuild their connections with others in secure and trusting learning communities (hooks, 2003a).

Building trusting learning communities involves finding out what similarities we have, as well as what divides us and creates differences. Many students, and teachers, avoid facing up to difference because they think this will lead to discord. However, hooks (2003a) argues that it is our refusal to encounter the existence of difference that creates continuing discord; instead she suggests we should connect with, and celebrate, our differences and confront any frictions as they are encountered. She promotes therefore the creation of learning communities which have 'unity within diversity' (hooks, 2003a: 109). She cites the dominator culture as blameworthy for students and teachers preferring uniformity over difference. In its place we should discover what aspects connect us and also rejoice in our differences. This in turn will bring individuals nearer to each other with a set of shared values to form meaningful learning communities, both inside classrooms and in the world (hooks, 2003a).

Her latest book of the teaching trilogy (hooks, 2010) makes links with engaged pedagogy, critical thinking, learning communities and what she calls practical wisdom. This is the awareness of the interconnections between theory and knowledge and the fact that knowledge cannot be detached from experience. Engaged pedagogy and critical thinking encourage us to think for ourselves and to be self-critical, which are essential for practical wisdom. By being critical and reflective about our lives and the world we live in:

> Practical wisdom shows us that all genuine learning requires of us a constant open approach, a willingness to engage invention and reinvention, so that we may discover those places of transparency where knowledge can empower ... learning to reflect, to broaden our vision so that we can see the whole picture. (hooks, 2010: 187)

The notion that knowledge is embedded in experience affects not only how we came about our knowledge, but also how we utilise such knowledge (hooks, 2010). Furthermore, practical wisdom helps us combine knowledge, theory and personal skills in a practical approach to learning (hooks, 2010).

The use of dialogue is central throughout all hooks' notions of learning. She particularly emphasises the significance of language and voice in education as a practice of freedom. In her own writing she uses autobiographical narrative to uncover the realities of the marginalised, in so doing enlightening her readership about significant issues of social justice, and also 'how the personal is fundamentally political' (Carolissen et al., 2011: 158). It is the English language which she feels is used in a political context by the dominant culture and 'what the oppressors do with it, how they shape it to become a territory that limits and defines, how they make it a weapon that can shame, humiliate, colonize' (hooks, 1994: 168). She criticises the reality that, in teaching and in writing, and in academia as a whole, there has been scant endeavour to use black colloquial speech or anything that is not 'normal' English. Furthermore, she contests that those students who come from ethnically diverse or working-class backgrounds can be disadvantaged, as she explains:

> To insist on speaking in any manner that did not conform to privileged class ideas and mannerisms placed one always in the position of interloper. (hooks, 1994: 182)

Despite these possible disadvantages, hooks has always encouraged and enthused about the use of student voice as being a vital part of engaged pedagogy within trusting learning communities (hooks, 2003a).

Throughout her works hooks stresses the significance of well-being for teachers and students, and interweaves notions of care, love, spirituality and imagination as underpinning such well-being and personal growth (Sewell, 2010). She likens teaching to a caring profession but considers that, like other caring professions in the United States, teaching is unappreciated. Moreover, she proposes that those teachers who care for their students in the wider sense are usually acting in conflict with their institutions because, she argues, these establishments are places where knowledge has been designed to bolster the dominant culture (hooks, 2003b). hooks' claim that teaching involves love goes against conventional wisdom, which states that teachers should remain emotionally detached from their students. For hooks, the idea of love in teaching ought to 'be a practice that validates the whole person and not only that which they can produce in a test' (Carolissen et al., 2011: 159). She argues that teachers should not be anxious that love will result in favouritism or rivalry, because love will act as a deterrent to domination: 'love will always challenge and change us' (hooks, 2010: 163).

Central to her idea of care are the aspects of the human spirit such as kindness, tolerance and forgiveness. All of these aspects can create a classroom environment where learning becomes meaningful and worthwhile, and students develop a sense of self-determination and take responsibility for their growth as learners. By involving these aspects of the human spirit students have an insight into the emotional and caring features of their inner self, which helps to create spirituality in the classroom (hooks, 2010). Imagination, like spirituality, is not encouraged within the dominant culture of higher education establishments, which value information over the process of learning. Even though young children are encouraged to use their imagination, as they get older 'imagination is seen as dangerous, a force that could possibly impede knowledge acquisition' (hooks, 2010: 60). For the most part, university discourages imagination in favour of data and information gathering. The dominant culture, hooks contends, is trying to quash imagination as a way of repression; arguing that, 'imagination is one of the most powerful modes of resistance that oppressed and exploited folks can and do use' (hooks, 2010: 61). These sentiments of resistance over oppression, and the notion of democratic education, are in common with other progressive educational thinkers and social activists.

LINKS WITH OTHER THEORISTS

Possibly the most influential thinker to promote democratic education was John Dewey in his 1916 seminal text: *Democracy and Education: An Introduction to the Philosophy of Education*. Like Dewey, hooks advances the notion of a democratic education which embraces experiences from real life and the world at large. Also, for both of them, education is not limited to the formal curricula of schools and universities, rather learning takes place in the real world and is a continual process (hooks, 2003a). Her ideas are also very comparable to those of Dewey, who argued for a move away from the traditional passive notion of teaching to a more active, participatory practice which valued difference and the building of democratic learning communities (Dewey, 1938). hooks and Dewey advocated a progressive and democratic form of education where experiences from different cultures were used to resolve problems through discussion, and where students learned from each other (Dewey, 1938).

The thinker who has had the most influence upon hooks was Paulo Freire, the Brazilian educational philosopher. When she discovered Freire, she 'found a mentor and a guide, someone who understood that learning could be liberatory' and not a process of 'banking' information given (hooks, 1994: 6). Undoubtedly, Freire has had an overwhelming impact on hooks' practice and her writing, especially concerning language and consciousness (Burke, 2004). It was Freire's notions of freedom from oppression (Freire, 1970 [1996]) which inspired hooks to generate approaches to her teaching which were aligned to his idea of 'conscientisation' – a term she interpreted and associated with her notions of engaged pedagogy and critical thinking. She was thereafter convinced that it 'was crucial for me and every other student to be an active participant, not a passive consumer' (hooks, 1994: 14). Both also considered education should be rooted in hope. Like Freire, hooks saw hope appear from 'places of struggle where I witness individuals positively transforming their lives and the world around them' (hooks, 2003a: xiv). Although hooks considered Freire's philosophy was in many ways attuned with her own feminist thinking, she did censure his use of sexist language apparent in his earlier writing (Irwin, 2012).

There are many similarities between Henry Giroux and hooks in their standpoints on education and teaching practice. Giroux's critical pedagogy emphasises the need for teachers to reach out to all students by taking into consideration matters of gender, race and class (Giroux, 1992). Giroux also stresses the importance of situating students' experiences and cultural differences in the process of learning. He also highlights the significance of encouraging the student voice, else otherwise students become passive recipients of the dominant and oppressive culture (hooks, 1994). Giroux, similar to hooks, also felt that feminist activists should not concentrate entirely on issues of gender differences but look at how they overlap with other sources of power, especially with respect to race and class (Giroux, 1992). hooks' view that traditional education and the curriculum were constructed and controlled by the dominant culture to maintain the status quo is very much aligned with Foucault's ideas outlined in *Discipline and Punish: The Birth of the Prison* (1979). This, hooks argues, thwarts opportunities for critical thinking and students soon learn 'via a model of discipline and punish that it is better to choose obedience over self-awareness and self-determination' (hooks, 2010: 8). hooks' progressive ideas have influenced other educational thinkers, and her inclusive and caring approach to teaching have had a positive impact on engaged classroom practice.

CRITIQUING THE THEORY

hooks attracts censure because her work does not conform to the conventions of academic writing (Cheng, 1997). This is a matter which hooks herself acknowledges, and she regrets that students are discouraged from citing her work as their professors do not consider it of a scholarly quality, this she puts down to her standpoint on issues of gender:

> Any of us who create feminist theory and feminist writing in academic settings in which we are continually evaluated know that work deemed 'not scholarly' or 'not theoretical' can result in one not receiving deserved recognition and reward. (hooks, 1994: 72)

Non-compliance to the conventions of academic writing includes her not citing scholarly sources and a style of writing which, as we have seen, is very personal and confessional in its nature. Therefore, by using this personal style of writing there is a danger that she could be accused of exaggeration and giving an excessive degree of bias to her ideas. In doing so she risks losing the regard from those in academia who would prefer a more reasoned and critically logical analytical approach (Cheng, 1997).

There are very real practical problems as well in the telling of stories and divulging personal experiences in the classroom, which hooks fully concedes. This can be seen by some students as an opportunity to try and divert the lesson away from the designated course reading and planned content, which can result in some students dominating whilst others are passive (hooks, 2010). She has also been criticised as a teacher, as well as during her time as a student, 'for having too much passion, for being too emotional' (hooks, 2003a: 127). She makes a strong case for promoting a notion of love between students and teachers as being a component of caring and open relationships; as long as that love is contained within the appropriate boundaries. However, there is a very real concern for some teachers who might feel overwhelmed at being too emotionally involved in students' problems (hooks, 2003a).

The practice of engaged pedagogy, ensuring all students are participating, is very tiring. It is made worse by an ever-increasing number of students entering her classrooms. When this happens engaged practice becomes impractical: 'overcrowded classes are like overcrowded buildings – the structure can collapse' (hooks, 1994: 160). There is also a risk, with large groups, of teacher over-exhaustion and consequently a return to the traditional didactic method of teaching (hooks, 1994). Moreover, there is a question over the validity of her emphasis on the use of an equity of dialogue between teacher and student. Berry argues that 'engaged pedagogy does not alleviate the historical power of the teacher/professor and thereby can limit the freedom of speech in the classroom' (Berry, 2010: 21).

A regular criticism of hooks' essays, in all three teaching trilogy books, is that they offer an abundance of passion and insight about gender and race issues but little in the way of concrete advice for practical application (Thomas, 1997; Carolissen et al., 2011). Irrespective of these criticisms, hooks' work offers a range of inclusive and progressive ideas which can be adapted for practice to create participatory learning opportunities.

APPLYING HOOKS' IDEAS IN PRACTICE

Although hooks may not propose a set of detailed guidelines for pedagogical practice, it is argued that her notions of engaged pedagogy, critical thinking, and the use of student experience and voice presents practitioners with a plethora of ideas for classroom practice. These ideas emerge from her optimistic and passionate vision of the liberatory form of higher education teaching, which is highlighted in the concluding paragraph of the first book of her teaching trilogy:

> The academy is not paradise. But learning is a place where paradise can be created. The classroom with all its limitations, remains a location of possibility. In that field of possibility we have the opportunity to labor for freedom, to demand of ourselves and our comrades, an openness of mind and heart that allows us to face reality even if we collectively imagine ways to move beyond boundaries, to transgress. This is education as the practice of freedom. (hooks, 1994: 207)

She emphasises that the engaged pedagogy approach has also had benefits for her as a developing intellectual and teacher because at the core to this approach is critical thinking. To do this requires teachers to employ a range of learning and teaching strategies to promote an active learning community. However, she accepts that at times students become quite uncomfortable when teaching deviates from the passive 'banking' system (hooks, 1994).

To encourage and embrace the active learning which is embedded in the spirit of engaged pedagogy teachers must act as performers, although not in the conventional meaning of the term. Such performances should endeavour to create flexibility and spontaneity to allow opportunities which empower all students. However, empowerment invites students to take risks, for example taking part in confessional discussions which could possibly expose their vulnerability. According to hooks, teachers should not ask students to take risks that they are unwilling to take themselves, if they do the teachers are 'exercising power in a manner that could be coercive' (hooks, 1994: 21). Therefore, it is this willingness on behalf of teachers to be at one with the students, to be open and share each other's vulnerability which is the essence of engaged pedagogy.

Engaged pedagogy, for the teacher, is the belief that the most valuable learning takes place when there is a shared and active rapport with the students. For this to happen the teacher must determine what the students already know as well as what it is they wish to learn. This in turn means that the teacher must delve deep to uncover the different levels of emotional awareness and consciousness that exist in the classroom. In practice, this takes a considerable amount of time, and can be quite disconcerting for teachers who are anxious about ensuring that they cover the assigned material that is expected of them. However, hooks contends that we should take the time to get to know the students at the start of programmes of study, by making time to let them introduce themselves and to share with the rest of the group where they have come from and what their expectations and aspirations are. Making time to do this, she argues, creates a more favourable and positive learning environment; the start of an engaged and active learning community (hooks, 2010).

She offers some practical examples of how she ensures such engagement and sharing of experiences, so teachers can begin to understand who the students actually are and where they stand emotionally. To do this she frequently asks students to write a brief paragraph (an activity in which she also takes part):

> We might all write a spontaneous paragraph beginning with a phrase like 'My most courageous moment happened when ...' or we might bring a small object to class and all write a short paragraph about its value and importance. Reading these short paragraphs aloud to each other, we have the opportunity to see and hear each unique voice... Writing and reading paragraphs together acknowledges the power of each student's voice and creates the space for everyone to speak when they have meaningful comments to make. (hooks, 2010: 20)

Another strategy she employs to build a learning community where every student voice is valued, is that she asks the students to keep journals and she encourages them to write in them during her classes and then to read them to one another. This practice ensures that no student is passive and hidden within the classroom. This she maintains also encourages active listening and a recognition of each other's voice and viewpoints (hooks, 1994).

The use of voice, and in particular active listening, she stresses is a crucial component of engaged pedagogy and in the promotion of critical thinking. The use of voice, hooks argues, is more than about the telling of stories of experience, it is about developing a voice so students can speak openly about other topics. hooks maintains that many students from working-class backgrounds believe their lecturers think that they have nothing of worth to say. The teaching strategy she offers to overcome this belief is to reduce the emphasis on her voice as a teacher and to encourage students to actively listen to each other. From her experience she feels this happens quite rapidly when students share their experiences in union with the academic topic in question (hooks, 1994). She does accept, however, that although the use of encouraging student voice through conversation and discussion enhances the notion of a learning community, it can in practice lead to what could be conceived as quite disruptive and argumentative behaviour. For many students from a middle-class background such behaviour is seen as aggressive. Nevertheless, she states that 'those of us from working-class backgrounds may feel that discussion is deeper and richer if it arouses intense responses' and, as such, teachers should continue to be open to such frank exchanges (hooks, 1994: 187).

A further consideration for practice is hooks' notion of the importance of the body in teaching and how the body is employed as a means of power in the classroom. She suggests that many teachers think it does not matter where they position themselves in the classroom. However, there are those teachers who, quite understandably, feel a loss of control if they move from behind the lectern or desk. Conversely, hooks feels more comfortable when she is among the students and being close to them. For her, accepting that both teachers and students are bodies is a crucial aspect of engaged pedagogy in her 'efforts to disrupt the notion of professor as [an] omnipotent, all-knowing mind' (hooks, 1994: 138). This idea of the teacher as the font of all knowledge who is always right, hooks argues, has no place in engaged pedagogy. She calls instead for an openness to recognise what teachers do not know and a 'radical commitment to openness which maintains the integrity of the critical thinking process and its central role in education' (hooks, 2010: 10). These are all linked to hooks' viewpoint on the importance of trust and love in the classroom.

One of the major facets of engaged pedagogy is the promotion of students' self-esteem; this for hooks is done by demonstrating appropriate approval, and a recognition of, students' capabilities. This she suggests is not achieved through lavish and uncritical praise. However, it does mean that teachers should provide feedback to students which recognises strengths, which in turn builds their confidence and leads to their self-esteem as learners. hooks' own practice encourages students to self-evaluate their progress so they are working for themselves rather than trying to satisfy the wishes of their teachers (hooks, 2010). Students:

are empowered by working in a manner where they recognize their responsibility and accountability for the grade they receive. That empowerment reinforces healthy self-esteem. (hooks, 2010: 125)

This empowerment then, not only raises the student's self-esteem but promotes the concept of critical thinking. These ideas form a basis for the application of an active engaged pedagogy and what hooks calls education as the practice of freedom.

REFLECTIVE TASK

hooks' notion of engaged pedagogy promotes the idea of encouraging student voice, and also the idea that all students should play an active part in the classroom. From your experiences as a student, answer the following two questions:

1. What are the barriers, both practical and philosophical, to achieving these aspects of engaged pedagogy?
2. If you had a free hand, and the opportunity to do so, how could these barriers be overcome in the future?

SUMMARY

bell hooks has had a profound impact as a social activist, feminist and scholar, her work has also been of great significance for educators throughout the world. Her ideas of democratic education have been shaped by her beliefs, which are rooted in the inequalities she still sees in matters of gender, race and social class. These viewpoints have arisen, and are deeply embedded, by her own experiences growing up as a black female in the South of the United States, as well as her experiences as a pupil first in a segregated school for black children and later as a black child in an integrated school. Her experiences as an undergraduate and postgraduate student affirmed for hooks the oppressive and controlling nature of the dominant culture of the 'imperialist white-supremacist capitalist patriarchy' (hooks, 2003a: 166).

hooks is a prolific writer, and wrote a trilogy of teaching books which offers a series of essays regarding education as a practice of freedom. These essays cover a range of topics which advocate a progressive, and somewhat radical approach to teaching, especially, in higher education. Her particular contributions to teaching are the notions of engaged pedagogy, critical thinking, creating learning communities and practical wisdom. Throughout all these ideas are the threads of active student learning through participation and the recognition of student voice and experience. Furthermore, she promotes aspects of love, spirituality and imagination which are quite radical and innovative strategies in higher education teaching.

Her ideas of education have strong associations with John Dewey and democratic education which espouses the concepts of embracing the student experience, and encouraging active participatory learning. However, she was greatly influenced by Paulo Freire and his writing on overcoming oppression. She found Freire's works an inspiration which helped shape her ideas on engaged pedagogy and critical thinking, despite her criticism of his sexist language. Her views on teaching practice and issues of gender were very much in tune with Giroux's critical pedagogy. She also shared with Foucault her aversion to the over-controlling and punitive systems in place in education to ensure the dominant culture maintains the status quo. The criticisms of hooks' work focus on the lack of scholarly application to her writing, her overly emotional approach to her pedagogical ideas and the risks involved in teachers being too close to their students. Furthermore, she receives criticism that her writings offer little practical guidance for classroom practice. This final point is contested; although she does not set out a prescribed step-by-step guide for teachers, her emphasis on every student participating and the promotion of the student voice offer many inclusive and refreshing ideas for practice in university classrooms.

 ## FURTHER READING

Atkinson, E. (2006) 'Sexualities and resistance: Queer(y)ing identity and discourse in education'. In: Lauder, H., Brown, P., Dillabough, J.-A. and Halsey, A. (Eds) *Education, Globalization and Social Change*. Oxford: Oxford University Press.
This chapter explores the notion of gender and sexuality as a process of resistance to the oppressive dominant culture in education.

hooks, b. (1996) *Reel to Real: Race, Sex and Class at the Movies*. London: Routledge.
A series of essays in which hooks considers the value of films in a pedagogical sense, and the ways in which watching films can teach the viewers about race, gender and class.

hooks, b. (2000) *Where We Stand: Class Matters*. London: Routledge.
Using her experiences as a child and an adult hooks presents a personal account of how the issues of class and race are interlocked, she also offers approaches to move these matters forward.

Scapp, R. (2002) *Critical Perspectives on Education, Politics, and Culture*. London: Routledge.
Written by a close friend and colleague of bell hooks, this work explores value-based teaching and learning in opposition to traditionalist models of education and includes an affirmation of the role of citizenship.

REFERENCES

bell hooks Institute (2015) About the bell hooks Institute. www.bellhooksinstitute.com.
Berry, T. (2010) 'Engaged pedagogy and critical race feminism'. *Education Foundations*, Summer–Fall: 19–26.

Burke, B. (2004) 'bell hooks on education'. *The Encyclopaedia of Informal Education*. www. infed.org/mobi/bell-hooks-on-education.

Carolissen, R., Bozalek, V., Nicholls, L., Leibowitz. B., Rohleder, P. and Swartz, L. (2011) 'bell hooks and the enactment of emotion in teaching and learning across boundaries: A pedagogy of hope?' *South African Journal of Higher Education*, 25(1): 157–67.

Cheng, C. (1997) 'A review essay on the books of bell hooks: Organizational diversity lessons from a thoughtful race and gender heretic'. *The Academy of Management Review*, 22(2): 553–64.

Cole, S. and Knowles, J. (Eds) (2001) *Lives in Context: The Art of Life History Research*. Lanham: AltaMira Press.

Collins, J., Harkin, J. and Nind, M. (2002) *Manifesto for Learning*. London: Continuum.

Dewey, J. (1916) *Democracy and Education: An Introduction to the Philosophy of Education*. New York: The Macmillan Company.

Dewey, J. (1938) *Experience and Education*. New York: Kappa Delta Pi.

Foucault, M. (1979) *Discipline and Punish: The Birth of Prison*. London: Penguin.

Freire, P. (1970 [1996]) *Pedagogy of the Oppressed*. London: Penguin.

Giroux, H. (1992) *Border Crossings: Cultural Workers and the Politics of Education*. New York: Routledge.

hooks, b. (1982) *Ain't I a Woman: Black Women and Feminism*. London: Pluto Press.

hooks, b. (1994) *Teaching to Transgress: Education as the Practice of Freedom*. London: Routledge.

hooks, b. (2003a) *Teaching Community: A Pedagogy of Hope*. London: Routledge.

hooks, b. (2003b) 'Confronting class in the classroom'. In: Darder, A., Baltodano, M. and Torres. R. (Eds) *The Critical Pedagogy Reader*. London: RoutledgeFalmer.

hooks, b. (2010) *Teaching Critical Thinking: Practical Wisdom*. London: Routledge.

Irwin, J. (2012) *Paulo Freire's Philosophy of Education*. London: Continuum.

Lim, L. (2011) 'Review: *Teaching Critical Thinking: Practical Wisdom*'. *Education Review*, April: 1–7.

Sewell, A. (2010) 'Review: *Teaching Community: A Pedagogy of Hope*'. *International Journal of Children's Spirituality*, 15(2): 341–3.

Thomas, R. (1997) 'Review: *Teaching to Transgress: Education as the Practice of Freedom*'. *Contemporary Education*, 68(3): 204.

14

JACK MEZIROW

TRANSFORMATIVE LEARNING

LEARNING OUTCOMES

Having read this chapter you should be able to:

- Appreciate Mezirow's background and his contribution to adult education
- Understand and identify his development of transformative learning and the implications for adult educators and their learners
- Appreciate the links between his work and other educational thinkers
- Critically appraise Mezirow's works
- Recognise how his work could be applied in practice

KEY WORDS

Transformative learning; emancipatory education; reflection; critical reflection; critical self-reflection; meaning schemes; meaning perspective; instrumental learning; communicative learning; frames of reference; discourse

INTRODUCTION

Jack Mezirow, who died in 2014 aged ninety-one, had a profound effect on the development of adult education theory. Before his notion of transformative learning was published the main focus for adult education was ensuring students mastered basic skills; the theoretical basis for adult learning centred on self-directed learning and the notion of andragogy (Brookfield, 2005). The theory of transformative learning acted as a catalyst which generated far-reaching changes and heated discussions in adult education, and also in other areas such as higher education, professional development, health and social activism (Columbia University, 2014). Mezirow's 1978 book *Education for Perspective Transformation: Women's Re-entry Programs in Community Colleges*, set out his initial thoughts regarding transformative learning. This notion was originally prompted by Mezirow's wife Edee's experiences when she went to college to study in middle age; it was also very much influenced by Habermas' earlier work on transformation. The research for Mezirow's transformative learning theory was based on a wide-ranging study in the United States of women returning to community colleges (Mezirow, 2006).

Transformative learning involves experience, critical reflection and personal change. The development of transformation starts with an experience, followed by critical reflection on that experience and then a discourse to allow for a change in the learner's actions (Hutchings, 2013). Mezirow noted that emotion and critical reflection on beliefs and attitudes are important features in an adult's transformative learning 'which involve changes in self-awareness and learner identity' (Carlile and Jordan, 2012: 101). The idea of transformative theory is that adults may be empowered to learn and that they can free themselves 'from unexamined ways of thinking that impede effective judgement and action' (Mezirow, 1998: 73). Furthermore it foresaw a 'society composed of educated learners engaged in a continuing collaborative inquiry' (Mezirow, 1998: 73). Overall, for Mezirow transformative learning was a democratic process which used critical reflection and critical action to enable adults to change and develop as learners.

The basis of Mezirow's work in adult education is embedded in the efforts taken in the United States to encourage community cohesion by integrating people from differing ethnic and social backgrounds. Moreover, Mezirow came from the state of Minnesota which had been very strongly influenced by 'Scandinavian social-democratic and even socialist ideas [therefore] his concern with community development in a social perspective is quite natural' (Finger and Asun, 2001: 54). Even though his professional background was as an educationalist rather than a sociologist his work placed a significant degree of emphasis on social justice, and aligned adult learning with social development and progression (Finger and Asun, 2001).

Mezirow's notion of transformative learning is a contested concept that has drawn considerable criticism, some of which has come from fellow adult educators mainly because it is seen by a few as being 'complex and multi-faceted' (Kitchenham, 2008: 104).

Nevertheless, as a result of his work a number of transformative learning groups were formed which involved global conferences, numerous journal articles and books being published, and the concept of transformative learning was the main focus for many a doctoral thesis (Mezirow, 2006). Mezirow published many articles which developed and defended his theory of transformative learning. He also wrote a number of books which mapped and demonstrated the progression of his ideas. These included: with Darkenwald and Knox *Last Gamble on Education: Dynamics of Adult Basic Education* (1975); with associates *Fostering Critical Reflection in Adulthood* (1990); *Transformative Dimensions of Adult Education* (1991); with associates *Learning as Transformation: Critical Perspectives on a Theory in Progress* (2000); and, with Taylor and associates *Transformative Learning in Practice: Insights from Community, Workplace, and Higher Education* (2009). To understand further the manner in which Mezirow's ideas emerged and how his theory developed, we now need to consider his background and his progress as an academic in the field of adult education.

MEZIROW, THE PERSON

'Jack' was born John D. Mezirow in 1923 in Fargo, North Dakota, USA. His career as an adult educator began in a teaching capacity working with communities, a role which he never relinquished even when he achieved a high degree of academic acclaim (Finger and Asun, 2001). Mezirow gained his first degree, and then his masters degree in social sciences from the University of Minnesota. Next, after prompting from Malcolm Knowles, who was at the time the Director of the National Adult Education Association, Mezirow went on to study for his doctorate in adult education at the University of California at Los Angeles. Following graduation he worked internationally in adult education and community development in Asia, Africa and South America. In this capacity he worked for the following organisations: the United Nations Development Programme; the United Nations Educational, Social and Cultural Organisation (UNESCO); the United States Agency for International Development; the Asia Foundation; and World Education. He became an associate dean for a number of extension and human resource programmes at the University of California, before joining Teachers College, Columbia University in 1968 as the Professor of Adult and Continuing Education (Mezirow and associates, 2000; Finger and Asun, 2001; Columbia University, 2014).

His ideas on transformative learning grew from his wife's experience when she enrolled at Sarah Lawrence College in the early 1970s to complete her undergraduate degree. The experience, for both Jack and Edee, was truly 'transformative'. Moved by Edee's experiences Mezirow set out on his seminal research work, which sought to uncover the factors which helped and hindered learning for women who were returning to study at community colleges in the United States. What he found, for most of the women returners to study, was that they had gone through an individual transformation and had experienced a staged process of personal growth and change. This process included the questioning of taken-for-granted assumptions and an examination of the possibilities for new opportunities. This in turn led to the development of competence and self-assurance (Columbia University, 2014). These outcomes were the beginning of Adult Education Guided Intensive Study (AEGIS), a distinctive and innovative adult education doctoral programme established by Mezirow in 1982 at Teachers College, Columbia University. The idea of AEGIS has since been reproduced internationally (Columbia University, 2014).

At AEGIS he endeavoured to promote the creation of a learning community which valued collaborative inquiry (Mezirow, 2006), and the learning and teaching methods Mezirow encouraged at AEGIS will be explored later in this chapter. To further this collaborative theme AEGIS took in postgraduate students from a variety of disciplines and areas, which included private and government sector employees from adult education, school education, healthcare, social and community work as well as religious organisations. In recruiting this variety Mezirow was trying to get students together so that they could question their fundamental beliefs and develop an appreciation of the viewpoints and beliefs of others. Apart from the work with AEGIS, Mezirow continued to develop his notion of transformative learning, particularly in regard to other disciplines. In the latter stages of his career he became interested in the chemistry of the brain, and after retirement he kept in touch with academics worldwide who were interested in transformative learning (Columbia University, 2014). The meaning, and development, of his notion of transformative learning will be explored in the next section.

MEZIROW AND HIS THEORY OF TRANSFORMATIVE LEARNING

This section will firstly define the key themes involved in Mezirow's ideas, and secondly explore some of the significant aspects of his work before considering the origins and influences of the theory of transformative learning. Core to Mezirow's notion of transformative learning was emancipatory education with its emphasis on 'effecting social change [to] modify oppressive practices, norms, institutions and socio-economic structures to allow everyone to participate more fully and freely' (Mezirow, 2006: 30). For Mezirow, emancipatory education required a combination of key themes. Before the main thrust of his ideas is discussed in more detail it is useful to define these key themes, even though the terminology used may be unfamiliar at this early stage:

Meaning perspective: The structure of assumptions that constitutes a frame of reference for interpreting the meaning of an experience.

Reflection: Examination of the justification for one's beliefs, primarily to guide action and to reassess the efficacy of the strategies and procedures used in problem solving.

Critical reflection: Assessment of the validity of the *presuppositions* of one's meaning perceptions, and examination of their sources and consequences.

Critical self-reflection: Assessment of the way one has posed problems and one's own meaning perspectives.

Transformative learning: The process of learning through critical self-reflection, which results in the reformulation of a meaning perspective to allow a more inclusive, discriminatory and integrative understanding of one's experience. Learning includes acting on these insights.

Emancipatory education: An organized effort to precipitate or facilitate transformative learning in others.

(Mezirow and associates, 1990: xvi)

Mezirow's notion of transformative learning is centred upon adult learners' use of experience, critical reflection and discourse. Discourse here signifies a dialogue which engages with learners' evaluation of beliefs, emotions and values. This discourse concerns matters raised from a specific frame of reference (Mezirow, 2003). According to Mezirow:

> Frames of reference are the structures of culture and language through which we construe meaning by attributing coherence and significance to our experience. They selectively shape and delimit our perception, cognition and feelings by predisposing our intentions, beliefs, expectations and purposes. These preconceptions set our 'line of action'. Once set or programmed, we automatically move from one specific mental or behavioral activity to another, we have a strong tendency to reject ideas that fail to fit our preconceptions. (Mezirow, 2009: 92)

For Mezirow, transformative learning begins with the manner in which problematic frames of reference are tackled – 'to make them more inclusive, discriminating, open, reflective and emotionally able to change' (Mezirow, 2009: 92). Mezirow offered two frames of reference which could be considered in unlocking these problematic frames and beginning the process of transformative learning; these were meaning schemes and meaning perspectives. The term 'meaning', here is significant to transformative learning, as it is a process of how learners understand, use and change their perceptions: 'transformative learning is an adult dimension of reason assessment involving the validation and reformation of meaning structures' (Mezirow, 2009: 93).

Mezirow differentiates between the two dimensions of meaning schemes and meaning perspectives. Meaning schemes are 'habitual expectations governing if–then, cause–effect'; for example, 'we expect food to satisfy hunger … that the sun will rise in the east and set in the west – they are habitual, implicit *rules* for interpreting' (Mezirow and associates, 1990: 2). On the other hand meaning perspectives are of a much higher order; they comprise theories, concepts, values, beliefs and evaluations. Meaning perspectives also concern the specific ways a learner interprets experience, which includes the phases of reflection before making value judgements. Mezirow cites the women's movement as an exemplar of meaning perspectives and transformative learning.

> Within a few years, hundreds of thousands of women whose personal identity, self-concept, and values had been derived principally from prescribed social norms and from acting out sex-stereotypical roles came to challenge these assumptions and to redefine their lives in their own terms. The women's movement provided a support climate for this kind of personal reappraisal by publicizing the constraints on personal development, autonomy, and self-determination imposed by such stereotypes and by providing support groups and role models. (Mezirow and associates, 1990: 3)

Both meaning perspectives and meaning schemes which are considered not viable can be transformed by reflection. Meaning perspectives which establish what, how and why we learn may be transformed through critical reflection – 'reflection on one's own premises can lead to transformative learning' (Mezirow and associates, 1990: 18). This reflection 'on one's own premises' involves the learners delving deeply into well-established beliefs and expectations which are both socially and culturally formed over the learner's lifetime. The resultant transformation could be radical in the way the learners regard themselves and the world they live in; it could also enable them to have a deeper insight into their long-standing values and beliefs (Hutchings, 2013). This emphasis on profound change taking place in transformative learning is a constructivist process and an outcome of personal intellectual conflict (Dennick, 2008). The role of reflection is crucial, creating a transformation of perspective as it enables learners to critically appraise their learning as well as being more creative and open and receptive to new knowledge and experiences (Mezirow, 1991; Kennett, 2010).

Transformative learning could happen suddenly, which is often associated with important life-changing crises, or it could occur in an accumulative manner, which is manifested by a series of understandings which in turn produces different points of view. 'Most transformative learning takes place outside of awareness; intuition substitutes for critical reflection of assumptions' (Mezirow, 2009: 94). The role of the adult educator is to facilitate learners to bring awareness into the process. This in turn will enhance the learners' competence and encourage proactive involvement in the transformative learning process. Using the outcomes from his study regarding women returners to college education, Mezirow (2009) identified ten sequential phases of meaning and becoming which learners followed in their transformative learning journey. Apart from the first – 'a disorientating dilemma' the other phases are quite self-explanatory. According to Taylor, a disorientating dilemma is 'some experience that problematizes current understandings and frames of reference' (Mezirow, Taylor and associates, 2009: 155). The phases are:

- a disorientating dilemma;
- self-examination with feelings of fear, anger, guilt or shame;
- a critical assessment of assumptions;

- recognition that one's discontent and the process of transformation is shared;
- exploration of options for new roles, relationships and action;
- planning a course of action;
- acquiring knowledge and skills for implementing one's plans;
- provisional trying of new roles;
- building competence and self-confidence in new roles and relationships;
- a reintegration into one's life on the basis of conditions dictated by one's new perspective.

(Mezirow, 2009: 94)

Mezirow reinforces the two central elements of transformative learning necessary during this phased process: 'First, critical reflection or critical self-reflection on assumptions ... second, participating fully and freely in dialectical discourse to validate a best reflective judgement' (Mezirow, 2009: 94).

Much of Mezirow's work, particularly the overarching theory of transformative learning, originates from, and has been influenced by, the German sociologist and philosopher Jürgen Habermas. This is specifically the case with Habermas' ideas on the differences between instrumental and communicative learning. For Mezirow, instrumental learning concerns controlling and influencing the environment with the intention of enhancing performance and outcomes. In essence, instrumental learning is about appraising assertions of truth. It is about measuring 'changes resulting from our learning to solve problems in terms of productivity, performance, or behavior ... canonized by natural sciences, that we all use or misuse in learning how to *do* things' (Mezirow and associates, 1990: 8). Conversely, communicative learning is deemed of greater importance to adult learning as it is about '*understanding the meaning* of what others communicate concerning values, ideals, feelings, moral decisions and such concepts as freedom, justice, love, labor, autonomy, commitment, and democracy' (Mezirow and associates, 1990: 8). Central to both communicative learning and Mezirow's transformative learning is the concept of discourse. Mezirow gives two very fitting examples of the application of discourse and understanding involved in communicative learning:

> This understanding involves being aware of the assumptions, intentions and qualifications of the person communicating. When a stranger strikes up a conversation on a bus, one needs to know whether he or she is simply passing the time, intends to proselytize, or is trying to pick you up. When a stranger recommends a new medicine or an investment, one needs to know whether he or she is qualified to make such recommendation or judgment. (Mezirow, 2003: 58)

Transformative learning may happen in either instrumental or communicative learning. In instrumental learning it normally entails task-orientated activities, whereas in communicative learning it demands critical self-reflection (Mezirow, 2009).

Dirkx and Smith provide a thought-provoking description of what transformative learning means to them:

> There is a kind of mystery to the idea of transformative learning, a way of learning that is more an expression of the creative and artistic dimensions of our being rather than the rational, literal and scientific. Like the unfolding and metamorphosis of the caterpillar into a beautiful, majestic, and soaring butterfly, the process of transformative learning touches on and reminds us of the fundamental mystery that is being human. (Dirkx and Smith, 2009: 65)

Mezirow's ideas regarding personal change, reflection and democracy in the learning process can be linked to other like-minded educational thinkers.

 ## LINKS WITH OTHER THEORISTS

The significant influence of Habermas' instrumental and communicative learning domains on Mezirow's theory of transformative learning has already been covered. At the heart of Mezirow's thinking was John Dewey's progressive and democratic notion of learning, which contested the traditional didactic methods of learning and teaching, and emphasised the primacy of the student in the education process (Columbia University, 2014). Mezirow was also guided by Thomas Kuhn, particularly by his seminal work *The Structure of Scientific Revolutions* (1962). In his work Kuhn explored the paradigm shift that happens in the revolution of ideas to progress the understanding of science. As Mezirow explains, these paradigm shifts can also be associated with the way we interpret the meaning of experience:

> As we encounter new meaning perspectives that help us account for disturbing anomalies in the way we understand our reality, personal as well as scientific paradigm shifts can redirect the way we engage the world. (Mezirow and associates, 1990: 13)

These paradigm shifts of Kuhn's, which influenced Mezirow's thinking, were seen as a progressive and transformative processes; old theories were considered dated and redundant, while new theories were being developed (Dennick, 2008).

Mezirow was also influenced by the radical educator Paulo Freire who was responsible for setting up emancipatory adult education programmes in Brazil as a prelude to a broader revolutionary mission with the aim of achieving social empowerment of the people (Mezirow and associates, 1990). Mezirow considered that the concept of 'conscientisation', which Freire introduced in his book *Pedagogy of the Oppressed* (1970 [1996]), was a significant factor in transformative learning. Conscientisation was the raising of the people's consciousness with a view to being freed from the oppression of the established social order; this Freire felt was only feasible through the process of critical reflection, dialogue and problem-posing learning (Freire, 1970 [1996]; Mezirow and associates, 1990). Although not considered such a revolutionary educator as Freire, Knowles' concept of andragogy, the teaching of adults using learner experience, has links with Mezirow's thinking. Knowles, like Freire and Mezirow, has altered the relationship between the adult student and the teacher; becoming less about the delivering of information and more about creating a dialogical process (Preece and Griffin, 2006).

Core to Mezirow's transformative learning is the idea of personal change in individual students. This is comparable, and indeed evident, in Kolb's theory of experiential learning and constructivist theory. Mezirow, like Kolb, stresses the importance of critical reflection for the process of change. In Kolb's experiential learning cycle learners are encouraged to reflect, and with the help of their teachers, transform their own points of view and create their own ideas (Mezirow and associates, 2000). Like Kolb, and Mezirow, Schön places great emphasis on the use of reflection as a social action. Additionally, Schön advocated the use of reflection on experience in understanding and solving problems. He used the terms 'reflection on action', and 'reflection in action'. Both of these are cyclical, ongoing processes where learners can discover their own theories and in so doing develop their personal transformative learning (Mezirow and associates, 1990). It is evident that Mezirow has been heavily influenced by other thinkers in his development of transformative learning theory, this could be the basis of some of the criticism that he encountered.

CRITIQUING THE THEORY

Some of the criticism which came Mezirow's way was from other adult educators who felt that he had abandoned his stance on social activism. This criticism centred on their perception of his notion of transformative learning increasingly focused on the growth and development of the individual at the expense of the wider principles and effects involved in the social activism of adult education. Finger and Asun (2001) argue that Mezirow's ideas of transformation have not truly incorporated the notions of Freire and Habermas regarding social change. They state that, more accurately, Mezirow's transformative learning focuses on how the 'learners adapt to rather than criticise society' (Finger and Asun, 2001: 59). There was also some disquiet from community and other not-for-profit bodies that adult education was being taken over by corporate business organisations with a view to gaining an advantage over their competitors. Mezirow himself was associated with, and acted as a consultant for, corporations and his ideas were taught at Harvard Business School (Columbia University, 2014).

There was also censure that the teaching and learning of transformative learning were not for everyone. There were certain challenges for both teachers and adult learners. These included aspects of ethics, confidentiality and conflicts between students (Cooper, n.d.). Undoubtedly, some adults find the notion of transformative learning stimulating and inspirational. Conversely, many adults strongly anticipate what they need, what they want, and how that education should be taught (Cross, 1981). Furthermore, there is some anxiety about the elusive nature of the teaching in relation to transformative learning. Taylor offers a warning about the practice of transformative learning from a teacher's point of view:

Much of it remains unknown and poorly understood. Like any other educational approach, it is rooted in ideals, and when the realities of practice are explored, it becomes difficult to get a handle on how it plays out in the classroom. It is laced with contradictions and oversights. (Taylor, 2009: 3)

Taylor also argues that using transformative learning involves 'personal risk, a genuine concern for the learners' betterment, and the ability to draw on a variety of methods and techniques' (Taylor, 2009: 14).

Finger and Asun contest that Mezirow's ideas are an amalgamation of differing notions and philosophies which require further development to validate the claims made (Finger and Asun 2001). Mezirow was quite aware of the criticism. He wrote a number of articles, particularly in *Adult Education Quarterly*, accepting these criticisms and sometimes defending his ideas. However, there are some aspects of his theory which he acknowledged as requiring further development. Possibly the main area, for Mezirow, which needed further work was the explanation and importance of the role played by emotions, intuition and imagination in the process of transformation. He confessed that this is a difficulty in his work because the process we use to interpret our own beliefs may encompass assumed values (Mezirow, 2009). Notwithstanding these criticisms the process of transformative learning has profound implications for the practice of emancipatory adult learning.

 ## APPLYING MEZIROW'S IDEAS IN PRACTICE

This section will firstly explore an overview of the practice of transformative learning before offering some specific examples for application. Although Mezirow was an adult educator and his major work of transformative learning was focused around the adult learning experience, there are, it is argued, many elements of his ideas which could be applied in universities, colleges and even schools. The idea that effective learning relies on effective teaching is an accepted concept, and educational thinkers such as Mezirow have 'argued that effective learning is self-actualising, self-directed, self-planned and transformative' (Griffin, 2006: 83). According to Moon there are five progressive phases, with transformative learning being the most valuable; these five phases are:

- noticing;
- making sense;
- making meaning;
- working with meaning;
- transformative learning.

(Moon, 1999 [2000]: 16)

Moon further explains that a learner at this transformative phase will be:

> Self-motivating and self-motivated, but may derive support from discussion and an environment in which their ideas can be tested by others... In formal education terms, 'transformative learning' is a place of intellectual excitement and of deeply satisfying discourse that can occur in good-quality tutorial work. (Moon, 1999 [2000]: 146)

Most teachers and students have experienced the moment in their learning when something has 'clicked'; this, it is suggested, is where learning shifts from being the accumulative to a transformative process. At this stage the topic is being considered from a changed perspective. When something 'clicks' it does not mean that the student has a greater knowledge of the idea than his or her peers, 'but, rather, that he or she has put it together in new ways that transformed the idea' (Cross, 1981: 232).

Mezirow argues that the function of the adult educator is to nurture the manner of transformative learning which enables students to make informed judgements and take valuable and applicable actions. A teacher's role is to assist students 'to think, judge, and learn – and to act – with greater insight not to prescribe what they think and learn' (Mezirow, 1998: 73). Moreover, for transformative learning to be successful Mezirow advocated collaboration not only between students but, possibly more importantly, between students and teachers. Although in many instances at the start of the learning process the teacher will have more knowledge than the student, what the teacher needs to do is to:

> Relearn what is known in the context of the learners' efforts to interpret these insights in terms of their own lives. This is what adults mean when they write of collaborative learning... The educator actively seeks to know learners' expectations and aspirations to enable the educator to understand learners' levels of perception, their language, and the difficulties they may have understanding the academic language or the nature of the instruction. (Mezirow and associates, 1990: 368–9)

What is also required when nurturing collaboration in transformative learning is for the teacher to take into consideration what the student wishes to learn. This will then instigate a discourse which in turn will lead to a critical exploration of the assumptions which underpin the value judgements of both student and teacher. Mezirow thought that for true transformative learning to occur there should be an unlocking of the traditional power relationships created between teachers and students. At the heart of adult education for Mezirow was the process of facilitating students in developing their awareness of their understandings and values and to be 'more critically reflective on their assumptions and those of others, more fully and freely engaged in discourse' (Mezirow and associates, 2000: 31).

Mezirow borrowed from Habermas' ideal foundations for conditions for adult learning. These conditions also offer a medium for adult educators to provide a social commitment for students to participate freely and fully in discourse. For these conditions to be met, students must:

- have accurate and complete information;
- be free from coercion, distorting self-deception or immobilizing anxiety; be open to alternate points of view – empathetic, caring about how others think and feel, withholding judgement;
- be able to understand, to weigh evidence and to assess arguments objectively;
- be able to become aware of the context of ideas and critically reflect on assumptions, including their own;
- have equal opportunity to participate in the various roles of discourse;
- have a test of validity until new perspective evidence or arguments are encountered and validated through discourse as yielding a better judgement.

(Mezirow, 2009: 92)

One of the attributes which Mezirow argues is crucial for students to acquire in the transformative learning process is the ability to 'imagine how things could be different' (Mezirow, 2009: 103).

Cooper (n.d.) outlines the characteristics and roles which teachers and students need to facilitate successful transformative learning:

Teacher characteristics and roles which facilitate transformative learning

- Encourage students to reflect on and share their feelings and thoughts in class.
- Be holistically oriented, aware of body, mind, and spirit in the learning process.
- Become transcendent of his [or her] beliefs and accepting of others' beliefs.
- Cultivate awareness of alternate ways of learning.
- Establish an environment characterised by trust and care.
- Facilitate sensitive relationships among the participants.
- Demonstrate ability to serve as an experienced mentor reflecting on his [or her] own journey.
- Help students question reality in ways that promote shifts in their worldview.

Student characteristics and roles which facilitate transformative learning

- Students must be free to determine their own reality, as opposed to social realities defined by others or by cultural institutions.
- Students must be ready for and open to change.
- Those with a wider variety of life experiences, including prior stressful life events, are likely to experience more transformation.
- Cultivate the ability to transcend past contexts of learning and experience.
- Students must be willing and able to integrate critical reflection into their school work and personal life.
- Students must be able to access both rational and affective mental functioning.
- Have sufficient maturity to deal with paradigm shifts and material which differs from their current beliefs.

(Cooper, n.d.)

Mezirow explains how he facilitated transformative learning in his graduate AEGIS doctoral programme at Teachers College, where great significance was placed on the establishment of learning communities for collaborative inquiry (Mezirow, 2006). Students on the programme were required to take part in a number of transformative learning-related activities. For example, they were asked to write papers which posed arguments on both sides, describing each viewpoint as well as their own, and then analyse their own beliefs. Topics offered on the programme included 'assumption analysis, involving comparative assessment of key turning points in the lives of the students' (Mezirow, 2006: 36). Art, literature and the work of adult educators such as Paulo Freire were used to inspire students to consider alternative methods of interpreting experiences. Methods such as critical incidents, life histories, media analysis, metaphor analysis, action learning sets and journal writing were all found helpful in developing critical self-reflection of assumptions and discourse (Mezirow, 2006).

The use of self-assessment in adult and higher education is very closely associated with the notion of transformative learning. Taylor argues that self-assessment encompasses much more than students being autonomous in their own marking and progression. The proficiencies students develop when self-assessing include: the use of deep questioning, and understanding and framing of the benchmarks for them to make judgements regarding their own learning. The use of self-assessment 'is likely to lead to habits of questioning criteria for performance and noticing the extent to which one's work meets these criteria' (Taylor, 2000: 177). Taylor suggests that students can use self-assessment to: check progress, self-diagnose and self-remediate, consolidate learning, and gain self-knowledge and self-understanding (Taylor, 2000).

Finally, it is interesting to note that transformative learning in the form of collaborative inquiry can take place online, in the form of emails and blogs, as well as in classrooms. Dirkx and Smith found that online collaborative inquiry provided an environment which promoted deep levels of discourse and reflection from students whose previous experiences of group work were not always positive (Dirkx and Smith, 2009).

REFLECTIVE TASK

Reflecting on your own learning as an adult in relation to Mezirow's transformative learning theory:

1. Give examples of the aspects of the theory that you are comfortable with in your own learning, and suggest ways you could enhance these further.
2. Give examples of the aspects of the theory you are anxious about, and suggest ways you could overcome such anxieties.

SUMMARY

Jack Mezirow was an adult educator whose notion of transformative learning has not only added to the theory of adult education but has also changed the way in which teachers perceive their practice. Transformative learning is now embedded in adult education, higher education, professional development, and health and social activism (Columbia University, 2014). Critical reflection, experience and discourse are all fundamental to successful transformative learning. The foundation for Mezirow's theory came from Habermas' previous work on transformation. Mezirow's research involved a wide-ranging study in the United States which explored the transformations evidenced by women who returned to community colleges. He worked as an adult educator and community developer in the United States and internationally. In 1982 he set up the renowned AEGIS adult education doctoral programme in Teachers College, Columbia University, where transformative learning was core to the learning and teaching process.

Apart from being influenced by Habermas' prior work on instrumental and communicative learning domains, Mezirow's notion of transformative learning was also shaped by Kuhn's idea of paradigm shifts. Dewey's concept of a democratic pedagogy was at the heart of Mezirow's work as well as his drive for social activism. Like Knowles' idea of andragogy, Mezirow added to the growing repertoire of adult education theory. Mezirow was inspired by Freire's concept of conscientisation and the need for critical reflection, discourse and problem-posing learning. There are also quite close links, particularly related to the importance of social interaction, with Kolb's experiential learning theory and Schön's notions of reflection on action and reflection in action.

Mezirow's work has drawn considerable criticism, mainly from adult educators. He has been accused of abandoning his social activism principles, and some see his work on transformative learning as a blend of theories. There has also been censure about the lack of research underpinning some of his ideas on transformative learning, especially regarding the processes of emotion, intuition and imagination. It is contested that transformative learning can be an emancipatory experience for many learners in adult education. However, transformative learning is not for everyone; it is a practice which requires experience from the teacher, and a willingness from the learner to undergo personal change. Nevertheless, despite these criticisms Mezirow's work still has the potential to make positive changes to the lives of adult learners.

FURTHER READING

Habermas, J. (1975) *Legitimation Crisis*. Boston: Beacon Press.
This is a review of what Habermas considers as two general forms of learning: non-reflexive and reflexive. It is a notion which Mezirow adopts throughout his theory of adult transformative learning.

Schön, D. (1983) *The Reflective Practitioner: How Professionals Think in Action*. New York: Basic Books.
This is a helpful book for teachers working with adults. It explains the value of the reflective process in enhancing students', and teachers', development in their professional lives.

Welton, M. (Ed.) (1995) *In Defense of the Lifeworld: Critical Perspectives on Adult Learning*. Albany: State University of New York Press.
A very informative text on the relationship and engagement of Mezirow with Habermas in regard to the distinction concerning technical, communicative and emancipatory knowledge.

REFERENCES

Brookfield, S. (2005) *The Power of Critical Theory for Adult Learning and Teaching*. Maidenhead: Open University Press.
Carlile, O. and Jordan, A. (2012) 'Learning'. In: Arthur, J. and Peterson, A. (Eds) *The Routledge Companion to Education*. London: Routledge.
Columbia University (2014) *In Memoriam: Jack Mezirow*. www.tc.columbia.edu/news.htm?articleID=9698.
Cooper, S. (n.d.) *Transformational Learning*. www.lifecircles-inc.com/Learningtheories/humanist/mezirow.html.
Cross, K. (1981) *Adults as Learners: Increasing Participation and Facilitating Learning*. San Francisco: Jossey Bass.
Dennick, R. (2008) 'Theories of learning: Constructive experience'. In: Matheson, D. (Ed.) *An Introduction to the Study of Education* (third edition). London: Routledge.
Dirkx, J. and Smith, R. (2009) 'Facilitating transformative learning: Engaging emotions in an online context'. In: Mezirow, J., Taylor, E. and associates. *Transformative Learning in Practice: Insights from Community, Workplace, and Higher Education*. San Francisco: Jossey Bass.
Finger, M. and Asun, J. (2001) *Adult Education at the Crossroads: Learning Our Way Out*. London: Zed Books.
Freire, P. (1970 [1996]) *Pedagogy of the Oppressed*. London: Penguin.
Griffin, C. (2006) 'Didacticism'. In: Jarvis, P. (Ed.) *The Theory and Practice of Teaching* (second edition). London: Routledge.
Hutchings, M. (2013) 'Arriving in a new place: The ecology of learning'. In: Ward, S. (Ed.) *A Student's Guide to Education Studies* (third edition). London: Routledge.
Kennett, K. (2010) 'Professionalism and reflective practice'. In: Wallace, S. (Ed.) *The Lifelong Learning Sector Reflective Reader*. Exeter: Learning Matters.
Kitchenham, A. (2008) 'The evolution of John Mezirow's transformative learning theory. *Journal of Transformative Education*, 6(2): 104–23.
Kuhn, T. (1962) *The Structure of Scientific Revolutions*. Chicago: Chicago University Press.
Mezirow, J. (1978) *Education for Perspective Transformation: Women's Re-entry Programs in Community Colleges*. New York: Teachers College, Columbia University.
Mezirow, J. (1991) *Transformative Dimensions of Adult Education*. San Francisco: Jossey Bass.
Mezirow, J. (1998) 'Transformational learning and social action'. *Adult Education Quarterly*, 49(1): 70–3.
Mezirow, J. (2003) 'Transformative learning as discourse'. *Journal of Transformative Education*, 1(1): 58–63.

Mezirow, J. (2006) 'An overview of transformative learning'. In: Sutherland, P. and Crowther, J. (Eds) *Lifelong Learning: Concepts and Contexts*. London: Routledge.

Mezirow, J. (2009) 'An overview on transformative learning'. In: Illeris, K. (Ed.) *Contemporary Theories of Learning*. Abingdon: Routledge.

Mezirow, J. and associates (1990) *Fostering Critical Reflection in Adulthood*. San Francisco: Jossey Bass.

Mezirow, J. and associates (2000) *Learning as Transformation: Critical Perspectives on a Theory in Progress*. San Francisco: Jossey Bass.

Mezirow, J., Darkenwald, G. and Knox, A. (1975) *Last Gamble on Education: Dynamics of Adult Basic Education*. Ann Arbor: University of Michigan, Adult Education Association of the USA.

Mezirow, J., Taylor, E. and associates (2009) *Transformative Learning in Practice: Insights from Community, Workplace, and Higher Education*. San Francisco: Jossey Bass.

Moon, J. (1999 [2000]) *Reflection in Learning and Professional Development: Theory and Practice*. London: Kogan Page.

Preece, J. and Griffin, C. (2006) 'Radical and feminist pedagogies'. In: Jarvis, P. (Ed.) *The Theory and Practice of Teaching* (second edition). London: Routledge.

Taylor, E. (2009) 'Fostering transformative learning'. In: Mezirow, J., Taylor, E. and associates. *Transformative Learning in Practice: Insights from Community, Workplace, and Higher Education*. San Francisco: Jossey Bass.

Taylor, K. (2000) 'Teaching with developmental intention'. In: Mezirow, J. and associates. *Learning as Transformation: Critical Perspectives on a Theory in Progress*. San Francisco: Jossey Bass.

15

LINDA DARLING-HAMMOND

EQUITY IN EDUCATION – POLICY, TEACHERS AND TEACHING

LEARNING OUTCOMES

Having read this chapter you should be able to:

- Be aware of Darling-Hammond's background and her contribution to education
- Understand and identify her ideas regarding educational policy for equitable education, teaching and teacher development
- Appreciate the links between her work and other educationalists
- Critically appraise some of Darling-Hammond's notions
- Recognise how her ideas could be applied in schools and classrooms

KEY WORDS

Teacher preparation and education; teacher professionalism; standardised testing; performance assessment; education reform and policy; collaboration; Professional Development Schools

INTRODUCTION

Linda Darling-Hammond, the renowned American educator, is one of the most influential, respected and active leaders calling for an equitable education system for all learners, which includes reforms of schools and teacher education. Although her work is internationally known, and she uses extensive data from other developed countries' educational systems, her main aim is to strive to inform and create inclusive educational policies in the United States. Her talents embrace the ability to relate her scholarship to school reform by way of her writing, and her determined efforts to facilitate policies that support successful learning for students regardless of their background. Darling-Hammond has provided educators and policy-makers with the leadership and insight needed for schools to be seen as democratic communities, resulting in a 'more just and equitable society' (Lieberman, 2001: 289).

One of the most significant policy documents she was involved in was as the director of the National Commission on Teaching & America's Future, which maintained the need to generate educational policies which would reinforce innovative pedagogies and professional practices. The Commission (NCTAF) report was published in 1996 and her own book, *The Right to Learn: A Blueprint for Creating Schools That Work*, which related to her work on the Commission, was published in 2001. Both the report and Darling-Hammond's companion book were very well received by educators. The report offered the country a proposal for rethinking the manner in which teachers and school leaders were recruited, prepared, supported and inducted. Educators throughout the United States were enthused by its brief, but forthright, recommendations:

- get serious about standards, for both students and teachers;
- reinvent teacher preparation and professional development;
- fix teacher recruitment and put qualified teachers in every classroom;
- encourage and reward teacher knowledge and skill;
- create schools that are organized for student and teacher success.

(Lieberman, 2001: 288)

Her book *The Right to Learn: A Blueprint for Creating Schools That Work* (2001) augmented the findings of the report in that it explored the research practice involved in the production of the Commission report, the possible policies to be implemented and the rationale behind creating a more democratic system of schools. The outcomes of the report still remain the basis for her ideas for educational reform.

Darling-Hammond has fought to foster the notion of teacher professionalism. She has spurned the use of older mechanistic, tick-box methods in teacher assessment and evaluation for a more rigorous and professional set of teaching standards. Darling-Hammond has worked closely with many schools, and school authorities in the United States in her research into educational policy. Disturbed by the poor state of many urban public schools, she was inspired to become an activist in enhancing teacher professionalism and championing the cause of students from disadvantaged backgrounds. As a new teacher she acknowledged that she was inadequately equipped for teaching. Furthermore, she considered that the 'factory model' schools she taught in had an unequal allocation of resources and funding, and the paucity of assistance for teachers' development was discouraging (Amrein-Beardsley, 2011).

Overall Darling-Hammond's interests and work have focused on education policy, teaching and assessment, and teacher professionalism and education. She has forged an extraordinary career path which encompasses two apparently opposing standpoints, that of social activist/researcher, and policy-maker (Lieberman, 2001). To appreciate how she reconciled and managed to blend these two seemingly conflicting positions we need to have an understanding of her upbringing and her progress in academia and her role in educational policy.

DARLING-HAMMOND, THE PERSON

Linda Darling-Hammond was born in Cleveland, Ohio in 1951. She came from a working-class family and when she was a young child the family moved home several times so that the children could attend, what the parents thought were, better schools. During the 1950s and 1960s schools in Cleveland were supported to offer students greater choice, and problem solving activities and project work were encouraged at the expense of rote learning. The curriculum movement of the 1960s appealed to teachers to consider realistic methods of teaching which offered learners the opportunity to experience authentic experiences, such as being an engineer, geographer or scientist. Darling-Hammond was an excellent student who benefited from a progressive educational system and the interaction of considerate and skilful teachers. She was the first woman in her family to go to college, she was also one of the first women to attend Yale University. Although she attributed her own experience of public education as the inspiration to become a teacher, it was during her time at Yale that she noticed the very dissimilar schooling experiences of her fellow students, many of whom had had a private education (Lieberman, 2001; Amrein-Beardsley, 2011).

Furthermore, while she was at university the United States was embroiled in the Vietnam War, and protest rallies were staged on many university campuses, it was also a time of an increasingly active civil rights movement. University then, for Darling-Hammond, was a potent experience of protest and fostered a growing awareness of the inequities in social justice. She knew from her own education that life prospects could be determined by having entry into a quality educational experience; this matter of universal access to quality education was to be at the heart of her future work. Despite the distractions of protests during her undergraduate years, she was a hard-working student who graduated from Yale in 1973 with distinction. Following this she trained as a public school teacher and became a student teacher in a large urban school in Camden, New Jersey, an experience which further strengthened her conviction of the inequities of the public school system. She achieved her doctorate in urban education from Temple University in 1978 (Lieberman, 2001; Banks, 2010).

Apart from leading the NCTAF, Darling-Hammond has been involved in numerous research and policy-making organisations such as: the American Educational Research Association, the National Board for Professional Teaching Standards and the National Academy of Education. She has also been a member of the White House Advisory Panel's Resource Group for the National Education Goals and the Foundation for the Advancement of Teaching (Darling-Hammond, 2010). She was also the leader of President Obama's education policy transition team. She was seen by some as a probable choice for the Secretary of Education position in President Obama's new government. However, this idea was of concern to many politicians who were in favour of corporate-type educational reforms. They thought Darling-Hammond was a champion of teacher professionalism, a close ally of the teacher unions, a supporter of teacher tenure and a critic of the fast-track teacher education programme Teach for America (Sadovnik et al., 2013). She has written extensively, both journal articles and books. Apart from *The Right to Learn: A Blueprint for Creating Schools That Work* in 2001, some of her other major works include: *Authentic Assessment and School Development*, with Ancess, in 1994; *Powerful Teacher Education: Lessons from Exemplary Programs* (2006); *Preparing Teachers for a Changing World: What Teachers Should Learn and Be Able to Do*, with Bransford, in 2005; and in 2010, *The Flat World and Education: How America's Commitment to Equity Will Determine Our Future*. All of these works, and others, set out her ideas.

DARLING-HAMMOND AND HER IDEAS OF AN EQUITABLE EDUCATIONAL SYSTEM, TEACHERS AND TEACHING

Darling-Hammond's ideas evolve from her drive for an education system which has social justice at its core. Although the themes of her work are very much interrelated in seeking an equitable education for all, this section will firstly briefly explore the challenges faced by the public education system in the United States; then broadly consider the aspects of educational policy related to, and championed by, Darling-Hammond; examine her thoughts on teacher profession-alism and teacher education; and finally, appraise her notions of student-centred teaching and assessment.

There is an overriding view that the corporate model of schooling in the United States affects most aspects of education: teaching practice, curriculum content, and many features of education reform and subsequent policies. Those who promote such corporate school models also advocate privatisation and the deregulation of schools, they 'imagine public schools as private businesses, districts [education authorities] as markets, students as consumers, and knowledge as a product' (Saltman, 2012: 674). Darling-Hammond, writing in 1997, paints a gloomy picture of the state secondary schools in urban areas:

> Schools are huge warehouses, with three thousand or more students. They are focused substantially on the control of behaviour rather than the development of community. With a locker as their only stable point of contact, a schedule that cycles them through a series of seven to ten overloaded teachers... Most students are likely to experience such high schools, heavily stratified within and substantially dehumanised throughout, as non-caring or even adversarial environments. (Darling-Hammond, 1997: 333)

Unlike many other developed countries, the United States does not have nationalised healthcare or housing support systems. In other developed countries children are, for the most part, well supported by society as a whole; should it be needed, assistance is provided by the government for meals, healthcare and housing. This social support is not so evident in the United States, and as a result much of the funding which is allocated to schools, particularly in urban areas, is spent on food, healthcare and other aspects of social welfare assistance. Schools also pay healthcare benefits for teachers. Unlike the United States, in most other developed countries school funding is mainly dedicated to educational purposes (Collier, 2011).

Recognising that the state of public schools in many areas of the United States is frightful, Darling-Hammond in her 2010 book *The Flat World and Education: How America's Commitment to Equity Will Determine Our Future* calls for quality and equality in genuine school reform. In doing so she argues for a new model in educational policy formation, both nationally and in individual states. This new model should be driven by the dual assurances that it will '*support meaningful learning* on the part of students, teachers, and schools, and ... *equalize access to education opportunity*, making it possible for all students to profit from more productive schools' (Darling-Hammond, 2010: 279). From the premise of these two assurances she explores her vision of the ideal educational policy. She states that the policy should contain five key elements:

1. *Meaningful learning goals*: These learning goals should equip students with the knowledge and skills for success, using new and inventive methods of learning, and also by giving responsibility to schools to manage the curriculum and assessment so they have control in monitoring and enhancing student and teacher progress.
2. *Intelligent, reciprocal accountability systems*: This includes creating systems which assure that students will experience good teaching and have a variety of learning opportunities. The systems will also involve processes for evaluating teaching, learning and the curriculum.
3. *Equitable and adequate resources*: Funding to enable all students to meet the learning standards and have the opportunities for success. This will also include a fair system for the availability of well-trained teachers through the setting up of an organisation for the recruitment and preparation of all teachers.

4. *Strong professional standards and support*: This will ensure that all teachers have access to excellent teacher education and mentoring during their career. It should also include the opportunity for teachers to develop their own education, both practical and academic.
5. *Schools organised for student and teacher learning*: Intended to allow greater freedom for groups of teachers to have a say in designing curriculum content, this element envisages a collaborative approach in creating innovative teaching methods and realistic assessments of students' performance.

(Darling-Hammond, 2010)

Further to these key elements of a new model of education policy, Darling-Hammond also argues that students' basic needs should also be provided for, such as food, health and housing, so when they arrive at school they can focus on learning rather than just existing. She contends that the US education system will continue to be neglected at a huge cost to society, if policy is not revitalised to equalise access to high-quality schooling. 'The path to our mutual well-being is built on educational opportunity ... and an unquestionable entitlement [to] a rich and inalienable right to learn' (Darling-Hammond, 2010: 328).

It was Darling-Hammond's experiences with other policy-makers, her engagement with schools in New York City and her work with Teachers College at Columbia University which gave her the chance and stimulus to reflect on how to create robust structures to promote and sustain a strong base for teacher professionalism. Such structures would amalgamate teacher education, 'ongoing professional development in collegial settings and a system of professional accountability' (Lieberman, 2001: 288). According to Darling-Hammond, teacher professionalism needs to be embedded into new and reformed educational policies which clearly specify what teaching is and the manner in which schools are structured to enable teaching to take place. This she argues should contain three core categories:

> (1) Policies governing entry and continuation in the profession; (2) policies and practices defining what teachers do in schools and classrooms; (3) policies governing how – and by whom – decisions about professional membership and teaching practices are made. (Darling-Hammond, 1990: 33)

Apart from the need to embed professionalism into new educational policy reform, she outlines her own definition of professionalism, where:

> members of an occupation share a common body of knowledge and shared standards of practice in exercising that knowledge on behalf of clients. It incorporates conditions of specialized knowledge, collective self-regulation, special attention to the unique needs of clients, autonomous performance and a large dose of responsibility. (Darling-Hammond, 1990: 32)

A large element of teacher professionalism for Darling-Hammond is teacher education. She has championed the cause of high-quality teacher education, arguing that well-trained teachers are vital to student success. She has also lamented the fact that the United States, unlike other high-attaining countries, has not yet formed a vigorous and widely accepted structure for teacher education which ensures all new teachers are well-prepared for the classroom. She has also been an advocate for a standardised and thorough form of student teacher recruitment, teacher induction, teacher tenure, meaningful and recognised teacher certification and ongoing professional development (Darling-Hammond, 2012).

The involvement of and collaboration with universities in teacher education is seen as crucial by Darling-Hammond in producing highly capable and professional teachers. She contests that, especially in today's complex and diverse society, teachers need an in-depth education, both practically and academically, to cope and succeed in classrooms. She maintains that teachers need to 'teach for understanding and to teach for diversity ... to understand subject matter in ways that allow them to organize it so that students can create useful cognitive maps of terrain' (Darling-Hammond, 1999: 13). Teachers also need to evaluate and reflect on their own practice, and consider and learn innovative pedagogies and forms of assessment. They also need to know how to motivate, research information, and keep up with new technologies and curriculum changes. All these aspects of becoming a professionally educated and competent teacher involve experiencing practice in the classroom which is underpinned by a theoretical framework in collaboration with universities (Darling-Hammond, 1999). A core element for all aspects of teacher professionalism is collaboration: collaboration between teachers, school mentors and with students in teaching and assessments.

Darling-Hammond considers collaboration between educators to be fundamental to the fostering of high-quality teaching and assessment practice which would benefit all students. Such collaboration is evident in the manner in which teaching and assessment is modelled and shared in Professional Development Schools (PDS). The PDSs are small urban schools which become principal sites of best teaching practice and teacher education. Darling-Hammond was involved in implementing the PDSs and promoting their work. New teachers in the profession were partnered with accomplished practitioners where they learnt through rigorous supervision, and reflection, about advanced teaching and assessment methods. Within this environment accomplished teachers also acted as a nexus between PDSs and universities, which not only enabled close links to be made between practice and theory, but also offered opportunities for practitioner-based research, ideas which Darling-Hammond campaigned for (Hagger and McIntyre, 2006).

Darling-Hammond advocates the notion of equitable and democratic schools and the practice of child-centred teaching. For her such schools are environments where students are encouraged to 'own their own learning, to become efficacious in pursuing their own goals by helping others to participate in building a healthier and more just society' (Darling-Hammond, 2013: xii). Her vision of these schools includes the notion that students take part in challenging and real-life learning activities which involve problem solving. Also, that these schools foster trusting relationships between teachers, students and the students' families, as well as with the local community. Rather than being overburdened with the preoccupation with test scores and school league tables, her idea of school is one where students experience support, encouragement, self-worth and an enthusiasm for learning. These schools are also places where students have opportunities to show their understanding and learning with the use of diverse and authentic methods of assessment (Darling-Hammond, 2013).

These authentic assessments are, for Darling-Hammond, a needed alternative to the standardised testing systems employed by many schools. She promotes the notion of performance assessments. This allows students to demonstrate the more developmental and higher-order intellectual levels of learning, rather than the regurgitation of facts or the recognition of possible right answers evident in much of the standardised testing. 'Performance assessment must construct an answer, produce a product, or perform an activity' (Darling-Hammond, 2013: 15). Bloom's taxonomy is the concept underpinning performance assessment. Students' progress through the mastery levels of knowledge, understanding and application – to the higher-order or developmental levels of analysis and synthesis to evaluation (Bloom, 1956). The use of performance assessment in schools, she argues, would also enable the United States to develop the required skills and knowledge to compete with other developing nations (Darling-Hammond, 2014).

Overall her ideas are quite closely linked with other educational thinkers, particularly those whose concepts focus on democracy, equity, collaboration, teacher professionalism and teacher education.

LINKS WITH OTHER THEORISTS

Darling-Hammond's notion of an equitable and democratic education is very much in tune with John Dewey. He challenged the older traditional methods of teaching and learning in favour of a more child-centred approach to practice. Dewey also stressed the significance of schools as collaborative environments, which should structure the curriculum to meet the needs of students in preparing them for the real world. There is also a striking parallel between his Chicago Laboratory School and Darling-Hammond's involvement in the PDSs. Dewey used the Laboratory School 'as a force for changing our existing schools and school systems' (Sarason, 1990: 66). There are also close links between Lave and Wenger, and their socially situated learning and communities of practice, and Darling-Hammond's notion of the importance of collaboration in the process of learning for students and teachers. For them, like Darling-Hammond and her championing of the PDSs, true learning involves a communal experience where people learn from their more experienced colleagues.

Learning, therefore, becomes an active process where knowledge and skills are accomplished and refined, which is very fitting for practice-based professions such as teaching.

Her views on innovative and challenging learning activities, which are embedded in the social and cultural background of the students, are associated with Freire's notion of problem-posing learning. The foundation of all of Freire's work is also based on aspects of equity and social justice. In the same vein as Darling-Hammond fighting for equity for the students in urban schools, Freire also argued for meaningful educational opportunities for those he considered were the *oppressed* (Freire, 1970 [1996]). Another educationalist who has strong connections with the notions of Darling-Hammond is Lawrence Stenhouse and his ideas of professionalism, the active engagement of teachers in curriculum research and design, and the benefits of forming collaborative partnerships between schools and university departments of education. His model of extended teacher professionalism resonates with what Darling-Hammond advocates for practitioners working actively and collegiately to improve and develop their practices. His idea behind the Centre for Applied Research in Education (CARE) at the University of East Anglia is aligned with the PDSs, as both afforded opportunities for teachers to be active researchers of their own practice in classrooms and to become involved with collaborative projects between schools and universities (Stenhouse, 1975). Another contemporary kindred spirit was John Goodlad, a leading educator who had, like Darling-Hammond, an alternative concept of what education should be, based on notions of ethics, social justice and democracy. Goodlad (1984 [2004]) also strove to convince both teachers and policy-makers to adopt his progressive ideas in education and create schools as better places for students to learn. Even though Darling-Hammond's ideas are in tune with other educationalists who strive for social justice, some of her ideas have attracted levels of censure.

CRITIQUING HER IDEAS

There are two major themes of criticism regarding Darling-Hammond's work, the first is to do with the practical aspects of her policy ideas and practice, the second relates to her socio-political stance. The practical aspects involve concerns about cost, matters of accountability and the sustainability of her ideas for school reform, and the enhancement of teacher professionalism. It is considered that these ideas would create 'expense, unclear lines of authority and confusion' (Darling-Hammond, 1990: 43). Her idea of schools being given more autonomy might lead to damaging educational decisions being made; also collaborative decision-making may not be a practical option as 'ultimately, no one will be in charge, and chaos will reign' (Darling-Hammond, 1990: 45). Furthermore, the high staff ratio needed to support new entrants to the teaching profession in the PDSs is a somewhat idealistic concept which is neither cost-effective nor sustainable for all schools or even all urban schools (Sarason, 1990).

There is also some disquiet on the topic of performance assessment; this concerns matters of cost, technical issues, and the demands upon teachers and students. Performance assessment has also attracted criticism because of anxiety about its trustworthiness, in particular around aspects of the reliability and validity of what is being assessed. Many of those teachers who have been involved in performance assessment have voiced their concerns. These concerns relate to whether performance assessment actually assesses the learning that it is meant to, and to what extent consistency of assessment is achieved between schools, assessors, students and assessment activities (Darling-Hammond, 2014).

The second theme of criticism is associated with her socio-political viewpoint. It is suggested that despite her impassioned ideas for improving the public schooling system, she has failed to address and challenge the underlying causes at the root of the educational inequity in the United States. These are fundamental 'problems and struggles that are inextricably bound up with the intersection of cultural politics and political economy' (Saltman, 2012: 680). According to Saltman, Darling-Hammond should have adopted Giroux's critical pedagogical approach to her work, which would explore the deeper struggles of class and culture which are blighting the educational opportunities for students in urban schools. Furthermore, he suggests that Darling-Hammond

> accepts the neoliberal framing of public schooling as principally serving the ends of global economic competition … education is for competition in a corporate-dominated capitalist economy; the goal of schools is to include more students into the existing social order, not to produce critical citizens who can challenge and transform that order. (Saltman, 2012: 681)

From this point of view, Darling-Hammond has not challenged the political and class injustices which are embedded in the public school system, rather she has cooperated with the system. Regardless of these criticisms there are aspects of her ideas which can be embraced in both the way we think about education, and the manner in which professionals work in schools.

APPLYING DARLING-HAMMOND'S IDEAS IN PRACTICE

After briefly exploring Darling-Hammond's thoughts on successful schooling and teaching, this section will consider her ideas for collaboration, including how they can be applied in teacher evaluation and induction, engaging students in learning, and finally performance assessment. For Darling-Hammond, the best schools are those which create structures that empower teachers to get to know their children, and the children's families. These schools are also places which build close relationships between students and teachers. In such schools, she argues, students not only attain higher grades but they become more confident about themselves as people (Darling-Hammond, 1997). She contends that there is a clear correlation between successful schools and successful teaching. For this to happen,

> teachers must have both the knowledge about teaching and learning needed to manage the complex process of getting diverse students to learn well and the discretion to practice variability rather than routinely. Successful education can occur only if teachers are prepared to meet rigorous learning demands *and* the different needs of the students... Teachers must be able to develop learning experiences that accommodate a variety of cognitive styles, with activities that broaden rather than reduce the range of possibilities for learning. They must understand child development and pedagogy as well as the structures of subject areas and a variety of alternatives for assessing learning. (Darling-Hammond, 1997: 335)

Successful teaching, she argues, is associated with the creation of collaborative opportunities where students can learn from each other in small group work activities. Collaboration is also at the heart of her thinking when she advances her notions of teacher development and professionalism.

She advocates the use of 'team teaching' where instead of one teacher being responsible for large groups of students, teachers share the task. This form of collaboration offers a number of possibilities, such as supervision opportunities, sharing ideas for lesson planning and teaching methods, and developing approaches for meeting the needs of individual students (Darling-Hammond, 1990). Such practice also allows teachers to work with other practitioners to help solve problems and develop skills together in supportive and progressive teaching communities. Successful schools which have robust teaching communities have a shared agreement concerning classroom practice and how to take practice further (Collier, 2011). By teachers working together in this manner, they are much better placed to share their knowledge of individual students with one another and, if appropriate, relay that knowledge to the student's family. In this way, 'the rewards of teacher communities go beyond individual teachers to benefit students, families, and society as a whole' (Collier, 2011: 14). Furthermore, by forming partnerships with university education departments, akin to the practice with the PDSs, teachers would broaden their collaboration network and develop their practitioner research skills.

Darling-Hammond extends her notion of collaboration for use in teacher induction and teacher evaluation. Induction of new entrants into the teaching profession usually means a series of lesson observations as a form of periodic evaluation of the inductee's skills in classroom practice. These evaluations are in the form of mechanistic checklists which record to what extent the teaching and learning standards were met, or not met, by the inductee. This process is then followed by a brief post-lesson feedback discussion between the inductee and the observer. This process, she argues, is not ideal and she offers an alternative practice. Her idea is that induction should be a process where inductees have mentoring by expert, experienced practitioners who have substantial time to provide continuous supervision to new practitioners, helping them learn to make the thousands of important decisions that a teacher must confront every day. This function can be best performed by mentor teachers providing expertise specific to the subject area, or grade level taught. (Darling-Hammond, 1990: 36)

This method of evaluation can also be employed for qualified teachers, and is very evident in highly successful collaborative settings. This takes the form of the evaluation of lessons through peer review. Teachers observe each other's teaching to highlight possible difficulties, and share classroom practice. The openness of the process of peer review, she argues, enhances teaching practice 'by decreasing teacher isolation and providing directly relevant opportunities for professional growth' (Darling-Hammond, 1990: 42).

Although the focus of Darling-Hammond and Ifill-Lynch's 2006 article concerned encouraging secondary age students to engage in homework, it also provides a number of practical *and* stimulating ideas which can be applied to engaging students in the classroom as well. They found that many of the students who did not engage in tasks set were unsure of what was required of them. They set out a series of applied ideas which teachers could use to encourage students to engage with their school work. These include suggestions for how practitioners can facilitate engagement:

1. *Give students work that is worth the effort*: Allocate tasks which are based on real life, and topics which students are interested in. Long-term projects which students become deeply involved in are productive activities.
2. *Set work which is achievable*: Give clear directions as to the needs for completing tasks, including how the task relates to the learning outcomes. Ensure feedback from the task is timely, and developmental in nature.
3. *Discover what the students need*: Endeavour to create challenging and meaningful tasks which meet individual student's needs by finding out what their aspirations are, and how they are best motivated; then implement individual learning plans to enable learning to take place.
4. *Allocate the time and space*: Be flexible with creating learning opportunities by using spaces such as libraries and by the use of classrooms during break times; if appropriate allow time extensions for students to complete tasks.
5. *Disseminate students' work*: Display the work of students that meets the required standards to demonstrate to others that such tasks are achievable. This also enables students at differing levels to work together to encourage peer tutoring and social collaboration.

(Darling-Hammond and Ifill-Lynch, 2006)

This final suggestion of displaying and disseminating students' work can also be used as part of performance assessment. Students' projects can be exhibited and presented to a panel for assessment; this panel could include members of the local community, fellow students and teachers. Students who exhibit their work have the opportunity to talk, use multimedia or display products and portfolios that have been created as part of their projects. According to Darling-Hammond,

> As students repeatedly develop and revise projects and exhibitions evaluated according to rigorous standards, they internalize standards of quality and develop college- and career-ready skills of planning, resourcefulness, perseverance, a capacity to use feedback productively, a wide range of communication skills, and a growth mind-set for learning – all of which extend beyond the individual assignments themselves in shaping their ability to learn in new contexts. (Darling-Hammond, 2014: 29)

Darling-Hammond's ideas are very much related to schooling and teaching in the context of the US educational system. However, it is maintained that many of her ideas for teacher evaluation, collaborative practice, engaging children in learning and performance assessment can be adapted by practitioners outside of the United States.

REFLECTIVE TASK

Darling-Hammond contends that 'effective schools ... are those that create structures for caring ... that enable close, sustained relationships among students and teachers' (Darling-Hammond, 1997: 333).

Reflecting on your own experiences of school, college or university:

1. List the structures or opportunities that were/are in place to enable and foster such close relationships.
2. What other structures or opportunities could be added to the above to strengthen these relationships?

SUMMARY

Darling-Hammond remains one of the most influential champions for educational reform in the United States. Her work spans a number of areas, but it is her quest for parity in the public school sector that stands out, particularly for children in urban areas. She has been involved in many persuasive and significant national educational policy initiatives as a social activist and policy-maker, where she sought to move away from the corporate model of schooling towards a more equitable model. Her prominence as a reformer and policy-maker was recognised when she was appointed to lead President Obama's education policy transition team. Within this drive for more equitable education she advocated a much deeper notion of teacher professionalism which included a more robust teacher education that combined both the practical and intellectual aspects of being a teacher. At the heart of the idea of teacher professionalism is collaboration – collaboration between teachers, between teachers and university staff, and between teachers and students. Darling-Hammond's view is that teaching should be interactive and involve project work, problem solving and be connected to the real world. She also advanced the idea of performance assessment as an alternative to standardised testing.

Darling-Hammond's ideas have similarities with other educationalists, especially those who have stood up for a democratic and equitable education, as well as those who supported the call for teacher professionalism and collaboration. These include Dewey's ideas of schools being democratic and collaborative environments; there are also close associations between his Chicago Laboratory School and Darling-Hammond's involvement with PDSs. There is further evidence of links with Lave and Wenger's socially situated learning and communities of practice, with her call for collaboration. Her idea that teaching should involve real-life problem solving is also associated with Freire's notion of problem-posing learning. Her interest in teacher professionalism and teacher education have resonance with Lawrence Stenhouse and John Goodlad. There are criticisms of her works, which are based on practical and socio-political issues. The practical issues are around cost, accountability and that her ideas are not sustainable for all schools. The disquiet about socio-political issues relates to her not addressing the root causes of the inequity in schooling, such as struggles of class and culture which impair equal opportunities for all students.

There are, despite these criticisms, a number of her ideas which can be put into practice in schools and classrooms for the benefit of students, teachers' professional development and the community. These include seeking opportunities for collaborative practice, using more problem solving and group projects in teaching, and finally, by raising the profile of using alternative forms of assessment which are authentic and measure all-round performance in students' learning.

FURTHER READING

Darling-Hammond, L. (Ed.) (2010) *Next Generation Assessment: Moving Beyond the Bubble Test to Support 21st Century Learning*. San Francisco: Jossey Bass.
A comprehensive review of assessment in the United States which argues for the adoption of performance testing that measures the higher-order cognitive skills, instead of large-scale standardised testing.

Goodwin, A. (Ed.) (1997) *Assessment for Equity and Inclusion: Embracing All Our Children*. London: Routledge.
Very much aligned with Darling-Hammond's ideas, this text challenges the use of standardised testing and offers inclusive alternatives for a diverse range of students.

Osguthorpe, R., Harris, R., Fox Harris, M. and Black, S. (Eds) (1995) *Partner Schools: Centers for Educational Renewal.* San Francisco: Jossey Bass.
This book explores the positive opportunities for teacher education and development that arise when schools and universities become full partners in striving for educational renewal.

REFERENCES

Amrein-Beardsley, A. (2011) *Interview with Linda Darling-Hammond.* http://insidetheacademy. asu.edu/linda-darling-hammond.

Banks, J. (2010) Foreword. In: Darling-Hammond, L. *The Flat World and Education: How America's Commitment to Equity Will Determine Our Future.* New York: Teachers College Press.

Bloom, B. (Ed.) (1956) *Taxonomy of Educational Objectives, Book 1: Cognitive Domain.* London: Longman.

Collier, L. (2011) 'The need for teacher communities: An interview with Linda Darling-Hammond'. *The Council Chronicle*, November: 12–14.

Darling-Hammond, L. (1990) 'Teacher professionalism: Why and how'. In: Lieberman, A. (Ed.) *Schools as Collaborative Cultures: Creating the Future Now.* London: Falmer Press.

Darling-Hammond, L. (1997) 'Restructuring schools and student success'. In: Halsey, A., Lauder, H., Brown, P. and Stuart Wells, A. (Eds) *Education: Culture, Economy, Society.* Oxford: Oxford University Press.

Darling-Hammond, L. (1999) 'The case for university-based teacher education'. In: Roth, R. (Ed.) *The Role of the University in the Preparation of Teachers.* London: Falmer Press.

Darling-Hammond, L. (2001) *The Right to Learn: A Blueprint for Creating Schools That Work.* San Francisco: Jossey Bass.

Darling-Hammond, L. (2006) *Powerful Teacher Education: Lessons from Exemplary Programs.* San Francisco: Jossey Bass.

Darling-Hammond, L. (2010) *The Flat World and Education: How America's Commitment to Equity Will Determine Our Future.* New York: Teachers College Press.

Darling-Hammond, L. (2012) 'The right start: Creating a strong foundation for the teaching career'. *Phi Delta Kappan*, 94(3): 8–13.

Darling-Hammond, L. (2013) Foreword. In: Steele, D. and Cohn-Vargas, B. *Identity Safe Classrooms.* Thousand Oaks: Corwin.

Darling-Hammond, L. (2014) *Next Generation Assessment: Moving Beyond the Bubble Test to Support 21st Century Learning.* San Francisco: Jossey Bass.

Darling-Hammond, L. and Ancess, J. (1994) *Authentic Assessment and School Development.* New York: National Center for Restructuring Education, Schools, and Teaching, Teachers College, Columbia University.

Darling-Hammond. L. and Bransford, J. (2005) *Preparing Teachers for a Changing World: What Teachers Should Learn and Be Able to Do.* San Francisco: Jossey Bass.

Darling-Hammond, L. and Ifill-Lynch, O. (2006) 'If they'd only do their work!' *Educational Leadership*, 63(5): 8–13.

Freire, P. (1970 [1996]) *Pedagogy of the Oppressed.* London: Penguin.

Goodlad, J. (1984 [2004]) *A Place Called School.* New York: McGraw-Hill.

Hagger, H. and McIntyre, D. (2006) *Learning Teaching from Teachers: Realizing the Potential of School-based Teacher Education.* Maidenhead: Open University Press.

Liebermann, A. (2001) 'Linda Darling-Hammond, 1951–'. In: Palmer, J. (Ed.) *Fifty Modern Thinkers on Education: From Piaget to the Present*. London: Routledge.

National Commission on Teaching and America's Future (NCTAF) (1996) *What Matters Most: Teaching for America's Future*. New York: NCTAF.

Sadovnik, A., Cookson, P. and Semel, S. (Eds) (2013) *Exploring Education: An Introduction to the Foundations of Education* (fourth edition). London: Routledge.

Saltman, K. (2012) 'Why Henry Giroux's democratic pedagogy is crucial for confronting failed corporate school reform and how liberals like Ravitch and Darling-Hammond are making things worse'. *Policy Futures in Education*, 10(6): 674–87.

Sarason, S. (1990) 'What are schools of education for?' In: Lieberman, A. (Ed.) *Schools as Collaborative Cultures: Creating the Future Now*. London: Falmer Press.

Stenhouse, L. (1975) *An Introduction to Curriculum Research*. London: Heinemann.

INDEX